Peter Nazareth
Toronto 26/6/93
Toronto 28/6/9?

$ 7.95

It Ain't Necessarily So

It Ain't
Necessarily So

AN AUTOBIOGRAPHY

Larry Adler

GROVE PRESS
New York

Published by Grove Press, Inc.
920 Broadway
New York, N.Y. 10010

The quotation from *The Last Hero: Wild Bill Donovan,* by Anthony Cave Brown,
is reprinted by permission of Times Books, a Division of Random House, Inc.
Copyright © 1982 by Anthony Cave Brown.

Library of Congress Cataloging-in-Publication Data

Adler, Larry.
It ain't necessarily so.

1. Adler, Larry.   2. Harmonica players—Biography.   I. Title.
ML419.A3A3   1987   788'.9 [B]   86-33485
ISBN 0-394-55757-3

Manufactured in the United States of America
First Edition 1987
Designed by Irving Perkins Associates

10 9 8 7 6 5 4 3 2 1

Acknowledgments

I WOULD LIKE TO THANK these friends for their help: Victoria Lownes, Selina Hastings, Gloria Leighton, Ken McCormick, E. J. Kahn, Jr., John Weity, Tatiana von Saxe, and Fred Jordan.

I made good use of the Epson PX8 computer and word processor and the Brother EP44 electronic typewriter, because their portability made it easy to write on planes, trains, in hotel rooms, and even while floating in a swimming pool.

Preface

SOMETHING THAT MUST WORRY any autobiographer is the treachery of memory. I find in too many instances that it's completely unreliable. I think I'm writing the truth; I'd even swear to it, but how can I be sure?

In 1945 I was in Munich and was entertained by a group of OSS men, a dirty tricks outfit, founded by Wild Bill Donovan. The leader, John Weitz, told me he'd had word that eight German soldiers had escaped capture and were holed up in a house whose address was known. Weitz and his men were going to raid the house early the next morning and invited me to go along. I found the idea exciting and accepted. I met Weitz at 5:30 A.M., got into a jeep with him and his men and we were off. When we reached the house, the men left the jeep, broke down a door and entered the house. The Germans started firing, the Americans fired back, two Germans were killed, the others surrendered.

That's John Weitz's version.

Here is mine: when the men entered the house they found two old women. There was no firing, no one was killed or captured. My

vii

main memory is of the Yanks opening drawers, flinging the contents about and generally wrecking the place while the women wept. I felt ashamed, felt that our side was acting like Nazis.

So there you have two stories, both eye-witnessed by two men who were there. John Weitz has become a famous fashion designer, we are friends and John delights in having people listen to our conflicting accounts of the same incident. What to make of that? Neither of us is lying but which account is the truth? I think mine is the more likely to be because mine is duller, no story at all.

But there is, so help me, still another account. In Anthony Cave Brown's biography of Bill Donovan, the following occurs:

> There remained only the task of cleaning up the Munich Were-wolf. That was done at about the same time as the destruction of the Tessman organisation. Werner (accompanied by the har-monica player Larry Adler, who was in Munich for a concert) had his last, long frightening walk down the dark alley to the SS lodging house. At a given hour the house was surrounded by armed troops, and all approaches were blocked by weapon carriers. Then, with the house bathed in searchlights, the Munich OSS and CIC burst in and arrested sixteen SS men all of whom were asleep.

Well, there you are. Three different accounts of the same incident. Take your choice but I'd stick with mine if I were you, reason being that I'm such a coward that had there been any SS men around I'd have run like hell. One final point: the report by Anthony Cave Brown in his book gives the date as April 1946 and says I was in Munich for a concert. The raid that John Weitz invited me on happened in July 1945.

A final (I hope) footnote. I sent the Cave Brown book version of the Munich raid to John Weitz. His reply arrived the day I was to turn in the completed manuscript of this book. Here it is:

Dear Larry; Yes, I am Johannes Werner (or was). I really did not know until The Times, *who published Donovan's biography, asked me if I'd seen the story on me, then they asked me to look under Werner. They got the time wrong but the general outline is almost like my story*

in the letter I wrote you before this one. You will also discover derring-do
of mine in an earlier Werner episode.

The Cave Brown story was sort of correct. His timing was not. But
then, when one writes so long after the fact, it's hard to research things
which were secret in the first place. In case you are wondering why
Werner, my middle names are Hans-Werner.

Warmly, John.

That should settle it. There were eight German soldiers, one jeep-
load of OSS men and one mouth-organist. There were two grand-
mothers, no German soldiers, and one mouth-organist.

There were sixteen German SS men captured in a raid involving
armed troops, weapons carriers and floodlights. There were OSS
men and one mouth-organist.

Are you calling me a liar? And if not, why not?

Another example. I toured Newfoundland entertaining U.S.
troops. At Harmon, my last stop, the commander of the base fell for
our acrobatic dancer. Suddenly there was no transport to get us back
to Gander, and the reason was obvious. I had a nightclub date in
New York and it looked as if, thanks to the commander and the
dancer, I wasn't going to make it.

In the canteen I noticed a British airman, an unusual sight on an
American base. We got into conversation and I told him of my
plight; he said he could get me to Gander if I could be ready in an
hour. I was and met him on the tarmac. He had a C-47 cargo plane
and a glider and he was conducting an experiment, to try towing a
glider across the Atlantic. If it worked, the method would be valuable in saving cargo from being sunk by German submarines. He put
me in the glider with the pilot, got into the C-47 with his co-pilot
and crew, and took off.

It was immensely exciting but the best part came when we were
over Gander. Then the C-47 pilot released the glider to make its own
landing. The feeling of free-floating, away from the noise of the
C-47's engine, is indescribable, at least by me. It was the ultimate
escape from reality. I wished that we could remain like that, just
floating, never having to land, but gravity doesn't work that way. I
thanked my friend, we had a final drink and I caught a commercial
plane to New York.

It was an exciting experience and I told a lot of people about it.

Then, a few years ago, I found a diary dating back to the Newfoundland tour. Here are two excerpts:

27 Apr. 1943. Harmon.
  Met RAF Captain who had set world's glider record that day. He flies to Gander tomorrow. I asked him to take me along.

28 Apr. Harmon to Gander.
  Got up early, retrieved my passport, had breakfast with RAF captain and then to hangar. I rode in huge C-47, a cargo plane. The squadron leader rode in the glider which, amazingly, carries very few passengers. Reached Gander very soon.

There is a discrepancy, wouldn't you say, between the story I've been telling for years and the account, written on the day it happened? Obviously I wasn't in the glider at all. In fact I've never been in a glider in my life.

Well, after that, how can you believe anything I say? Am I a congenital liar? No more than most people. I am, of course, a ham with a ham's wish to make a good story better. It would have been more exciting if I had been in the glider. It is obvious that I wished I had been in the glider. And, after a while, I damned well *was* in the glider.

Remember, when I told the glider story, I wasn't lying. I believed what I was saying, probably would have sworn in court to the truth of it. Only, it wasn't true.

Tolstoy anticipated me (well, to coin a phrase, he would, wouldn't he?) in *War and Peace*. A young man, back from a major battle, is telling his war experiences to some young ladies in a Moscow drawing-room. But he had been behind the lines, had seen no action and, as he went on he saw that he was beginning to lose his audience. So, he began to embellish his story with details that he'd heard from front-line soldiers, making these personal, as if they had happened to him. Then Tolstoy writes: "And as he spoke he felt the truth slipping away from him and soon he would no longer know what the truth was."

I think this applies to anyone's anecdote about anything. Alan Jay Lerner told me that Dirk Bogarde, in his autobiography, takes credit for introducing Lerner to Rex Harrison. "But I had known Rex for years," said Lerner, "long before I'd met Dirk!"

So the next time you are challenged, beware the "Are you calling me a liar" syndrome. Do what I'd like you to do while reading my story, sing an occasional chorus of "It Ain't Necessarily So." I have suggested to my publishers that with each copy the reader get a grain of salt.

Caveat, you should pardon the expression, *emptor.*

It ain't necessarily so,
It ain't necessarily so,
De t'ings dat yo' li'ble
To read in de Bible,
It ain't necessarily so.

Ira Gershwin

It Ain't Necessarily So

CHAPTER
One

THE FIRST WORLD WAR and I began at about the same time, a fact that somebody in the future will, I hope, find to be of significance. Baltimore was an awful place to be born and I spent my first fourteen years plotting my escape. Nobody seemed to like anybody. Catholics, Protestants, Poles, Negroes, Jews, cordially detested or feared one another, and there was hardly any contact between the groups. I was called "Jew bastard" my first day at school but was also cautioned by my parents not to play with "the little nigger boys." I didn't, and don't, see the logic of either position. Far too much time was spent by the Gentile boys assuring me that I had killed Christ and they could prove it. My alibi did me no good. I doubt whether even the strictures of Pope John XXIII have penetrated the hard-line fundamentalism of Baltimore. Lenny Bruce said it all. "Okay, we killed him. But after 2000 years shouldn't there be a statute of limitations?"

My father was a plumber with his own truck (Adler's Plumbing Shop on Wheels) and I would sometimes go out with him on jobs. Watching as he dug a ditch in which to lay a drainpipe convinced me that, whatever my future, it did not include a career in plumbing.

We lived in 774 Columbia Avenue, later to acquire the higher-class name of Washington Boulevard which it didn't deserve. Trolley-cars ran past Adler's Plumbing Shop, the one without wheels, and their rumbling shook the whole house. We lived in rooms at the back of the shop and also occupied the floor above. The top floor was rented to Mrs. Schallenberg, who spoke with a heavy German accent. She was a kind lady, always giving me nickels and sometimes even dimes, who felt keenly the anti-German feeling that was around. The kids made fun of her, burlesquing her accent, and I hated them for it.

My full name was Lawrence Cecil Adler and my brother, born five years after me, was named Hilliard Gerald. I don't know where mother got those names but she did us no favor. Lawrence was considered a sissy name and as for Cecil, pronounced "seesil,"—wowee! Other kids would shout. "Oh Lor-rents," in fag style. How I envied the Chucks, Buzzies and Heckies. I had a nickname at home, Butzie, but it never reached the kids. When my name was pronounced without caricature it was Larnts. That was Baltimorese and Baltimore was, and still is, pronounced Ballmer.

My grandparents on my father's side—I scarcely remember my other grandparents—lived in another part of town, on Baltimore Street. They spoke no English, yet my grandfather—Zadie, in the Yiddish phrase—ran Adler's Dairy. Bubbim, the Yiddish word for grandmother, was an imposing lady who looked the way a matriarch ought to look. She was really the head of the family, all disputes were referred to her. Zadie was nondescript.

How did we get to be Adler? Zadie came from Russia and Adler is German. One uncle told me our name was really Zelakovitch but nobody would confirm this. Recently I saw my brother—he's been Jerry for years, having shed Hilliard as I did Lawrence—who said yes, we were indeed Zelakovitch to begin with but Zadie got tired of waiting in immigration queues, always last to be called because his name began with Z. Thus he changed to Adler.

Mother and Dad were both born in Russia but were brought, as infants, to the U.S. and their idiom was Baltimorese. They used Yiddish as a secret language to keep me from knowing what they were saying. I resented this and, instead of trying to learn Yiddish, I backed away from it. It was my loss, as Yiddish is the best language for jokes—even among Gentiles. *Schmuck, schtumm, megilleh, schmeer, nebisch, oy vay, hassle, chutzpah* are all in general usage, especially in the cosmopolitan centers like New York, Chicago and San Francisco.

Mother was beautiful, with long black hair that reached to the ground. She had a Spanish beauty. I never thought I looked like Dad but as I grow older I see more and more of him in me. Mother had the nasal intonation of Baltimore. Dad had a high, almost strangulated, way of talking and Jerry does an accurate imitation of him.

I was always sensitive to sound, couldn't stand eating noises and would leave the table when soup was slurped. Whistling is still the sound I find most irritating and I will cross a street rather than walk near a whistler. Dad used to call me into the house by a family whistle —three short blasts with a rising inflection on the third—and I didn't like being whistled for, like a dog, so perhaps my phobia is Freudian.

When I was five I entered a singing contest sponsored by the Public Parks Municipal Band. This band, conducted by E. V. Cupero, played in the Baltimore parks every summer and that year my mother's sister, my Aunt Annie, taught me "I've Got Those Profiteering Blues." The words were:

> Do you remember when prices were low?
> Oh that was so long, long ago.
> Gone are the days
> When free lunches went with beer,
> Gone are the days
> It fills my eyes with tears.

I was doing well in this contest but toward the end, caught a bad cold, so never reached the finals. Not surprising, considering that, while other contestants sang once a week when the band came to their neighborhood park, I insisted that my parents take me to each park. My only souvenir of this is a clipping from the *Sun* with a photograph of me, hairier than Paderewski, wearing overalls and a sickly grin. The caption reads: "Follows Park Band to win gold medal," and was my first press notice.

If there is any credit for my musical ability, a lot of it must go to Aunt Annie. Still active at the time of writing, she is a Joycean character, ribald, profane, vulgar and very funny. She taught me to sing before I learned to talk.

We had a wind-it-yourself Victrola—all gramophones were called Victrolas, the way all facial tissues today are called Kleenex—and records of Al Jolson, Eddie Cantor, Sophie Tucker, Cantor Josef Rosenblatt (singing "Eli, Eli"), Mischa Elman (playing Humoresque) and Sergei Rachmaninoff (playing Prelude in C Sharp Minor). For Jews we were fairly catholic. I was taken to see and hear Jolson in *Sinbad* when I was five and knew even then that this was a very special fellow. The same year I heard Cantor and he just didn't hit me in the belly the way Jolson did. Harry Jolson, a distant cousin, had a tailor's shop near us and Dad got him to make me a costume like Jolson's. I wore it to a Halloween party, blacked up like Jolson, and drove my host's father nuts by constantly checking my makeup with him.

We had a piano, a Kimball upright, which mother had won by supplying the last line in a limerick competition. I wish I knew what that line was. I could pick out tunes "by ear" and even harmonize them. When I heard Rachmaninoff at the Lyric Theater I was sure that what he did was what *I* wanted to do. It never occurred to me that Rachmaninoff must have practiced like crazy to *be* Rachmaninoff. I coasted on my facility for picking up tunes, and even two years of piano lessons did me little good. I either wouldn't or just couldn't practice. Scales and exercises bored me, nor could I ever hold my hands or place my fingers the "correct" way. Many years later Arthur Rubinstein stared at my hands as I played the piano and said flatly that it was impossible. Nobody could get a sound out of the piano by doing what he saw me doing.

I was supposed to start piano lessons when I was six. Dad drove me in the truck to my first lesson but on the way another truck, carrying a protruding log, backed out of an alleyway. The log went through our window, missing Dad but knocking me cold. Dad ran with me to a nearby hospital where I stayed for weeks. This came to court a year later and we lost the case. The defending lawyer implied that I was a congenital liar and I was shocked, when court adjourned for lunch, to see *our* lawyer go out for a bite with him. How could nice Harry O. Levin have anything to do with such a monster? It was disillusioning.

That should have been the end of music lessons but the matter came up again when I was ten. I was in the habit of going to piano recitals, especially those of my hero, and became dissatisfied with our

Kimball upright. Rachmaninoff, Cortot, Paderewski—*they* didn't play any old upright, no sir, *they* used a grand. One Saturday I went downtown to Howard Street where the music stores were and tried Steinway, Estey, Chickering, Baldwin. None seemed right to me, even though the great Sergei played a Steinway. Then, at the Hammann, Levin shop I tried a Mason and Hamlin and that was *it*. I grandly told Mr. Levin himself to send it to me, Lawrence Cecil Adler, gave him my address and went home.

A few days later a van arrived to deliver a piano. My father told the driver he hadn't asked for one. I remarked that I had. Dad gave me a baleful look, phoned the store and spoke to Mr Levin who told Dad that he was impressed that a ten-year-old kid could tell one piano from another. He felt I should have that piano. Dad asked how much it cost.

"Twenty-five hundred dollars," said Mr. Levin.

"I'm a plumber," said Dad, "and I can't afford that kind of money."

Mr. Levin asked, "Could you afford fifty cents a week?" And on that basis we kept the piano. Can you imagine a similar thing happening today?

When Dad let me keep the piano, I promised to practice at least an hour each day. I couldn't live up to it and that was the first sign of my long-term vice, laziness (plus procrastination).

About this time Dad felt we were doing well enough to move to Bryant Avenue near Druid Hill Park, where every house had a flight of stone steps and a porch, or "stoop." The streets were broad and I longed for a bicycle. There was a magazine advertisement showing a Ranger bicycle "with the New Departure coaster brake" and a kid looking up adoringly at a beaming adult; a balloon coming out of the kid's mouth read, "Gee, Dad!" I wanted to be that kid. Then I found that if you sold subscriptions to *Liberty* magazine you not only made money, you got coupons which could be redeemed for goods. I sent away for details, because one of the prizes you could win was a Ranger bike. I soon found that, at the rate I sold subscriptions, it would take me about twenty years. In the in-house magazine *Liberty* sent to its subscription salesmen, *everybody* seemed to win a bike. What was wrong with *me?* I made a pitch at every relative and got fairly good support but my best results were in the apartment houses around Eutaw Place, on the other side of the park from where I lived. I would take the lift to the top and work down, canvassing every apartment. I sold a few hundred subscriptions but I could see I'd never get that bike. I gave up and settled for a carom board, a game like pool but with wooden rings instead of balls.

One day I came home from school and Dad told me to look in the garage; I did, and there was a Ranger bike. It even had the New Departure coaster brake. Gee, Dad! I took the bike out and rode around the streets, Bryant Avenue, Whittier Avenue, Mondawmin Avenue, Auchentoroly Terrace and into Druid Hill Park. It was sunset, the weather was warm and it is one of the most beautiful moments I can remember.

When I began at grade school No. 60 in Baltimore I found that I had very bad eyesight. Although I could read books all right I couldn't see the blackboard clearly. I was taken for an eye examination and had to be held down by force to have eyedrops inserted. I couldn't bear anything approaching my eyes. I was short-sighted and the glasses I had to wear from then on got me the usual nickname: Four Eyes.

One day a kid at that school tried to take my marbles away from me. Another kid, a bigger one called Reese Whittemore, came along, made the first kid give me back my marbles and told me that if I was bothered again, I should come to him and he'd beat the shit out of anybody who picked on me.

It figures that the big boy, my rescuer, was a hero to me and, when he let me into his gang, it was like winning the Manliness Medal. When I was nineteen I read that Reese Whittemore had been executed in the electric chair in Maryland for murder. Had I stayed in the gang, I might have been in on the job that ended in murder and an execution. But I went on the stage when I was fourteen.

At the Sha'arei T'filoh Synagogue, on Auchentoroly Terrace (don't we have great names in Baltimore?), I went every Friday evening and Saturday morning to sing in the choir. At the end of the high holidays each choir boy was given a gold watch and chain. One night, after the synagogue service, while walking back home (I wouldn't even ride a bicycle on *Shabbos* I was that religious) I heard some exciting piano music as I was passing a house. I walked up the steps to the porch—all houses in that part of Baltimore had porches —and looked in. A boy, about my age, was playing four-hand duets with a lady. I don't know how long I stayed there, fascinated, until suddenly my left ear was gripped hard by the lady.

"Vot you doing hot here?" she asked.

I explained (not easy when your ear is grabbed) that I was listening to the music.

"So? Den dunt stand hotside like tremp, com heen." Still gripping my ear she led me into the drawing-room and sat me in a chair, after which I heard Schubert, Schumann and Tchaikovsky. The boy was Shura Cherkassky, who had just come from Russia and spoke no English, the lady was his aunt. She invited me to play with Shura the next day but it was difficult because we couldn't talk to each other. He had a sensitive face and a mane of black, bushy hair.

A few months later Shura gave a solo recital at the Lyric Theater, which was Baltimore's concert hall. He played his own piece, Prelude "Pathétique" and, though Shura has forgotten it, I can still play it on the piano.

I was deeply jealous of Shura, despite our friendship. Here he was, just a year or two older than me, giving a recital. I couldn't match that. Zadie took Shura's success to heart. He said to Dad: "Look at Shura Cherkassky, only twelve years old and already giving concerts. And look at Lawrence, ten years old and what has he accomplished? Nothing!"

I didn't like being made to feel a has-been at ten and I resented Zadie for making me look small.

After junior high I went to study the piano at the Peabody Conservatory of Music at Mount Vernon Place in Baltimore. I was never a good student. I tried really hard to do what teacher said, but it just wasn't in me. For the students' recital, which was obligatory after two terms, I prepared a Grieg waltz, based mainly on my imitation of Rachmaninoff's recording. I was nearly twelve by that time and it seemed to me that my interpretation compared quite favorably with that of the Master.

The supervisor, big tits and pince-nez, called my name and, as I sat at the piano, said: "And what are we going to play, my little man?" Goddammit, *we* weren't going to play *anything,* I was, and I didn't like being patronized. To hell with the Grieg waltz. I went into a stride version of "Yes, We Have No Bananas," glaring at tits and pince-nez to the cheers of the other students. She stopped me after about twelve bars. "That will do. We have heard *quite* enough."

She sent me to my seat and later my parents got a letter saying, in effect, don't send him back. I was expelled and it is still a unique distinction.

My parents then arranged private lessons with Miss Virginia Fore, but the practicing got no better. Many years later she told me she knew I'd never make it as a pianist. My musical ear was too good— I coasted on it. Miss Fore learned never to play for me any piece I was expected to learn. If she played it, I'd pick it up by ear, could reproduce it fairly well and thus wouldn't bother practicing it. My friend Earl Steinberg was also learning the piano and he hated practice as much as I did. The year before I'd become interested in hypnotism, because I'd read that Rachmaninoff, in a depression that was ruining his music, was cured by hypnotic treatment under A. Moll, to whom he dedicated his Second Piano Concerto. I tried hypnotizing Earl and made piano-practicing out to be more fun even than girls. From then on Earl did indeed practice and actually seemed to like it. I tried autohypnosis but it didn't work.

I was stagestruck, had been since my exposure to Al Jolson, and used to hang around the various stage doors. The Loew's theater played a film plus a stage show, the RKO Hippodrome played straight music-hall, twice a day, no films. Ford's played legitimate theater and there was a burlesque house where the famous "Sliding Billy" Watson often starred. Some first-class comedians came from burlesque, whose main attraction was the stripper. Jackie Gleason, Abbott and Costello, Phil Silvers, all learned the hard way, getting laughs from crowds who would rather be yelling, "Take it off!"

I was fascinated by Singer's Midgets, would follow them to a restaurant and peer at them from outside. The Hilton sisters, Daisy and Violet, Siamese twins who were joined at the waist, did an act where they sang, danced and played the violin. They are also known for another legend in show business. They were in the lobby of the Manger Hotel on Seventh Avenue in New York when Nils Asther, the film star, came out of a lift. The sisters, with the dreadful sidling walk they had to adopt, accosted him and said (in unison?), "Mr. Asther, we were on the bill with you at the Scollay Square Theater in Boston—we don't know if you remember us or not."

George Jessel came to Baltimore in Samson Raphaelson's play, *The Jazz Singer*. The cheap seats were all sold and I couldn't afford the expensive ones. I went backstage and Jessel, who was very kind, took me through the pass door and put me in a box seat. I never forgot that.

The Jazz Singer was not only a stage hit all over the U.S. but saved the fortunes of Warner Brothers film studio by being the first talking picture. It was taken for granted that George Jessel would play in the film the role he had created on the stage, but then there was an item in *Variety,* the theatrical trade paper. The part would be played by Al Jolson. Jolson was my hero but I felt badly that Jessel should be brushed off. The Warners were afraid to take a gamble on a comparative unknown, while Jolson was guaranteed box-office. Jolson wanted $25,000. The Warners, near bankruptcy, offered him a percentage, a piece of the action. No, Jolson not only wanted the money, he wanted it "up front," meaning he got his full salary as soon as the contract was signed.

Jolson was Jolson and Warner Brothers needed him more than he needed them; they raised the money. The irony is that if Jolson had accepted the percentage deal he would have made millions. In Baltimore, at the Metropolitan, which normally changed films every week, *The Jazz Singer* ran nineteen weeks and I saw it four times.

When I wasn't watching films, I was playing the mouth-organ in a band led by Fred Sonnen, who worked for the Hohner Company, who made the instruments. We practiced at the City Hall, where I discovered that the men's toilet was great for acoustics. My playing sounded livelier and more resonant than it did in the hall. I raised my hand to be allowed "to leave the room" as often as I dared. Sonnen had us playing in four-part harmony from instruction books which we had to buy, and we also had to buy the mouth-organs. I would go by streetcar to the rehearsals. There was a wooden seat, near the motorman, that held three. I always tried to get that seat because I liked the sensation of almost being the driver. If I got it, I'd take out the mouth-organ and begin practicing. This ensured that I had the seat to myself all the way downtown; it must have driven the motorman nuts.

Once, on a crowded streetcar, somebody got up, making a seat vacant near me, which I made a dive for. Then I realized that a Boy Scout had got up to give his seat to a lady. Embarrassed, I retreated, while the scout favored me with a smile which I could draw right now. Never did I try to be a Boy Scout. I was delighted with Jack

Benny's description of a scout troop: "Twelve little kids dressed like *schmucks* following a big *schmuck* dressed like a kid."

Sonnen sold the *Evening Sun* and the mayor on sponsoring a mouth-organ contest, which I entered. I have said that I started to play the mouth-organ at fourteen. But a press cutting exists, a photo of me at nine, entered in a mouth-organ competition. There it is and I have no memory of it. There were preliminary heats, held in the schools, and I got to the finals. As the day drew near I developed an abscessed tooth and my jaw looked as if I were chewing on a baseball but nothing was going to keep me from those finals. I remembered how I'd lost the singing contest by developing a cold. Maybe both instances were psychosomatic but nobody knew that word yet and certainly my aching tooth and swollen jaw were both real and painful.

In the finals there was one winner for the boys and one for the girls. They would be Baltimore's male and female champions. Then they could compete against each other and the victor would be the Maryland *State* Champion, or champeen. (I didn't know there was any other way to pronounce it.)

I played the Minuet in G by Beethoven, because it was easy. The notes lay right next to each other, no jumping about; the middle section was more complicated so I skipped it.

The other kids played popular tunes, like "Black Bottom" or "St. Louis Blues." The judges included Gustav Strube, conductor and, in fact, founder of the Baltimore Symphony Orchestra. I could see that my Beethoven Minuet impressed him. I *know* that two other boys played a lot better than I did; Melvin Vogel, who had a much cleaner technique and a purer tone, and Jerome Flinkman, whose "St. Louis Blues" delighted the audience.

After the judges conferred, Gustav Strube addressed the audience:

"Ve haf given de avord," he said, "to Lorenz Cecil Aidler mit an average of ninety-nine und nine tents." He shrugged, apologetically. "No von is pairfect."

It wasn't a popular win. No one actually booed but I sensed a murmur of discontent. Based on applause, Flinkman should have won with Vogel second. Mind you, with my abscessed tooth I rated an award for stoic heroism.

Then there was the play-off against the winner of the girls' section, but that was easy. I received a medal for winning the boys' section and a silver-plated cup for being State Champion.

Next day it was in the *Sun,* photo and all, and that made it official.
Of course, my fame went to my head; whereas before I had been
obnoxious, I was now unbearable. At the harmonica band rehearsals,
I acted as if I were Sonnen himself, giving orders, advising others
how best to play a particular piece. My fellow members, perhaps in
awe of a winner, let me get away with it but they must have loathed
me.

The letdown came later. There was another mouth-organ contest
at the Hippodrome Theater, this one with cash prizes. I entered,
figuring I was sure to win. The winner was chosen by applause and
you don't have to be psychic to predict the results: first Jerome
Flinkman; second Melvin Vogel; third Lawrence Cecil Adler. Flinkman and Vogel were very kind and considerate. They tried to con-
sole me, telling me that this contest wasn't important. What mattered
was that I was still champion of Maryland. It was good of them and
I was grateful, but it hurt just the same, more so because I knew that
they were better players than I.

A few weeks later a friend of mine named Bernard Needle called
me up. He lived on Mondawmin Avenue, which, though only one
block above Bryant where I lived, was a smarter neighborhood,
more of a boulevard with the two sides of the street separated by a
grassy area where the rich kids played: I envied them that little
stretch of grass. Bernard said that a musician from New York, a
friend of the family, was at his house. Why didn't I bring my mouth-
organ over? I did.

The friend was Nat Brusiloff, the lead violinist at NBC. He heard
me play and said: "You're okay, kid. If you ever come to New York,
look me up." He didn't know what he was letting himself in for.

CHAPTER
Two

*I*BADLY WANTED TO GO to New York. I had seen a poster for the New York show *Good Boy* that starred Helen Kane, and Borrah Minevitch and His Harmonica Rascals were also in it. I'd never seen him perform, but if you played the mouth-organ, you knew who Minevitch was. He had formed a band and created a great act, using the astonishing mime of Johnny Puleo, a dwarf whose eyes expressed more pathos than Chaplin's.

I had money that my parents knew nothing about. I had accumulated about $35, mainly from selling subscriptions to *Liberty,* but also from the odd amateur contest or singing in a nightclub. I went to Union Station and got on a train to New York without telling my parents. At the end of the four-hour ride I got off at Pennsylvania Station and phoned Nat Brusiloff who was in and, in keeping with his word, had to invite me over. He made me phone home; my parents arrived next day but I refused to go back, saying that I'd just run away again. They had already spoken to Dr. Friedenwald, the family doctor, who advised them to let me stay. I was sensitive, he said, highly nervous—what today we'd call neurotic—

and forcing me home could bring on a nervous breakdown. They didn't want *that!* I stayed.

Brusiloff arranged an audition for me with Minevitch, backstage at the Manhattan Theater during a matinee of *Good Boy.* While I waited I stood in the wings and heard Helen Kane sing "I Wanna Be Loved by You." She was unique: she invented baby-voiced singing and her "boop-boop-a-boop" at the end of a phrase was a boon to impersonators and as recognizable as Cantor's big eyes.

Puleo and other members of the band stood in the doorway of Minevitch's dressing room while I played to the great man himself. I chose Minuet in G, the piece with which I'd won the mouth-organ competition in Baltimore. Minevitch scowled at me with obvious irritation, which was no help, and when I had finished, said simply, "Kid, you stink."

People have suggested that I was too good and that Minevitch didn't want competition. I'd like to think that too but I don't. Several of his boys could play better than me: Leo Diamond, later a famous soloist; Freddie Zimbalist; and Ernie Morris, the black player, who had the finest tone I ever heard on a mouth-organ. So it wasn't that. I think it was that I didn't produce the Minevitch sound, which depended on a throat vibrato. I never liked that sound, I wouldn't have used it, and I never would have fit in.

Minevitch was really doing me a favor. He paid his boys $18 a week, under scale, but the Musician's Union didn't recognize the mouth-organ so Minevitch could get away with it. Had he accepted me I'd have become used to being part of a group and it would probably have taken me a long time to become a soloist. Minevitch *made* me become a soloist, the first ever, but I didn't know that then. The "you stink" dazed me. I was near to crying. Puleo came in.

"Borrah," he said, "why don't you let the kid come on with us for the night show?"

"Aah, get him out of here," said Minevitch. Puleo and the other boys assured me that I played very well indeed. I was grateful to them but their words didn't help. I was lousy: an expert had said so.

It was back to Baltimore, and when I left Minevitch that was where I was headed. But my stuff was at Nat Brusiloff's, he was at NBC working, and it would be rude just to walk out. I got on a streetcar and sat there, thinking that I was fourteen and already through in show business. At 44th and Broadway I noticed the marquee of the

New York Paramount. The attraction was Rudy Vallee and His Connecticut Yankees. Vallee was the most famous singer of his time, people who think that mob hysteria over the Jaggers, Presleys, the various Donnys, Rods, Sonnys and Bobs is something new should have seen the reaction to Vallee. It took police guards to get him out of the theater: the girls tried to tear his clothes off. *In* the theatre they screamed, fainted and wet their pants. *Plus ça change.*

I got off the streetcar, went to the Paramount stage door, sneaked past the doorman and started walking up the stairs. It was a long walk before I found Vallee—he was on the twelfth floor. His dressing room door was open and he was making up for the next show. He saw me.

"What do you want, kid?" he asked.

I told him I played the mouth-organ.

"Look, kid, I'm just the master of ceremonies here—what you want is an agent."

However he did agree to listen to me.

"Tell you what," he said, "you come back tonight and I'll put you on at my club."

Wow! I couldn't wait to tell this to Brusiloff, who was equally excited, though he said that if he ever met Minevitch he'd kick his nuts in.

That night I called for Vallee. We left the theater with police protection all the way and it was needed because girls were completely blocking 44th Street. We went to the Villa Vallee on the East Side. There was another mob waiting for Vallee but his guards got us inside.

Vallee told me to hang around, he'd tell me when to go on. A musician got me some coffee. His name was Paul Denniker, the composer of one of Vallee's hits, "S'posin." (Vallee's biggest hit was "I'm Just a Vagabond Lover" to which Ring Lardner pointed out that "vagabond" meant "bum.")

At about 11:30 Denniker said: "The boss says go on now." The band was off the stand, the lights were up, there was a lot of talking. It was no way to go on but, as nobody was going to announce me, I walked out and began to play. (In those days there were no microphones, Vallee sang through a cardboard megaphone.) Nobody heard me and, when I finished playing, no one applauded. Zero.

I'd had my chance and I'd ruined it. I just left the club by myself. But I didn't feel too bad, certainly not the way I'd felt after the Minevitch audition. Vallee had noticed me, put me on, and Vallee was a *name.* I forgot about returning to Baltimore.

Brusiloff wasn't too surprised when I reported the evening to him. "You wait, kid," he said, "he'll be on his knees to get you back."

Brusiloff had good news. He was booked to conduct the music for a sound cartoon, *Pony Boy.* Toward the end a song was flashed on the screen, with a little white ball bouncing from word to word, guiding the audience as they sang. ("Follow the bouncing ball" was already a showbiz cliché.) The cartoon character played the mouth-organ and Brusiloff had got me the synchronizing job.

I knew the tune and couldn't wait for recording day. The studio was in the Paramount Theater Building and I noticed that the head-liner was now Paul Ash, who was famous for discovering talent. Among his discoveries was Ginger Rogers.

The synchronizing was easy and took two hours, for which I got $10, my first salary. When I left the studio I started down the stairs, hunting for Paul Ash.

I found him in Vallee's former dressing room. He knew who I was.

"Nat Brusiloff told me about you," he said. "Let's hear you play something."

When I finished playing ("When Day Is Done," a bit of ass-kissing as it was Ash's best-known hit), he took me up to the office of Jack Partington, the producer of the Paramount "units." (A unit was a bill of five acts plus a line of girls: this bill would travel all over the States playing the Paramount theaters.)

"Jack," said Ash to Mr. Partington, "you said you were short an act for a unit. Here's your act."

Partington didn't even audition me. If Ash okayed me . . .

Ash told me to get an agent and recommended Lou Irwin. With the prestige of Ash's name behind me, Irwin, with his office in the Bond Building on Broadway, saw me at once, and when he found that I already had a job, that he didn't even need to book me, he was delighted. He sent an assistant, Ben Lundy, back to the Paramount office with me and Lundy negotiated a forty-four-week contract for me at $100 a week, ten percent to be paid to the Lou Irwin Agency. In 1928 that was *money.*

In the office of Lou Irwin, I heard Ethel Zimmerman having a fit;
she was making a short subject at Warner Bros., they wanted her to
do a number in a tiger skin and she was shouting fortissimo she
wouldn't do no goddam number in no goddam tiger skin. I don't
know if she ever did the number or not: she later changed her name,
dropping the "Zim" part and leaving "Merman."

I was under age, of course, and it was illegal for me to be working,
but no questions were asked at Paramount. (A minor had to travel
with a parent and a tutor before he could get a work permit and the
Gerry Society existed to see that children weren't exploited. I
wanted to be exploited like crazy.)

I started to rehearse with the unit which was due to open in New
Haven. A unit was sandwiched between showings of a film; if the film
was popular, the unit might do five or six shows a day, as I had to
do with the Mae West film, *She Done Him Wrong*.

The units rehearsed for ten days on the tenth floor of the Paramount Building. One day Boris Morros came to see a rehearsal.
Morros was in charge of the entire Paramount unit operation, he had
an accent that would make a Jewish dialect comic sound like Basil
Rathbone. Later he was charged with being a double agent for the
U.S. and the USSR. I can't imagine any self-respecting espionage
system employing Boris. With that accent?

For some reason I resented auditioning for Morros. Instead of
doing my act properly, I coasted through it, holding the mouth-
organ in one hand, the other resting nonchalantly in my trouser
pocket. Morros listened to me and I could see horror mount on his
face.

"Check," he said to Jack Partington. "Who is dot keed? He
steenks." (It's amazing how often I heard that phrase used about
me.)

Partington, who thought I had talent, spoke rapidly to Morros, I
could not hear his words.

"Check," said Morros. "Are you trying to roon me? Get dot bum
out of here. I tell you, he steenks!"

Somehow Partington saved my job but he gave me hell after the
rehearsal. We opened in New Haven.

That is where I found out I was a snob. The chorus, the stage
manager and the smaller acts stayed in a boarding house while the
headlining act stayed in a hotel. Though I was the lowest-paid act on

the bill, I registered at the same hotel as the headliners used. I just didn't want to feel inferior to *anybody.*

Although it was exciting being in show business, having a long contract, I soon realized that five-a-day, let alone six, could be monotonous. We rehearsed with the pit band (we played a different city each week) on Monday. Once you'd rehearsed, that was your routine, and it couldn't be changed without another rehearsal, which you weren't going to get. My act had two numbers, "When Day Is Done" and "I Wanna Be Loved by You," and after two days of playing those two I got very tired of them.

At first Partington had me come out carrying a double-bass case, out of which I'd take a cello case, then a trombone case and finally a harmonica box, out of which I'd take a mouth-organ. Doesn't sound hilarious, does it? It wasn't. In fact, it was a flop.

Then Bill Clark thought up the gimmick of making me a local boy in whatever town we played, and for the master of ceremonies to say that he had found me outside the stage door, shining shoes and playing the mouth-organ. Each theater had its own M.C. Dick Powell was the resident in Pittsburgh; Vallee and Ash played the Paramount in New York and Brooklyn. Each would build up sympathy for me: "C'mon, give this little kid a great big hand, wuddia say folks, he's one of your very own." I would come on twisting myself into contortions of shyness and begin to play. There wasn't a dry seat in the house. As a local boy I mopped up and got more applause than anyone else on the bill. I think Bill Clark regretted his bright idea. I believed that all the applause was for my talent; I was benefiting from a sympathetic buildup but was so big-headed I didn't realize it. Revolting stuff but it couldn't miss. I was a local boy in forty-four cities, except Baltimore, where, I argued, I *was* a local boy and could imagine the raspberries from my classmates if they were given that "discovered bootblack" crap.

As the smallest act I got the smallest billing and never saw my name in lights—until Rockford, Illinois. There the theater had a huge marquee, big enough for the film title, the stars and every act. So my name was in lights and I wanted to photograph it. "Wait until it gets dark," said Ross. "It looks better lit up." I took his advice. But then someone discovered that a Ruth Etting short was on the bill. My name came down and Miss Etting's went up. So there is no record of the first time my name was in lights. That name was

Lawrence Adler; I don't know when I became "Larry." Maybe I figured there was more chance of getting in lights with a shorter name.

The headliners were Clark and Samuels, a comedy team. Bill Clark was almost as good a joke-teller as Lou Holtz, which is high praise. Lou Holtz was *the* Jewish comic; never vulgar nor did he ever stoop to the cheap laugh; he had real class. Bill Clark was like an uncle to me: made sure I ate regularly, reminded me to write home and guided me to a Jewish restaurant in the days when keeping kosher was still important to me. The Jewish habits, if not the real religion, hung on a long time. I would feel slightly guilty doing shows on Friday night or Saturday afternoons, the Jewish Sabbath, and very guilty when I did shows on the important Jewish holidays, especially *Rosh Hashanah* and *Yom Kippur,* the Day of Atonement. I tried to fast but I couldn't go the distance. I started out fine on *Yom Kippur* eve but next day, with fasting going on until sundown, I was weak with hunger by the second show of the day. I went out between shows and had a steak, waited for lightning to strike, it didn't, so I had dessert and coffee as well.

In the Paramount unit there was a brother and sister tap-dancing act called Peter and Zelda. Peter was, to hear him tell it, the greatest stud since Casanova. Curiously, he never scored with any of the chorus girls. (Both Bill Clark and Fred Samuels did better there.) He was short, blond and ferret-faced. I was in awe of his sophistication and sexual prowess. He would go to the red-light district in every town we played and his account never varied. The girl was nuts about him, so much so that she never let him pay. I waited for him to tell me that the girl ended up paying *him* but even Peter never went that far.

In New Orleans Peter and I walked through the red-light district. He talked to two black girls. I was amazed as, being from Baltimore, I had never spoken socially to any black—Negroes, they were called then: "black" would have been considered an insult—and just stood there. One of the girls tried to talk to me. Pointing to Peter she said, "What he do?" I told her he was a dancer. "Can you dance?" She measured me the way Jack Dempsey might have measured Luis Firpo.

"Ah kin *fuck,*" she said, leaning on the last word for emphasis. I reeled back and hit my head against a brick wall. I had never heard a girl swear before. Peter went off with his girl while mine, figuring

me for a dead loss, walked away. Had I followed through, I wouldn't have known what to do.

I had a real adventure at the Horn and Hardart restaurant near Times Square during our week at the New York Paramount. I went there after the last show and ordered corn flakes. (I was still trying to observe the kosher food laws.) Two girls sitting at a table overheard me as I gave the order and they burst out laughing.

"Little baby wants his corn flakes," one said, giggling. "C'mon over, little baby, and eat your corn flakes."

Oh boy, I was being picked up! I joined them, tongue-tied with embarrassment but excited too. They wouldn't let me pay the bill— I did try—and we left together, walking up Broadway, past the theaters. (The big hit was Noel Coward's *Cavalcade* and the advertisement read *"Cavalcade*—pronounced success," which must have confused foreigners.)

One girl left us and the other led me to her apartment. She undressed, so did I, I got into bed with her and had no idea what happened next. (As Sammy Cahn writes, "This is my first affair, so what goes where?") She must have been a very nice girl; she could have made fun of me, but didn't. She gave me a condom, but that killed whatever passion I might have felt. Again, she was sympathetic; she gave me her name and phone number and I left. When I told Nat Brusiloff what had happened, he called the girl, who came over. Nat screwed her while I watched in amazement. He then told me to take the girl home, which I did. Now I knew what to do, but there was no joy or excitement. It was too impersonal.

Back to New Orleans. I walked through the red-light district, girls sat at their windows or on verandas and said things like "Come in, honey." I thought them friendly and hospitable but was too scared to accept. After all, we hadn't been introduced.

On the way back to the theater a black man called to me from a doorway.

"Come on in, boy, and lemme suck 'at prick." This was so terrifying that I ran all the way back to the theater.

That was quite a week. On Saturday, the last day in New Orleans, the cast of *Radio Romance* joined with the acts on the bill at the Keith Orpheum Theater to hire a sexual circus. As I was not yet fifteen, I was allowed to come along without paying—my first freebie.

The cast was all black. There was straight fucking, lesbian sex, homosexual fucking (I remember that the man playing the passive role wore a grass skirt, which was endearing) and there was a donkey and a woman. She lay on a table, the donkey was guided to mount and enter the woman. For an encore some of the girls smoked cigarettes genitally—it can't be that easy. We put rolled-up dollar bills on the table edge and the girls would pick them up the same way they smoked the cigarettes. I was roused by all this flaunted sex but could do nothing about it. Very frustrating,

In Toledo I was asked to play at a high school assembly. I met a very attractive girl and invited her to see my show and have dinner. She wanted to bring a girl friend along so I asked Peter along to join us. He rented a car and, the night of the date, had a box of chocolates with him which he gave to me and asked me to pass around. He leered at me and I was suspicious; why that leer? I didn't offer the candy. Peter made a pass but was rebuffed. I wouldn't have dreamed of making a pass at mine.

After we had taken the girls home, Peter shouted at me.

"You goddamn fool, I spent twenty-five *bucks* on that stuff."

I looked at him. "Twenty-five bucks on *candy?*"

"Of course not, ya dumb bastard, for Spanish Fly."

Spanish Fly! Peter must have been insane. These were under-age girls, or as they were called then, jailbait. (Spanish Fly was supposed to be an aphrodisiac; that fable has long since exploded, but I didn't know that then. It *was* a drug and a dangerous one.) I kept the candy and put it in a drawer in my hotel room.

Next week we were in Cleveland. Peter asked me what I'd done with the candy. The candy! Oh my God, I'd left it in the hotel drawer. The unit that was behind us featured a Chinese tenor, Jue Fong. I phoned him at the Toledo Paramount. Fong said he'd go to the hotel, get the candy and destroy it. When I phoned him back later that day he told me that the candy wasn't there.

I bought the Toledo papers the rest of that week, expecting a story about a randy chambermaid raping six bellboys. No such story appeared and I never learned what happened to the candy.

In Chicago, where we played at the Oriental Theater, Bill Clark told me, the last night of the date, that a party was going on at the Croydon Hotel for all the showbiz people in town. I went along. A man came over and asked me how old I was and where I came from.

"You're a Yid, right?" he asked. I said yes, I was Jewish.

"Thought so. I can always tell. I'm Catholic myself. Ya go to *shule?*" No, I said, I didn't go to synagogue. He looked pained, wanted to know why not. I said that we did five or six shows on weekends, to get up early to go to synagogue would knock me out. He didn't like my answer. He asked if my parents were with me. No, I said, they're in Baltimore.

"But ya write to 'em every day, right?"

No, I said, maybe once a week, or every two weeks.

"Hoddia like that," he said, almost angrily, "what kind of kid are you, anyway? Look, kid, getcha coat, gowwan back to your hotel, this ain't no party for a kid like you anyway. When ya get back, siddown and write a letter to your mother and father, right?" I agreed.

"Suppin else," he said. "This Saturday you're gonna go to *shule,* I don't give a damn how many shows you got to do, right?" I nodded yes, got away from the man and asked Bill Clark who he was. Clark looked at me.

"Aw, come on, you're *kidding!*"

No, I said, I wasn't kidding. Who was the guy?

"Al Capone," said Clark.

Capone spoke to me again before I left. He told me he went to Mass every Sunday, then sent his mother flowers. He asked whether I sent my mother flowers. I said she was in Baltimore.

"So? Ya never heard of Western Union, ya can't wire 'em?"

Then he told me something that had happened recently. One of his men had shot and killed a man in daylight, on State Street, and there were several witnesses prepared to testify. It looked as if Capone's man would get a first-degree murder conviction, which carried an automatic death penalty.

"So," said Capone, "I had to get to the jury, right?" He found a bribable juror, paid him $25,000 to hold out for, not first-degree murder, but manslaughter, which carried a two- to twenty-year prison sentence. The jury, which was out for three days, brought in a verdict of manslaughter. Capone gave a banquet for the juror— "cost me another twenty-five G's"—and said to him: "How did you do it? I never thought you'd get away with manslaughter."

"Oh boy," said the juror, "you don't know what a dumb buncha bastards I hadda put up with—they wanted to *acquit* 'im."

I never saw Capone again but my memory is of a rather kindly Sicilian face, a gentle manner and a willingness to concern himself

with the religious habits of a fifteen-year-old kid. Other people see
him differently. But when the mayor of Chicago needed to have an
absolutely clean election, no corpses voting, no double entries, he
had to send for Capone, the only man who could do it.

After two tours I figured I had enough experience to get away
from that bootblack routine, I thought I was about ready to try being
a "class" act. So I had a smart double-breasted suit made, put together some classy patter and was booked at the Scollay Square
Theater in Boston. The first thing I got was stage fright. Though I'd
been in show business two years, I'd never before walked on cold,
without an M.C. to give me a buildup. That was the big difference
between cine-variety and straight music-hall. The two-a-day was the
test of how good you were. The act preceding me finished, my
introductory music began and I was on.

It was Disasterville. If there's such a thing as no personality, that's
what I had.

"Only connect," says E. M. Forster. Wuddia mean *only?* I *couldn't*
connect with that audience. If my music left them cold, my patter
made them hostile. Nobody threw anything nor was I booed but this
indifference was, in a way, worse. I was a flop and I knew it. All I
was doing was making things tough for the next act, which would
have to cope with the bad mood I was creating. My act came to its
finish ("Born in Baltimore, died in Boston," I thought to myself) and
I exited to nearly no applause at all.

The theater manager came backstage to my dressing room. I was
a young kid, he tried to let me down easily.

"You know how it is, kid, sometimes a bill is over-long, probably
our fault, booking one act too many, we're going to have to make
cuts. You know, we're not allowed overtime here."

Pure bullshit, I was sure. I knew what was coming.

"It's like, kid, well, you're really too good for them, they don't
understand that clever stuff, like, y'know?"

Yeah, sure, I knew. He was saying, politely, that he wanted me
out of his theater, preferably immediately, and probably had already
phoned New York for a replacement. So, that was that. End of class
act, end of double-breasted suit, end of sophisticated patter.

That was also the end of two-a-day straight vaudeville for me. Back
to the movie houses, with an M.C. to give me a buildup, which I
needed. You can guess what the buildup was. It was about the local

boy. "We found him outside shining shoes, wuddia say, folks, let's have a great big hand for your own hometown kid."

The worst of the Scollay Square debacle was that I wasn't even paid for the week, just for the one show I did. I was given one-twelfth of my full salary.

Much later, in 1939, I came back to the U.S. having made a big reputation in the UK. However, despite the occasional column mention and generally good reports about my British successes reported in the trade papers such as *Variety, Billboard* and *Zit's,* the public neither knew me nor knew about me.

And again, learning nothing from experience, I had the idea that I needed a class act, some witty patter. I just didn't think an American audience would keep quiet for a solo mouth-organist. I needed a writer, the wittiest, the funniest I could find. To me that meant S. J. Perelman, whom I'd been reading for years, since he did wood-cuts with captions such as, "I've got Bright's Disease and he has mine."

I located Perelman's agent, a lady, and this charmer was amenable to my suggestion that Perelman write for me. Her terms turned out to be fifteen percent of my earnings. For life. And whether or not I used Perelman's material. Well, the hell with that. I decided to approach Perelman direct and he was much nicer than his agent. He'd do me some material for a straight $1500. That was fine but Sid Perelman's material turned out to be literally unspeakable. It was wonderful to read, impossible to say. (Groucho Marx later said to me, "I could've saved you a bundle, kid. We always had to rewrite Sid.")

I can only remember one line. It had to do with me describing a young lady who attracted me. Perelman had written: "She was wearing a slim-pin Bemberg corselette, well-boned over the diaphragm." *You* try saying that!

The smart patter went just about as well in 1940 as it had at the Scollay Square Theater.

In 1929 I worked at the Palace. Gus Edwards stuck me in at the end of his act. I was a big hit, if I say so myself, and by now I'm about the only one left to say it. The bill had, besides Gus Edwards and his kiddies, Bill (Bojangles) Robinson, Ruth Etting and Lou Holtz. Holtz followed the Gus Edwards act, which meant he followed me.

I stopped the show on the first house, Monday, and was happily taking bow after bow. Gus Edwards, in the wings, said: "You'd better play them another chorus." I had already played two choruses of "If I had a Girl Like You," one of the songs Rudy Vallee featured. Holtz was in the wings and was getting impatient.

"Kid, go back in there, make a thank-you speech and get the hell off. Do you want me to stand here all day?"

I went back out and made a thank-you speech, all right. I seem to have said something like, "I'd like to play more for you but Lou Holtz is waiting to go on, and he's *fuming!*" which couldn't have endeared me to Mr. Holtz.

A few days later I passed Dave's Blue Room, on Seventh Avenue. It was a hangout for show people and columnists. I'd heard of it and read about it but had never been inside. I was afraid to go in. A man came out, he looked very prosperous.

"You the kid who plays the mouth-organ with Gus Edwards?" he asked.

I was recognized! The man was Dave of Dave's Blue Room and he said that there was someone who wanted to meet me.

I went in and Dave introduced me to a tiny man, hardly more than five feet high. "Hiya, kid," he said, "I caught your show, you were great. Seen this?" He showed me a show-business column, about me, my first big publicity. The columnist had caught the show where I made the remark about Lou Holtz and he'd run it.

I was delighted to get all this space but felt I should look as though this happened to me all the time. Pointing to the offending quote, I said, "I'd like to see the guy who wrote that!"

The little man smiled. "You would, eh? Okay, you're seeing him."

He was Sidney Skolsky, who wrote a column for the New York *Daily News,* the paper with the largest circulation in the U.S., very right-wing. Sidney and I became friends, he gave me column mentions from then on. Later he moved to Hollywood, ending each column: "But don't get me wrong, I love Hollywood."

In a world that had such characters as Walter Winchell, Skolsky was an anachronism. Everybody liked him, everyone trusted him and I've never heard that he betrayed that trust. It was Skolsky's idea to make a film about the life and career of Al Jolson. In *The Jolson Story* the part of Jolson was played, with amazing accuracy, by Larry Parks with Al Jolson himself providing the sound track (and appearing in one scene on the runway at the Winter Garden Theater on Broadway). Parks was set to become a star but it was his bad luck to be the first well-known actor to be called before the Un-American Activities Committee. He gave names to the committee but despite that he never got clearance nor really worked in films again.

Skolsky, in his column about me, remarked on my resemblance to Eddie Cantor. Cantor came to the Palace Theater to see my act and also, perhaps, to check for possible libel. He decided I *did* look like him—I still do. He talked Gus into letting me go on tour with him.

Cantor had five daughters—he made jokes about it—and that was why he wanted me in his act. I don't think I even played the mouthorgan; Cantor just wanted to make a joke. I came on, in Western Union uniform, and handed him a telegram. He looked at me, did a double take, and said to the audience: "Hey, this kid looks like me! How old are you, son?"

"I'm fifteen, sir."

Cantor would count on his fingers, murmuring to himself. Then: "Where you from, son?"

"I'm from Baltimore, sir."

More counting, more murmuring. "No, I was in Seattle."

For that one lousy joke Eddie Cantor paid me $125 a week—and this was in 1929!

I worked as Cantor's Western Union boy stooge at the Mastbaum Theater in Philadelphia, the largest in the U.S. (it was before Radio City), and at the Steel Pier in Atlantic City. My final date with him was at the RKO Theater in Brooklyn.

On the same bill, at the RKO, was Gus Edwards's kiddie revue with the same kids I had worked with at the Palace in New York. Well, I had to be a big shot. I bragged that Cantor was paying me $500 a week. The kids believed me, and complained to Gus Edwards, how come *they* weren't paid five C's a week? Edwards told Cantor and I was fired.

It was humiliating. I couldn't hide my disgrace. It was my own fault. Cantor had treated me with great kindness. I wish I hadn't been so stupid—I could have learned from a star like Eddie Cantor.

Around this time, when I was still in my teens, I developed a crush on Vera Milton, a British showgirl in the Earl Carroll *Vanities* at the

New Amsterdam Theater in Times Square, where the legend over the stage door read: "Through these portals pass the most beautiful girls in the world." I took her to a party at the Park Central Hotel where our host was the famous gambler/gangster Arnold Rothstein. (When Rothstein was shot and killed in his suite in the hotel, the legend was that all the lights in the sign went out save for "AR.") At about three A.M. Vera and I left the party and got a taxi. "Where to?" I asked Vera, hoping she'd invite me to her place. "Stage door of the New Amsterdam," she said. "Vera, it's three A.M.!" "Do as I say," she said. When we arrived she left the cab, went to a small car and rapped on the window. Someone, half-asleep, crawled out. "Who's that?" I whispered to Vera. "Hubby," she answered. Hubby looked at me and didn't like what he saw.

"This is a hell of a time to be running around the streets with a man."

"But, darling," said Vera, "it's not a *man*—it's *Larry*!"

Then I met Dorothy Fox. I was fifteen or sixteen at the time and I took Dorothy out for nearly a year. I wasn't making much money but I was still able to take her to expensive places. In the early thirties, a lot of hotels and clubs would have what they called "celebrity nights." The idea was that the celebrity would get up and do a number and, *noblesse oblige,* he wasn't given a bill. I got to know the routine, which place had a celebrity night and when, and I would take Dorothy. Sometimes there would be more than one place a night; the St. Moritz Roof, where they had Leon Belasco and his orchestra, and later, the Central Park Casino where the band was led by Leo Reisman but the real attraction was his pianist, Eddy Duchin. I was taking no risk by going with Dorothy to these places; I would always be called on by the M.C. to play a number. Sometimes I wouldn't get Dorothy home till three A.M. or later.

One day Dorothy called me from Neponset, Long Island, where her parents had a summer home, and suggested I come out for the weekend. I took the train and was met at the station by the family car and chauffeur. Dorothy's parents seemed less cordial than usual and I wondered why they'd asked me to come. After lunch Dorothy's father suggested we go for a drive. I sat in front with the chauffeur, Dorothy and her father sat in back.

"Larry," called Mr. Fox and I turned around to find him pointing a pistol at me. It didn't scare me, it just seemed silly.

"What's that for?" I asked.

"Dorothy is pregnant," he said.

"Well, why point a gun at me? Please put it away." Through all this the chauffeur kept his eyes on the road.

I told Mr. Fox that, if she were indeed pregnant, we would get married. Then came the kicker.

"Dorothy," he said, "is fourteen."

Oh, wow! Fourteen! I had no idea of that. Dorothy had the body of a girl of eighteen. If she were fourteen, why had they allowed her to stay out so late? They never criticized me for bringing her home late, nor had they ever given Dorothy a hard time over it.

It turned out Dorothy wasn't pregnant, so marriage wasn't necessary. To my surprise, Dorothy was allowed to go out with me as before, no pressure, no questions. However, we were a lot more careful from then on.

In many ways the best manager I ever had was Gus Edwards. It was Gus who, in 1931, got me the audition that led to my being in Ziegfeld's *Smiles.* The show starred Marilyn Miller and the Astaires, Fred and his sister Adele. For support there were Eddie Foy, Jr., Tom Howard and Harriette Lake. Miss Lake didn't last long; her song, "Blue Bowery," was too well received in Boston, where the show had its road try-out. Marilyn Miller told Ziegfeld that she wanted Miss Lake out and out she was. She went to Hollywood, changed her name to Ann Sothern and became more famous than Miss Miller.

"Blue Bowery" was a beautiful song which was dropped from the show along with the hapless Miss Lake. The score was by Vincent Youmans, who would show up for the musical rehearsals, lie down on a bench and go to sleep. He suggested that one of his songs, "I'm Glad I Waited," be my solo. It worked well on the mouth-organ and in fact was a show-stopper. (Apparently Marilyn Miller felt no threat from the mouth-organ because she didn't complain.) One day, I got a telegram from Mr. Ziegfeld. I was backstage, Mr. Ziegfeld was in front directing a rehearsal, but he had a passion for sending telegrams. Mr. Ziegfeld told me that Vincent Youmans wanted the ballad sung by Marilyn Miller and Paul Gregory in the first act as a reprise. There was no place for the song to be sung again, so Ziegfeld suggested that I use it to replace "I'm Glad I Waited."

"Mr. Ziegfeld, you're the boss and if you want me to change my solo, I'll have to. But it stops the show every night and that other one—well, it's pretty dreary."

"Suit yourself, kid," said Ziegfeld—I don't think he ever knew my name. "I agree with you. I just thought I'd try and please Vince."

The tune I rejected was "Time on My Hands," which, as the world knows, is pretty dreary.

With Harriette Lake fired, my number and one by the Astaires were the only ones to stop the show. The Astaires did their famous run-around, in which they just ran around the stage in rhythm. Doesn't sound like much but it was thrilling. I did a duet with Fred, "Young Man of Manhattan," in which he used his walking-stick as a machine-gun to mow down his fellow dancers and, finally, me. (It was that duet that gave me the idea, years later, to team up with the tap-dancer Paul Draper.)

Smiles was a mess. The story, about a Salvation Army lass who Does Good, was feeble and the dialogue was dreadful. Ring Lardner was sent for to doctor the show. After three days and nights, with nothing much happening, Ziegfeld said, "Ring, if we don't lick this book into shape, the whole goddamn show is going to be stolen by the kid with the mouth-organ."

"That," replied Lardner, "would be petty larceny."

Lardner did better out of the show than the rest of us. He used his experiences to create a portrait of Ziegfeld in the story, "A Day with Conrad Green," that made Ziegfeld a heartless monster who cheated his employees out of their salaries. Maybe. I never knew that side of Ziegfeld.

While we were rehearsing *Smiles,* I developed a crush on a chorus girl called Marian. (There were chorus girls and show girls in those days. The latter acted and were treated like stars—after all, Ziegfeld's slogan on each show was "Glorifying the American girl"—got big salaries, some as much as $500 a week, and all they ever had to do was stand still and look gorgeous. The chorus girls had to dance.) Marian had a virginal beauty and a shyness that brought out the protector in me—I was seventeen. Marian was unlike the other girls —I never heard her swear. I felt it was my duty to keep her away from the Broadway wolves. When we opened at the Shubert Theater in Boston, I would take Marian out every night for "night-lunch," then I would walk her back to her hotel and say good night. I never made a pass, it would have seemed like sacrilege. Marian liked me and seemed grateful for the attention.

We came into New York and had a week's rehearsal before opening at the Ziegfeld Theater on Sixth Avenue. (This was 1931 and Sixth Avenue had not yet graduated to being called Avenue of the Americas. I still call it "Sixth Avenue." Imagine hailing a cab, being in a hurry and saying: "Go to 57th Street and Avenue of the Americas.") The third day of rehearsal Marian didn't show up. Two of the show girls were her friends, one of them, Virginia Bruce, was later to become an MGM film star. The other, Gertrude Dahl, was a tough broad. I asked Virginia if she'd seen Marian anywhere: she looked at me oddly and, without answering, walked away. I found Gertrude Dahl and asked her if she'd seen Marian. Gertrude snarled at me, "Fa krissake, you kidding?" and started to cry. I didn't know what was going on. We broke for coffee and, on a news-stand, I saw a headline in the *Graphic* (Bernard MacFadden's paper, a scandal sheet). "LEGS" SHOT IN CHORINE'S BED, it read. I knew before I bought the paper who the "chorine" was going to be. Marian was called "Kiki" in the story. She was the mistress of Jack "Legs" Diamond, had been for a long time. Diamond had indeed been shot while in bed with Marian; he wasn't seriously hurt. Marian never showed up again in *Smiles* and I was one disillusioned teenager (although the term "teenager" hadn't yet been coined).

Years later, in a Greenwich Village bar, I heard my name called by a lady sitting on a barstool. I went over; the face was ravaged by now though you could see that it had once been beautiful. It was Marian, very drunk.

"Never forget you, kiddo," she said. "You're the only one ever treated me like a fuckin' lady." I could have wept.

At rehearsals of *Smiles,* when nothing else was happening, Fred Astaire and I would race to get to the rehearsal piano. Each of us thought ourselves the better player. Thus I was delighted when Adele Astaire asked *me* to accompany her on a radio program run by Alexander Woollcott. Woollcott, *The New Yorker* magazine dramatic critic, had a radio program that may have been the first chat show. He was to interview Adele Astaire and she would finish by singing one of the Vincent Youmans songs, "If You Would Always Be Good to Me," that she sang in the show. That was the plan anyway. When we rehearsed at the studio for sound balance Adele decided that the key was too low for her voice.

"Put it up a half tone," she said.

What an innocent phrase. Sounds easy, but not for me. I played the piano by ear, and my only key was C. Adele sang it in C in the show and I had been able to play it with her once before, at a party, but now she wanted it changed. Putting it up a half tone would make it not in C, which I could handle, but in C sharp, which I couldn't. It meant playing almost entirely on the black notes and black notes scared me. I tried to explain all this to Adele. "Nonsense," she said briskly, "you can play anything."

No, I couldn't. Even the composer wouldn't have recognized what I did. Adele left in tears, Woollcott just ignored me, not even saying thank you (for what?).

When I got to the Ziegfeld Theater that night Paul Lanin, the orchestra conductor, said, "For Christ's sake, what the hell *happened* to you?" He was a musician—I could tell him. He was sympathetic, the only one who was.

I got no sympathy from Fred. He left a newspaper in my dressing room, the *Herald-Tribune*. By cutting out letters and rearranging them, he had manufactured a front-page headline: LARRY ADLER IS A LOUSY CUNT. He never let me forget my disastrous performance and would introduce me to people as "Adele's great accompanist." Adele never asked me to play for her again.

This may sound as if we didn't get on well but it was a friendly company. Once Marilyn Miller and the Astaires took me to "21" for lunch. Confronted by that splendid menu I ordered boiled eggs. Fred stared at me.

"Larry," he said, gently, "this is '21.' You can have anything you like. Boiled eggs you can get at the Automat."

I was embarrassed but held out for boiled eggs and got them from a disapproving waiter. I couldn't bring myself to explain then but told Fred later, at the theater. I was trying to keep kosher. And by Spinoza-like logic I figured that the wicked goyim couldn't corrupt boiled eggs.

Once, in a rare burst of confidence, Marilyn Miller told me: "I would never wear a dress that cost less than a thousand." So when I met "Legs" Diamond once at Dave's Blue Room I wasn't so surprised when he gave me a piece of advice: "Never wear a suit costing less than two hundred clams, kid." In the early thirties $200 was like $2000 today.

Not even the genius of Ring Lardner could save *Smiles*. The book, by William Anthony McGuire, wasn't finished when we opened in Boston, nor was it when we got to New York. Ziegfeld added a song by Dorothy Fields and Jimmy McHugh to the Youmans score, which couldn't have pleased Youmans. The Fields-McHugh song, "I Can't Give You Anything But Love," was already a hit. The show had a salary list of over $20,000 a week; even sellout business wouldn't have kept it in the black and we never sold out. The opening night was a Ziegfeld event, Klieg lights, Duesenberg limousines, the mayor, the governor, Peggy Hopkins Joyce, Texas Guinan, Jimmy Walker, Arnold Rothstein, Tex Rickard, Jack Dempsey, it was a theatrical disaster. The Astaires' "run-around" stopped the show, my solo did okay, Marilyn Miller should have taken the night off. Her singing was off-key and her ballet pathetic. She was too fat. Pirouetting in her tutu, she just looked silly and the audience laughed where they weren't supposed to. The critics killed her, though they were kind to the Astaires. I got a mention from *Variety* and Walter Winchell. We ran seven weeks and it broke Ziegfeld.

One thing I have never understood. No show then had amplification. Performers like Al Jolson or Eddie Cantor didn't need mikes and Ethel Merman could have been heard two blocks away. Thus I played without a microphone, accompanied by a full pit orchestra, and they *heard* me or I must assume they did, because people applauded at the end of my number, and also, I got other engagements. Maybe in those days people simply *listened.* But I still can't figure out how they could hear a little mouth-organ, in a large theater. I wouldn't dare play under those conditions today.

On Sunday, our day off, there were benefits. Benefits were free charity shows, but you couldn't afford to turn them down. If one of the Hearst papers, or even Bernard MacFadden's *Graphic,* was sponsoring a benefit, you'd better show up for it, otherwise you were blackballed in those papers or, worse, the gossip columnists would turn on you. If Winchell was against you, you might as well quit.

Worse than the benefits were the rehearsals. If you were doing four benefits it meant four rehearsals in four different theaters and with four dreadful pit bands; musicians who had no other job. Fred Astaire suggested that we take the duet we did in the "Young Man of Manhattan" number and make a routine that we could use for benefits. This would at least spare us those goddamned rehearsals. Fine, and I thought we could do it in one rehearsal; I didn't know

Fred. We rehearsed for a fortnight before he thought it was good enough to use for the benefits. Now I knew what a perfectionist was.

Gus Edwards took me with him to a spectacular event in the Waldorf-Astoria ballroom in 1932, in aid of some charity. On the stage there were about two dozen concert grand pianos. At center stage front was one concert grand. When the curtain went up there were the great composers of the day, two at each piano. One would go to the central grand and play a chorus of his best-known melody and on the second chorus all the composers at the other pianos would join him. I've never seen anything like it. Imagine, George Gershwin plays "I Got Rhythm" and on the second chorus is joined by Jerome Kern, Sigmund Romberg, Noel Coward, Irving Berlin, Hoagy Carmichael, Harold Arlen, Sammy Fain, Johnny Green, Arthur Schwartz, Burton Lane, Harry Revel, J. Fred Coots, Benny Davis, Gus Edwards, Richard Rodgers, Jimmy McHugh, W.C. Handy, Duke Ellington, "Fats" Waller—and at that I know I'm leaving out some.

Gus Edwards had a reason for bringing me along. In the Green Room backstage he had me play; they all seemed interested. In 1931 the mouth-organ was a novelty, good for cowboy tunes or in comedy acts but nobody had tried to play music *qua* music on it; I tried.

It got results. Noel Coward had a revue going into production in London in about six months, George Gershwin was getting a show ready (it turned out to be *Of Thee I Sing*), and Arthur Schwartz was casting a musical revue he'd written with Howard Dietz for Max Gordon. I liked the idea of going to England for the Coward show but Edwards told me to take the Schwartz show because that was immediate (also, if I were in London he might have trouble collecting his commission). Schwartz wasn't offering a contract, contracts weren't his territory, but he wanted Howard Dietz and Max Gordon to hear me. Dietz first.

I went to their studio in the Essex House in Central Park South. Schwartz played the score and somehow I got the idea that, not only was I already *in* the show, but that the whole thing was being built around me. This seemed to me entirely logical. I liked "Alone Together," said I'd do that as my main solo, but let on that I'd be cooperative about playing the other tunes as well. Schwartz and Dietz looked at each other; they'd never come across such a bigheaded *schmuck* in their lives.

Despite their unfavorable impression (which Schwartz told me about later) they sold me to Max Gordon. *Flying Colours* had wonderful material; Clifton Webb, Tamara Geva, Patsy Kelly, Charles Butterworth, Philip Loeb (he was to die by suicide later, a victim of the McCarthy witch-hunts), and a team who, even in rehearsal, stole the show, Vilma and Buddy Ebsen.

As well as being a background for the Ebsens, I drove the horses in "Louisiana Hayride," a great stage effect with back-projection which gave such an impression of a real wagon going down a real road that the audience used to cheer it every performance. The number was sung by Monette Moore, a black singer (credited with discovering Billie Holiday) who sang a number, daring in those days, "Smoking Reefers." I played a dummy piano during that number; oh, I was the star all right.

Flying Colours was the first show to present a mixed chorus—mixed racially. A number called "Bless the Butler" featured Billie Worth, a black comedienne, stepping out of an otherwise white chorus line, to walk away with the number.

The opening number was called "Max Gordon Raised the Money" and for it Norman Bel Geddes had designed a stadium effect. The cast sat in the stands, stars on ground level, and the higher you sat the less your salary was. Where I sat, my nose would have bled, except I never got there. On our first rehearsal with the new set I started to climb up and felt it swaying. I turned and called: "Hey, this thing isn't safe." Bel Geddes's rage was almost tangible.

"You little shit," he shouted. "Who the hell are *you* to say my set isn't safe? You get your ass up there or get the hell out of the theater."

That scared me. I didn't want to get fired but the set *was* rickety. Arthur Schwartz came backstage, tried to talk me into going back up on the set but, when I refused, told me to stay out of Bel Geddes's sight. The rest of the cast mounted the set and the rehearsal went well. I prepared to get fired.

That night there was a dress rehearsal to an invited audience. The cast, with a certain exception, were in their places as the curtain rose, telling the people out front how Max Gordon raised the money. In the middle of the number the set collapsed. Two girls were badly hurt. They were taken to hospital, one later came back into the show, the other never did.

One of the show's backers was "Waxey" Gordon, no relation to Max. "Waxey" derived from his real name, Wechsler. Waxey looked like and acted the gangster he was. He gave an opening night party in Philadelphia and for it I invited my girl friend, Sally, to come from New York. Sally was beautiful; she had been on the cover of *College Humor* and was the model for some of James Montgomery Flagg's covers.

During the party a dark fellow with a thin face, striped suit, dark shirt and white tie, tapped me on the shoulder.

"Waxey says beat it, gowwan, get out of here, screw."

I gulped. "Okay." I wasn't going to argue with Waxey Gordon. I went to find Sally. The thin-faced man tapped me again.

"The broad stays," he said. "You—screw."

I am not now, nor have I ever been courageous. Card-carrying coward, that's me. But I wasn't going to leave Sally with those jerks. We got our coats and left, me expecting a bullet or knife in the back. It was the bravest act of my life.

I was disappointed that I had no solo. On opening night in New York, the piano was pitched higher than usual, the orchestra tuned to the piano, and I sounded flat. You can't tune a mouth-organ, it has a fixed pitch. I sounded awful but probably only Al Goodman noticed. The notices didn't mention me at all, they mostly went to Vilma and Buddy Ebsen. Walter Winchell had a crush on Vilma and mentioned her almost daily for the show's run, which was thirty-four weeks.

The stadium set had been scrapped and the cast now sang "Max Gordon Raised the Money" standing in two rows on the stage. One matinee I arrived late, the opening was already on. I went through the pass door and sat in a box seat in full view of the cast; they had assumed I was on the stage with them and seeing me sitting there, leering, they broke up. I was seized by the stage manager.

"What the hell do you think *you're* doing? Why aren't you on-stage?"

I looked up at him.

"I just wanted to catch myself from the front."

The stage manager didn't think that was funny. He reported it to Max Gordon and Arthur Schwartz had to save my job again.

CHAPTER

Three

IN 1933 I WAS APPEARING at the Chicago Theater, on the bill with the Radio Rogues. It was part of a four-week tour but I was told that the following three weeks were canceled, no reason given. I moaned to Henry Taylor, of the Radio Rogues, who showed me an item in *Variety*. At Grauman's Chinese Theater in Hollywood the impresario Sid Grauman was putting on a prologue to Eddie Cantor's film, *Roman Scandals*. Why not, said Taylor, ask Cantor to use his influence to get me into the show? I was shy of calling Cantor but there was nothing shy about what I did. I wired Grauman that the world's greatest mouth-organist (me) was appearing at the Chicago Theater and that he would be perfect for Grauman's show. I signed the wire Louis Lipstone. (Lipstone was the general manager of all the Balaban & Katz Theaters.)

The next morning I realized I had forged a telegram. I went to the office of the B & K chain and asked the receptionist if I could see Mr. Lipstone; no, I had no appointment but it was urgent. I waited a long time. Finally I was told, go on in.

Lipstone, cigar in mouth, greeted me with "Make it snappy, kid, I'm busy. What's on your mind?"

That made me even more nervous. Stammering, I started to explain what had happened. Before I could get going the phone rang.

"What? West Coast? Grauman? Put him on."

Had there been an open window I'd have jumped.

Lipstone put his hand over the mouthpiece.

"Grauman says I sent him a wire about you. What is this? I never sent no goddamn wire about you. . . ."

"*I* sent it," I said, bleating like a sheep, "and I signed *your* name."

Lipstone looked at me a long time. Then he turned back to the phone.

"Yeah, sure thing, Sid, the kid's *great!*"

Lipstone told me I was a little sonofabitch but with something like admiration.

At the end of that week I flew to California.

My agent, Abe Lastfogel, met me at the plane. I stayed at the Roosevelt Hotel, near Grauman's Chinese Theater. The first thing I did after checking in to the hotel was to go to the Chinese Theater forecourt to see the famous footprints, handprints and, in Mae West's case, breast prints.

I didn't really have an act. At the Chicago Theater I had played two numbers but here at Grauman's I needed something strong. At the Blackhawk nightclub in Chicago, I had played by ear Ravel's *Bolero* using Hal Kemp's dance arrangement, so I knew the number, or thought I did. I said I'd play it in the Grauman show. It turned out I didn't know it at all. Hal Kemp played it as a dance tune, a two/four foxtrot. Ravel had composed it in three/four and it might as well have been a new and unfamiliar composition. I just couldn't handle it. I was in a panic; this was my biggest break so far and I was about to destroy it. Why hadn't I ever listened to a classical recording of *Bolero?* Too late for that now, I was stuck. I took the shortened arrangement by Roger Branga back to the hotel and tried to study it, but I never was a good reader and I could see disaster ahead.

Opening night I stood in the wings and watched Nell Kelly do her Garbo impersonation; and the Piccianni Troupe, acrobats who turned triple somersaults off a teeter-board and ended up in a very high chair balanced on the strongman's shoulders—they never missed. I was afraid to go on but I had to. For about forty bars I kept in time with the orchestra; after that I got lost, couldn't tell where one phrase was supposed to end or the next to begin. What I heard from the orchestra seemed like something that got in by mistake. I felt that the orchestra was a few bars behind and, to get them to catch up, I waved one arm like a crazed semaphore operator while holding the mouth-organ with the other. The number, in its short arrangement, plus a few other cuts I'd made, lasted about four-and-a-half minutes—it seemed much longer to me—and finally, the famous climax was reached. ("Climax" is used advisedly; Ravel was commissioned by the dancer, Ida Rubenstein, to set sex to music.) I played the last note with a flourish and a swoop up the mouth-organ that Ravel never intended and certainly didn't need.

I couldn't believe what happened next. A roar of applause, shouts, cheers—the number was a big hit. It stopped the show and, after about ten curtain calls, the stage manager said that Grauman had called on the house phone to tell me to play it again. Well, I couldn't. I had swum my musical channel, and couldn't face a return trip. Despite the pleas of the stage manager I just kept taking bows until finally he put up the house lights, which usually meant the intermission. That stopped the applause; he then brought down the lights, leaving a lot of people to scramble back to their seats, and the show continued.

Next day the notices were about the kid who played *Bolero* on the mouth-organ. My agents phoned to congratulate me, said there were offers coming in already. I practiced hard that day, which I should have done all along, heard a recording of *Bolero* and had it down pretty well in my head. The performance that night was better. I played the right notes in the right time, I was relaxed and at ease. I was also a flop, getting only two curtain calls. Sid Grauman came backstage. "What's happened to you, kid? You lost your showmanship!" What showmanship? He meant flailing my arms in a frenzy, acting as conductor as well as soloist. I explained what had happened the previous night and that there was no longer any need for such histrionics; I knew the material now. Screw the material, said Grauman, put back the showmanship. (I didn't tell Grauman that the orchestra leader in the pit had threatened to knock my block off if I tried taking his job again.) Grauman was the boss, back in went the showmanship, out went the music and the orchestra leader never spoke to me again.

The other performers started scowling when the corny *stürm und drang* with the arms was put back; the audiences didn't know or care

if *Bolero* was played correctly; they were impressed by the way I
chopped an invisible tree.

One day, at the Brown Derby, lunching with Bill Perlberg, my
agent at the William Morris Agency (and later to become a film
producer), I noticed a man pointing me out to his table companions.
He got up and came over, said hello to Bill and told me he'd seen
my act the previous evening at Grauman's.

"Music's way too loud, kid," he said. "I told Grauman, take it
down. Better for you." Then he went back to his table. I asked Bill
who was the busybody?

Bill looked at me oddly. "That was Al Jolson."

Jolson! I couldn't believe it. If I had a hero, Jolson was it. I believe
he was the single greatest entertainer the U.S. ever produced. Al
Jolson had noticed *me!*

Grauman told me that Gloria Swanson had phoned saying she'd
like me to play at a party she was giving. Fine, I said, for $500. (I
was getting just $150 a week at Grauman's, where did I get off asking
$500 for a single performance?) Grauman told her what I asked and
Miss Swanson told him to shove it. Admittedly it was *chutzpah* on my
part; mind you, Miss Swanson was making $25,000 a week and this
was before the days of high taxes. But I should have realized; it was
a break for an unknown to play at a party given by a star.

Making a hit in a Grauman prologue didn't qualify me for putting
my footprints in cement in front of the theater: the success was small,
my head was big. I began to *act* like a bigshot and I must have been
insufferable to my fellow performers. One who seemed sympathetic
was Nell Kelly, who said she'd have made me take the Swanson
party.

"Fuck the money! Who needs it? You need to be seen around, get
people to know about you. I'd have done it for nothing."

The Morris Agency got me a film, *Operator 13,* a Cosmopolitan
production owned by William Randolph Hearst (on whom Orson
Welles based *Citizen Kane*) which was to star Marion Davies. Walter
Wanger was the producer, Raoul Walsh the director, Gary Cooper
was Miss Davies's co-star. There were problems; Wanger and Hearst
couldn't get on and both Wanger and Walsh were fired, also everyone under contract except Gary Cooper. I had been drawing a salary
for twenty weeks and hadn't seen the studio when I got a call from
the casting director, Ben Piazza—who could forget that name?—to
see him.

Piazza reminded me that I'd been drawing a salary for several months and had done nothing to earn it. Well, he said, the way things were going, nobody knew when the film would be made. There was a new producer, Lucien Hubbard; a new director, Richard Boleslavski; but no cast. *Operator 13* was about the American Civil War, which meant there'd be some Southern folk songs. The idea was that I should record some Stephen Foster and, said Piazza, "Later on we'll photograph some little nigger boy but it'll be your sound track."

I told Piazza that if my music were to be used it would have to be with me on the screen.

"Kid," he said, "you're not taking the right attitude."

I told all this to Bill Perlberg, who phoned Piazza, and with what were later to be known as deleted expletives, told him that Adler was to be shown playing, otherwise no music. As for what Piazza could do with his "little nigger boy"—well, it was physically impossible. They took me off the payroll. When the film was made there not only was no mouth-organ, there were no folk songs, either.

Before this, Wanger asked me to play at a party at his home. (I was more sensible by now and asked no fee.) Wanger considered me a genius and decided to spring me on the big brass at Metro-Goldwyn-Mayer.

I went out to his house the afternoon of the dinner party. The idea was, I'd be behind a curtain. At a signal from Wanger, I'd start to play, the guests would be startled by the music, the curtains would be drawn, they'd realize that all this sound was coming from nothing but a mouth-organ and, Wanger was sure, they'd fall flat on their asses with amazement.

Wanger's guest list had Louis B. Mayer, Irving Thalberg and Norma Shearer, Eddie Mannix and Benny Thau (two high-ranking MGM executives), Jeanette MacDonald and Bob Ritchie and the Orsatti brothers, the biggest agents in Hollywood.

I waited a long time behind that curtain, getting nothing to eat, either. Finally, as I peeped through the curtain during their coffee, Wanger gave the signal, I began to play, Wanger slowly drew the curtains, I was revealed—and no one looked up. No one at all. They neither knew nor cared where the music came from. Wanger looked at me and shrugged, hopelessly. There was nothing to be done; I went home.

At one point the MGM publicity office asked me to take a starlet to Grauman's Chinese (this was after my appearance there) and sent a limousine, picking me up first, then the starlet. When we got near Grauman's there was a queue of limousines. A bunch of kids rushed our car, one stuck his head in the open car window, turned and yelled to the others, "It's NOBODY!"

In Palm Springs, one rainy afternoon in 1933, I was at the villa belonging to Bryan Foy. Foy, a son of the theater star Eddie Foy (when I used to sing in the Baltimore parks I was named "Little Eddie Foy" by the *Sun*), was known as King Bee because he made successful "B" pictures, generally inferior to "A" pictures. Other guests included the team of Bert Wheeler and Robert Woolsey, an agent or two and a few hangers-on and gofers. Gofers were people happy to be stooges just so they could live in the shadow of the great. If Bert Wheeler wanted a coffee, one of the stooges would go for it, hence "gofer." Most of the men drank Scotch. I was nineteen and didn't drink hard liquor.

The conversation got around to the occult, to ghosts, fortune-tellers, psychic phenomena. Foy said to me, "Adler, anybody ever tell you you were psychic?"

No, they hadn't, but I had tried a few experiments in hypnotism. . . .

"There you go, what'd I tell you?" asked Foy. "I got an idea. Pick a winner in the first at Hialeah, race comes up in twenty minutes. Here, look at the card. . . ."

"Brynie, I don't know anything about horse racing. . . ."

"Ya don't *hafta* know anything, just look at the names and say the first one that comes to your mind."

I felt stupid doing this but everybody was looking at me expectantly.

"Well . . . this is silly . . . okay, Calaveras."

The others raised a stake of $100. Bryan Foy phoned a bookie, put the C-note on Calaveras . . . to win.

More drinking, some played poker or Klabiash, another card game. The phone rang and Foy picked it up.

"Yeah . . . yeah . . . yeah . . . hey, no kidding! By three lengths, huh? Okay, call ya back."

"Hoddia like that," said Foy, "your hunch paid off, kid. Eight to one shot, we're ahead eight C's and we're cuttin' you in for ten percent. Okay, now give us something in the second race."

I protested, feebly, that this was just coincidence, I could never do it again. Try, urged Brynie. I looked at the card.

"Bay Rum," I said.

"Aaahh," said Brynie, "that's no good. Bay Rum's an odds-on favorite. Pick another one."

"No," I said, "Bay Rum is my hunch. That's the name I see, Bay Rum."

Reluctantly Foy called the bookie, put the eight C's on Bay Rum.

Bay Rum won, the pot was now $1200. It went on like that all afternoon. I just couldn't lose.

By the end of the afternoon the stake was $20,000.

"Okay, kid," said Foy, "last race, last time around and we're all in clover, hey baby?"

I looked at the card. Twenty grand!

"Brynie," I said, "I don't get any hunch on this one."

"C'mon, kid, don't let us down now, you gotta come up with something. C'mon concentrate."

I concentrated.

"Brynie," I said, "I'm sorry, I just don't get a name, I get two names."

"Two names is no good, loverboy, pick one of those two."

"Brynie, you got twenty grand riding on this one, what if I pick the wrong one?"

"Wuddia mean, the wrong one? Ya haven't picked one stinker the whole day. Now come on, kiddo, one name . . . just one."

"Oh, it's awful . . . I keep seeing two names . . . Donatella and No Cigar . . . I wish you wouldn't do this . . . No Cigar."

Foy called the bookie. Twenty grand was too steep for him to handle, he'd have to spread it around, it would take a little time. Brynie was expansive. Take all the time you like, he told the bookie, just be sure it all goes on No Cigar, on the nose, to win.

I was in real panic. After all, my share of the $20,000 was $2000. Why couldn't they just quit?

The phone rang.

"Yeah . . . yeah . . . uh-huh . . . came second, eh? Who won? No shit! Donatella, eh? Ah well, ya can't win 'em all." He hung up.

"Don't feel bad, kid, it wasn't your fault. I probably shouldn't of pushed you. You had the right idea at that."

I felt as if a nervous breakdown was the next step. Twenty grand!

Six years later, in 1939, I was sitting with Charles and Elsa Laughton at Romanoff's. Across the room, in another booth, was Bryan Foy. He was pointing over at me and laughing. Then it hit me. The whole thing had been a practical joke. Foy hadn't placed a single bet, no money had been won or lost. Foy had just phoned a friend who was in on the gag and I had been played for a sucker. They'd carried it off beautifully.

Even if it had been genuine I would not have believed in my powers. "What is truth?" asked Pontius Pilate and, like a lot of other people I know, wasn't really interested in the answer. The theory of Ockham's Razor is one way of answering the question. If a given result has two explanations: one mysterious, complicated and contrary to the laws of nature; the other simple, understandable and verifiable by objective standards; the second is apt to be correct. If Uri Geller says, "Look, I have bent that spoon using only my psychic power," and a stage magician, James Randi, said, "Look, I bent a spoon too, you didn't see me do it because I'm a professional magician," Randi's explanation is more likely to be the true one.

The simple explanation is up against powerful opposition, the will to believe in the incredible. Many, maybe most people, would rather accept an assertion on blind faith than find the answer by thinking for themselves. Well, why shouldn't they? goes one argument. Who are you to say that faith is a bad thing? I answer that when faith leads to a closed mind, then it is indeed a bad thing. Faith's first cousin is gullibility; leading to belief in "Rev." Jim Jones, who, about to be arrested on criminal charges, told his followers to drink cyanide, and so help me, they drank it! I am against any dogma that puts the mind in blinkers, that forbids the free discussion of ideas. Question received wisdom and you'll never be Mr. Nice Guy.

Most of us see ourselves as thinking, logical people, no suckers, we. Yet the majority of newspapers run astrology columns and people who profess not to believe in astrology still peep at them. The claims of astrology are an insult to the intelligence; astrologers deal in duck-billed platitudes, glittering generalities. Yet there is more money spent on astrology, which doesn't work, than on astronomy, which does.

A friend of mine, E. J. Kahn Jr., a writer for *The New Yorker,* wrote a series about gypsies and, in the course of it, got to watch quite a few gypsy fortune-tellers at work. What astonished him was the amount of stuff that the sucker, without realizing it, was feeding the gypsy, who would, after a discreet interval, feed it back to the sucker, who was invariably amazed at the psychic ability of the gypsy.

Houdini, the greatest name in stage magic, devoted a considerable part of his career to challenging spiritualists who claimed to be able to produce psychic phenomena, contact the dead, etc. Houdini, together with the magazine *Popular Science,* offered $10,000 to anyone who could produce any paranormal phenomenon that he, Houdini, could not expose as a fake and, in fact, duplicate. Mediums tried to win that ten grand in every city that Houdini played; his money was safe, he never had to pay out.

In our own time James Randi, like Houdini a successful stage magician, carries with him a certified check for $10,000. Again, like Houdini, he will hand the check to anyone who can demonstrate a psychic phenomenon of any kind. Again, many have tried, none has succeeded. Randi's money is safe.

You have read of the psychic surgeons of the Philippines, who operate without knives or anaesthetics? Well, in my London home, Randi showed me how they work. He drew his finger across my extended arm and a line of blood appeared. He dug into my arm with his hand and extracted "diseased tissue." The blood was red wine (my own) and the "diseased tissue" was chicken liver, that Randi had thoughtfully brought along with him. Randi has filmed the Filipino fakes, and their methods are almost endearingly crude. They do *not* operate, they extract *nothing.* Randi has exposed them publicly on television programs and it hasn't hurt their business one bit, they merrily go on coining fees from hapless suckers. The cruel thing is that people with tumors are taken in by these racketeers, and actually think they've been cured.

Transcendental Meditation is another gimmick, promising much, delivering nothing. TM, to use its chosen label, does nothing that one cannot do for oneself by relaxing in a quiet place. That's all there is to TM, or would be if the famed Maharishi hadn't come up with a new gimmick. For $1500 he will teach you to levitate. The Maharishi has been teaching levitation since 1978 but nobody has yet been seen to rise in the air unassisted. I offer $5000 for proof that anyone has levitated.

You who read this have no doubt already come up with some psychic phenomenon that you witnessed personally and have asked yourself: "How does he explain THAT?" I suggest that what you are about to relate is an anecdote; one that you believe but an anecdote just the same, with no more or less value than any other anecdote.

I am not calling you a liar. I accept that you are sincere, I do say that you can offer no proof, in the way of verifiable evidence, that what you believe to be true is true in fact.

The Reader's Digest used to run a feature, "It's fun to be fooled; it's more fun to know." People, it appears, prefer to be fooled. An account of paranormal happenings is a natural big-seller. The exposé, showing that there is no evidence, has a hard time finding a publisher, and even when it does, the public isn't interested. Thus Eric Von Däniken writes books with such titles as *Chariots of the Gods?* (nice of him to allow the question mark), *Gods from Outer Space, The Gold of the Gods* and *In Search of Ancient Gods.* James Randi, in his book *Flim-Flam,* from which I've drawn most of the evidence for this chapter, writes: "The only facts in Von Däniken's four books that I depend on are the page numbers." Von Däniken has been exposed by Randi, by Ronald D. Story in *The Space God Revealed,* by Thor Heyerdahl and others. It won't affect his sales one bit.

The Washington Star had an editorial, admittedly written before the Jones tragedy, denouncing those who sought to expose the paranormal believers and practitioners. It said they lacked humor: "What had happened to their funny-bones?"

Perhaps, after the 950 dead in Guyana, the *Star* may see less humor in the subject. Or maybe not.

CHAPTER

four

MY NEXT ENGAGEMENT WAS to play a number in *Many Happy Returns,* a film that starred Burns and Allen and Guy Lombardo's orchestra. The romantic male lead was Ray Milland. I did something during the making of *Many Happy Returns* which still appalls me when I think of it. The director told me that I'd do a solo, set in a broadcasting studio, with Guy Lombardo's orchestra. I said I didn't like Lombardo's band.

"Who asked you what you *like*? This is what you're gonna *do.*"

I refused and was fired. The next day the producer sent for me. He tried to talk me into doing the number with Lombardo; again I refused and again I was fired. Then, incredibly, I was sent for by William LeBaron, the studio head. He was kind and patient with me. He pointed out that I had a contract and that I was reneging on a signed agreement. This could get me blacklisted in all the major studios. He said that while I was a comparative unknown, if I did just this one number, millions all over the world would hear and be aware of me. I said I didn't want to be heard with Guy Lombardo and his band. "You know who I like," I said, "I like Duke Ellington."

"So do I, Larry, so do I. We all like Duke Ellington. What is your salary for the film?"

It was $300.

"Do you know what we'd have to pay Ellington? About twenty grand. Does that make sense?"

Of course it didn't. But I still refused. LeBaron said good-bye to me. He had really tried to help, he had been patient and kind.

That night, quite late, my phone rang. It was William LeBaron.

"Well, you little prick, we've got Ellington for you."

And they had. He was, in fact, on the Paramount lot, appearing in a Mae West film, *She Done Him Wrong,* which had a fine score by Arthur Johnston. "My Old Flame" was the main tune.

My troubles with *Many Happy Returns* weren't over. After my Grauman date I had arranged a booking there for Paul Draper, the dancer with whom I had worked at the Radio City Music Hall. Paul was having a romance with a girl named Mona; she had come backstage to see me, but I was infatuated with somebody else and I introduced her to Paul Draper. Paul and I shared a rental car and, the night before my Paramount scene, I put everything in the car that would be needed, my white suit, my mouth-organs, etc. I left a call for five A.M. and, when it came, called Paul, who was going to the studio with me. No answer. I went to the hotel garage; the car wasn't there. I wasn't worried. I thought Paul had gone on ahead to the studio to lay everything out for me, like a good pal. I took a taxi to the studio. Paul wasn't there nor was the car, which meant I had no costume and, more important, no mouth-organ. Duke Ellington was already on the set with the band—in those days they did direct recording—and everyone was ready. Except me. I explained what had happened and the explanation didn't go down well. They had to send someone to a music store in Los Angeles for a mouth-organ, which took some time. I would do the number in the suit I happened to be wearing.

The mouth-organ eventually arrived and we went to work. I was going to play "Sophisticated Lady" with Duke, which required practically no rehearsal since I knew his arrangement from the famous record, with the sax solo by Johnny Hodges. A point: Duke couldn't be photographed; nothing racial but, as Guy Lombardo was one of the film's stars, no other band must be photographed. I don't think Lombardo can have known about Ellington playing behind my solo.

Had he done so, he would have raised hell. Recently, during a TV interview with me, they showed that sequence from *Many Happy Returns*. My showmanship was corny, deeply embarrassing to watch, but I would make no apologies for my playing; it has always been true for me. If I work with an Ellington, a Django, a Bill Evans, a Dizzy Gillespie, I play at the top of my form or even beyond it. I know that I could not duplicate the solos I recorded with Django Reinhardt—because there is no longer a Django to inspire me.

At about six-thirty Paul Draper arrived on the set and asked cheerfully if things had gone well. "They went well, no thanks to you, you no good sonofabitch!" Paul wanted to know what he'd done wrong. I reminded him that everything to do with my performance in the film was in the boot of the car we shared. Paul was contrite; he'd forgotten all about that. Well, why had he gone off with the car in the first place? Mona had phoned him at about six A.M., said there was a lovely sunrise in San Bernardino and he ought to see it. So Paul took the car, with my mouth-organs and everything else I needed, and went to see the sunrise with Mona.

Only one writer, to my knowledge, spotted the music of Duke Ellington behind my solo; that was Leonard Feather, then a jazz critic for the *Melody Maker* in London. As a result of his prescience I contacted him, we became friends and we still are. In 1982 Leonard Feather did a feature on me for the Los Angeles *Times* that made the front page of their arts section. Ellington's manager Joe Glaser liked the sequence in the film and proposed that I record with Ellington some two dozen titles at a fee of $25 a title. By ill luck I had read, that week, in *Variety* that Bing Crosby got five percent royalty on his records. I told Glaser I wanted the same. Glaser told me with gestures what I could do with my five percent royalty. The records were never made; one of my real regrets.

That winter I was appearing at the Palmer House in Chicago. Earl Hines ran the show at the Grant Terrace, on the South Side, where they had the best black talent, acts like the Berry Brothers whose entrance was a leap from a platform ending in a sliding knee drop. Duke and I went there one night and Earl Hines asked us to play a duet. Afterward Duke said, "I want you to meet somebody," and took me to a ringside table where a lady was sitting alone.

"Larry," said Duke, "Billie Holiday." I put out my hand and said, "How do you do?"

"Man," said Miss Holiday, "you don't play that fuckin' thing, you *sing* it."

And, if I'm allowed to choose my own epitaph, that's it.

When Paul Whiteman's orchestra played the Roxy Theater, on the bill with his film *The King of Jazz,* I used to stand outside the stage door and play my mouth-organ at whoever came in or out, hoping that someone would give me a job. One day the jazz saxophonist, Frankie Trumbauer took me inside to Whiteman's dressing room. "Paul," said Trumbauer, "listen to this kid." I played "When Day Is Done," my interpretation cribbed from Whiteman's own record of the piece.

"Lemme hear you play *Rhapsody in Blue,*" Whiteman said.

The piece was much too complex for me to handle, but, and this says more about me than I should be revealing, I couldn't admit this to Whiteman. Showoff as ever, I said, airily: "I don't like *Rhapsody in Blue.*" Whiteman turned to a young man I hadn't noticed before: "What do you think of *that,* Gershwin; this kid doesn't LIKE *Rhapsody in Blue.*" That's how I met Gershwin.

Shortly after this, I was on the bill at the Palace, the Palladium of New York, when C. B. Cochran, the British impresario, the Ziegfeld of England, came to see the show. Cochran was in New York producing a play with Pierre Fresnay and Yvonne Printemps so he might have come to see the headliner, Ben Blue, or he might just have wanted to get out of the rain. Whatever reason, there he was. He came backstage to see me and made a fan of me by calling me "Mr. Adler." This was rarer than you might think. The Shubert brothers called me kid; Lew Leslie, kiddo; and I don't think Ziegfeld ever knew my name.

Cochran didn't know whether I was a good mouth-organist or not —"I don't know anything about mouth-organs"—but he took the word of his musical director, Elsie April, who, besides her enchanting name, was a dead ringer for the figure of Punch. But something impressed him more than my musical ability: "You're the first mouth-organist I've ever seen in a dinner-jacket." He wanted me to come with him to London, sailing in a fortnight on the *Aquitania.* He offered me no contract, I paid my own expenses, I got no guarantee. "But," he said, "if C. B. Cochran comes back from America with a mouth-organist, it'll make news."

Hell, I would have paid *him!*

Curiously, I was dickering with N.T.G. (Nils T. Granlund) of the Hollywood Restaurant, to come in for a twelve-week run at $350 a week, the highest figure I'd reached so far. But the Hollywood was what Lenny Bruce would have called "a tits 'n ass" place. The showgirls were the feature, the talent not much more than fill-ins. It was a guaranteed $4200 with N.T.G. against a possible nothing at all with Cochran. I turned down N.T.G. Cochran as a man had what Jolson had on stage, Rachmaninoff on the concert platform: class. Class out-pointed money.

The best theatrical parties in New York at that time, the early thirties, were given by Jules Glaenzer, the vice-president of Cartier's. Jules had two concert Steinways in his town house in the East Sixties and you didn't refuse an invitation from him. I've even met Howard Hughes at Jules's house. Hughes was partly deaf and conversation with him was difficult. He would nod and smile while you were talking to him and it was only when you expected a response that you'd realize he hadn't heard a word.

The night before I sailed to London in the *Aquitania* with C. B. Cochran, Jules Glaenzer gave me a farewell party. He had assembled a roomful of talent. It was quite an evening, all the men in white tie except me. I provided most of the entertainment, playing "Body and Soul" with Johnny Green, "Blue Skies" with Irving Berlin, "Mountain Greenery" with Richard Rodgers and "But in the Morning, No" with Cole Porter. Then Jules shushed everybody—he was known as The Great Shusher—and announced: "Larry and George are going to play the *Rhapsody in Blue.*" I certainly hoped that I'd do a number with George but *Rhapsody?* I had never played it through but I knew the Paul Whiteman recording (Paul was also there that night) and had it in my head. George looked dubious; he didn't know whether I could handle it or not, nor did I. He sat at the piano, I began the run usually taken by the clarinet and George came in at the top of the run. It was one of those times when two musicians had complete rapport. I knew when to lay out and let the piano take over, George would signal me back in at the right moment. When we finished, with the piano taking the five chord climax while I held a high F, everybody cheered, Ethel Merman enveloped me in a bear-hug and Vivienne Segal kissed me. Gershwin looked at me oddly.

"Goddamn thing sounds as if I wrote it for you," he said. The goddamn thing still does. I can't count the times I've played it, either with piano or with full orchestra, but it always gives me goose-bumps. I'm sorry it went so well. Whenever, after that, I would raise the idea of George writing for the mouth-organ he'd tell me he already had.

Dorothy Fields (who wrote the lyrics to "I Can't Give You Anything But Love" and "Sunny Side of the Street") drove me to the pier where I was to board the *Aquitania*. My parents were there, my agent, Nat Kalcheim from the William Morris Agency, and two girl friends.

The whole thing was very exciting but I didn't realize that I was embarking—no pun intended—on the most exciting event of my life so far. The voyage wasn't a bad preparation; I entered the table tennis competition and was baffled when my opponent would cry, "Shot, sir!" or "Oh, well played, sir!" When he won a point he would say, "Sorry." He accepted his victory with regret if not sorrow, and implied that I was a spiffingly good sport to let him win when it was obvious that I could have walked away with the match. It was my first introduction to British sportsmanship.

Between the first and the last night of the crossing we dressed for dinner. If this was the British way of life, I liked it. Mr. Cochran was now calling me "Larry" instead of "Mr. Adler," and there was a warmth about him, a kindness, that I'd never found from a man so powerful in show business. No one called him Mr. Cochran, and his female stars called him "Cockie"; perhaps some of the men did too, but I never got to that familiar point.

Cochran was right about making news. There was a huge gathering of press at Southampton, where we docked, and when they came aboard they were interested in the American mouth-organist. Cochran, on previous voyages to the U.S. had returned with something glamorous. Cochran announced that my mouth-organ could replace an entire symphony orchestra and would do just that at the Royal Albert Hall. *The Times* couldn't quite accept my existence and called me a "trombonist" and C. L. Graves, in *Punch,* had a full-page poem in which he gloomily predicted mass unemployment in Denmark Street, where the musicians hung out, and the dissolution of Britain's major orchestras all made redundant by my mouth-organ. "This portent foreshadows the slumber of Steinways, the scrapping of Strads.''

The papers were full of Cochran's latest discovery, some on the front page, and it was my first taste of being a celebrity. I had had successes in the past, local ones at Grauman's Chinese Theater or at the Palmer House in Chicago: I had a certain standing in show business but was unknown to the general public. I had played choruses on records by Ruth Etting, Eddie Cantor, the Brunswick Orchestra and two sides with Salesman Sam, but I had yet to make a solo record.

Cochran had a revue running at the Palace Theater called *Streamline,* which was a lavish production, one scene being a pastiche of a Gilbert and Sullivan musical. There was Florence Desmond, as the first British mother to fly to the North Pole with her baby; Tilly Losch (called Lily Tosh by the chorus); Naunton Wayne; Sherkot, who brilliantly mimed an insane football goalie, playing a match alone on stage; a Hungarian flamenco dancer, La Jana, who was later shot by the Germans during the war as a spy; sets by Doris Zinkeisen and Rex Whistler; a score by Vivian Ellis with one hit, "Other People's Babies"; lyrics and sketches by A. P. Herbert. Despite that lineup the show hadn't caught on and a four-week notice had been posted. Cochran decided to put me into *Streamline* and A. P. Herbert wrote a sketch that had me playing in a BBC studio. This was in the days of John Reith, the autocrat who had made the BBC the most respected of broadcasting companies. In Herbert's sketch, after my first number, the announcer, played by a comedian, Billy Stephens, asks me what my second number was to be:

ME: What do you think they'd like?
BBC: Oh, Mr. Adler, we don't give them what they'd like but what is good for them.

I intended to play "Smoke Gets in Your Eyes" followed by Ravel's *Bolero* but we had problems. "Smoke Gets in Your Eyes" was from a musical, *Roberta,* that hadn't been produced in England, thus the score was not yet published. We didn't anticipate any objections but we were wrong; Chappell, the music publishers, who controlled the score, wouldn't let us use it. C. B. Cochran, Elsie April and I went to see Teddie Holmes, who ran the popular side of Chappell's.

Holmes was sympathetic and introduced us to Louis Dreyfus, who said he hadn't the authority to release "Smoke" but would call New York. We rehearsed the number and hoped it would work out. We got permission at five P.M. on my opening night.

For *Bolero* there was a large white screen behind me and a projector in the footlights beamed a huge shadow of me onto the screen. It was very effective. I closed the first half, and Cochran's judgment was justified; the show ran another fourteen weeks.

Cochran had a party for me at his house in Montagu Square. Mrs. Cochran, a lovable lady who always treated me as a not-too-bright nine-year-old, told me that A. P. Herbert would bring a lady to the party who, because of the obvious intimacy between the two, I might address as "Mrs. Herbert." But, warned Mrs. Cochran, I must be careful *not* to do that. Mr. Herbert had a wife elsewhere. "So you see, Larry, you mustn't call her Mrs. Herbert, because she *isn't* Mrs. Herbert."

Putting on my superinnocent face, I asked, "Then just what is she?"

Now Mrs. Cochran was distressed. She tried to find the right word, then she looked as though she'd found it.

"Well, Larry, she's . . . she's his . . . you see, Larry, she's . . . she's his *bit*!"

I later conceived a mild crush on the lady myself but even though I knew her name she was forevermore A. P. Herbert's *bit.*

I often practiced on the fine Broadwood grand piano at C. B. Cochran's home in Montagu Square. Mrs. Cochran told me that composers such as Gershwin, Porter, Rodgers, Coward, Vivian Ellis, had all composed music on that very piano.

"And do you know, Larry, their spirits seem to linger there and sometimes you even hear them sigh."

One day I was alone in the house, playing the piano when, in the middle of a tune, one of the spirits began sighing. Being a practical type I started to sound the notes by hitting each key once to see which caused the sighing. It was C above middle C. Hit that note and right away you got a sighing spirit. I checked over the piano and found that one leg had a loose metal ring around it. When high C was struck the ring would give a sympathetic vibration.

One of the nicest things I can think of to say about myself is this: I never told Mrs. Cochran.

As I was a latecomer into *Streamline,* all the dressing rooms were taken. Frank Collins, the stage manager, let me use his office on the fourth floor, fine if the lifts were working, hell if they weren't. On Christmas Eve Mrs. Cochran climbed the four flights to give me a present, a dozen monogrammed handkerchiefs. I had a silver baton made for Charles Prentice, the conductor and, for Cochran himself, a solid silver cigar-cutter in the shape of a mouth-organ.

One night, at the Shim-Sham Club, a man came to my table and told me he was going to photograph me. He made it sound as if I were lucky. I was impressed with his arrogance and went to his studio, which turned out to be just a flat. He didn't *have* a studio, all he had was a Leica camera and a few lights. With the photos he took he got a double-page spread in the *Bystander;* his name was Baron and these photos were the first he'd ever had published. His full name was Baron Nahum, the Baron part not being a title.

Through the publicity of my arrival, plus the notices in *Streamline,* I was in demand and found myself playing four places in one evening: first the show, then the Trocadero in Piccadilly, then the Empress Rooms in Knightsbridge, and finally the Savoy with Carroll Gibbons's orchestra. I also played in cabaret at the Berkeley and at the Dorchester.

One night, during the run of *Streamline,* the chromatic slide on my mouth-organ stuck. I had a spare in my pocket, and switched instruments without missing a beat, congratulating myself on my cleverness. The number died. Cochran, who had seen the performance, asked what had happened. When I told him, he advised me never to do it again, not to change instruments in full view of the audience. He said that they assumed I must have trick instruments for special effects. He was right, of course, and I never did it again. Once, with Pierre Monteux and the San Francisco Symphony, I was playing the Vivaldi A Minor Concerto (for Violin) and two notes stuck. I got through the movement, held up a warning hand to Monteux, scooted offstage, changed instruments, came back and finished the concerto. Afterwards Monteux asked me what had happened—"Deed you have to go to ze bassroom?" I explained the problem. But why, he asked, didn't I carry a spare? I gave him the answer you already know.

I played one engagement before my *Streamline* opening. Margaret Whigham's marriage to Charles Sweeney was the event of the season. I had had a suit of tails made at Kilgour and French, and this was my first chance to wear them. I didn't know how to tie a bow tie nor did I have any idea what went where. The reception clerk at the Mount Royal, Marble Arch, where I was staying, took pity on me, he tied the tie and put the studs and links in the right places. I thought I looked marvelous.

At the embassy every man was in tails, they were used to wearing them, which I was not, and, to my chagrin, they looked a hell of a lot better than I did.

The band was led by Bert Ambrose, who had the best band England ever produced. His arrangements were highly musical and his style unique. I never heard any band use brass better than Bert Ambrose's.

The Prince of Wales was there, so was his brother, the Duke of Kent. The prince was as well known in the U.S. as any film star. He had a talent for falling off his horse, each fall photographed and front-paged. The bride, Margaret Whigham, was the most beautiful woman I had ever seen; that was 1934 and today (1984) Margaret, Duchess of Argyll as she is now, is still beautiful.

Although I had an agent, Harry Foster, I let C. B. Cochran decide when and where I played. Cochran told me that Columbia wanted to record me. We recorded "Smoke Gets in Your Eyes," *Bolero,* "The Continental" and, with two pianos, "Londonderry Air" ("Danny Boy"), Kreisler's *Caprice Viennois* and de Falla's *Ritual Fire Dance.* On "Londonderry Air," I made an announcement, something about how it would sound jazzed up. Christopher Stone, reviewing the record, praised my playing but wondered why I inflicted my "execrable American accent" on the public. The first record released, "Smoke" and "The Continental," was the biggest seller of the year. That record made me a name throughout the British Empire.

Cochran arranged a charity concert ("benefit" in the U.S.) at Queen's Hall and I heard comedians like Ronald Frankau and George Robey. Frankau I couldn't take at all, I thought him obscene, vulgar and unfunny. I was charmed by George Robey; I didn't find him hilarious, in fact I doubt that I laughed at all, but his timing was as sensitive as the best of musicians. His opening lines were: "In the early days Mother and Father went up the river for a lark. I'm the lark." I did cabaret with Max Miller. His innuendoes were even more loaded than Ronald Frankau's, but he had charm and wit. In his loud suit (jacket and knickerbockers) and the white hat, Miller was an original. Miller, on a Royal Variety Performance, got himself banned from the Palladium for several years. With King George and Queen Mary in the Royal Box, he began a story which one knew in advance was going to be dirty. It began with a drunken sailor chasing a young boy up a dark alley. Just at the crucial point in the story Miller paused, looked up at the occupants of the Royal Box and said: "*Not* tonight . . . any other night but *not* tonight." I thought it funny and admired Miller for taking the risk. If you don't take risks, you are not an artist.

My parents came over at the time of the Jubilee of George and Mary. Dad saw all the heralds with GM displayed and thought that General Motors must be a very big company to afford all that advertising.

Streamline made me a name and it went to my head. I did the star bit, acting like Sinclair Lewis's *Babbitt.* I complained about everything: the coffee was lousy, no central heating, phones didn't work, couldn't get room service at night, couldn't get a hot meal after the show. Goddamnit, where *I* came from, back in the good ole USA, things were *efficient.* Many a Briton must have wondered why in hell I just didn't go back there.

One night, at Cochran's home he said, "I've very good news, Larry—I've booked you to appear on Henry Hall's 'Guest Night' on the BBC."

"For how much?" I asked.

Just writing those words gives me the shivers. How could I have done that to Cochran, of all people? He was hurt, that I could tell, but I lacked the quality which Hemingway calls "grace under pressure," to apologize immediately and admit my oafish behavior.

Next morning Evelyn Cochran rang. "Larry, what ever did you say to poor Cockie? He hasn't slept all night." I went to the house and apologized, but neither Cochran nor I really got over it.

The broadcast took place, Cochran introducing me on the air. I was to play two numbers with the orchestra; "Smoke Gets in Your Eyes" and Ravel's *Bolero.* Cochran gave me a fine intro and I played. After the first number Cochran was to announce *Bolero,* but he had mislaid his glasses. There was dead air while Cochran searched for them. The producer signaled him, beseechingly, for God's sake, forget the goddamn glasses, say *something*. Cochran launched into a complete ad-lib, anything at all, just to fill that silence.

To my horror, I heard him say: "Larry uses a new mouth-organ every time he plays, don't you, Larry?" No, I didn't but I couldn't contradict Cochran on the air. I said yes, sure, fine, that's right. What else could I do? Then I played *Bolero*. There were several thousand letters asking for my used mouth-organ. It was the beginning of a legend that has never died.

When I later lunched with Henry Hall and Eric Maschwitz, composer of the lyrics for "These Foolish Things" and then a radio producer, Henry Hall said, rather smugly, that one broadcast with him had made me a household word. I didn't accept that. I bet £20 that I could play as a street busker and not be recognized. Hall bet I'd be spotted.

I played to the queues outside the Holborn Empire, London's finest music hall (I preferred it to the Palladium). I was the headliner that week, the people were coming to hear *me*. I loaded the dice by dressing as a complete slob, mussing my hair so that it stood up wildly. Nobody paid much attention. I went on playing. Someone threw a coin. I wasn't wearing my glasses and without them I couldn't even see the coin. Some people in the queue were curious; What kind of a busker doesn't pick up his money? That's when someone recognized me. I felt I'd won; it was only on a technicality that I was spotted. There was disagreement as to who had won the bet and nobody paid. A press photo of the event showing me with my wild hairdo was in *Men Only*, which had a way of running juxtaposed photos. They had one of a black African tribal chief, captioned, "M'bongo M'bongo, King of the Zulus," and on the facing page, "Larry Adler, King of the Mouth-organ."

In a later issue, *Men Only* ran a cartoon drawing of a symphony orchestra playing frenziedly, the conductor waving his arms. In the audience a man says to a lady: "That's the piece Larry Adler plays on a mouth-organ." *Radio Pictorial* had a cartoon of an organist seated at an organ with huge pipes going up, right out of the drawing. Two ladies watch him and say, "And to think Larry Adler plays it with his mouth!"

CHAPTER

Five

IN 1935, I PLAYED AT the Alhambra in Paris on a bill headed by Lucienne Boyer. I featured Ravel's *Bolero* and, not exactly to Mademoiselle Boyer's joy, I stole the notices. The impresario was Kurt Robitschek, who had run a cabaret in Berlin, Der Komiker, and was famous for having put down Goering. Robitschek was making political jokes about the Nazis when Goering was at a ringside table. Goering said loudly: "I think this man is a Jew."

"No," said Robitschek, "it's just that I *look* so intelligent." He left Berlin shortly after.

Robitschek, after the notices were out, said he'd like to hold me over four more weeks.

"And my good friend Lahree, I will make for you a big *publicité.*"

Then his face seemed to ooze sadness, his lower lip trembled and I thought he might cry.

"I suppose," he went on, "that you will want *more* money."

There should have been violins behind that remark. Old heart-of-stone Adler said that, yes, more money was what he had in mind. I was held over. The headliner for the second program was Lys Gauty,

a singer of great force. I had a call from Jacques Lyon, who ran a
record shop, the Sinfonia, on the Champs-Elysées. He said he'd had
a call from Maurice Ravel, who had heard that I played his *Bolero* and
wanted to hear me. I couldn't stand before the *maître* playing without
accompaniment so I brought my record with me. We drove to Mont-
fort-L'Amaury, outside Paris and had a hard time finding Ravel's
house—no one seemed to have heard of him. When we did find it,
Ravel opened the door, took the record and before Jacques could
even introduce me, put it on. Until then I'd thought it was a good
record, it was a big seller and I was proud of it. Standing there while
its composer listened to it I was aware of imperfections, of mistakes
that I had never noticed. It sounded awful and, though it was on one
side of a 78 rpm record, it seemed interminable. When it finished,
Ravel spoke to Jacques.

"The master he say, you play it very fast. Why?"

Hell, *I* didn't know why. I hadn't ever known that I *did* play it fast.
Ravel spoke again.

"The master he says you have made cuts, you do not play the
whole thing. Why?"

I explained that, in music hall, my act ran fifteen minutes, which
was the length of *Bolero*. I loved the number, I meant no criticism
but, to include it, I had to make cuts.

Jacques said, "The master he ask, do you know Arturo Toscanini?"

Yes, I had met him.

Jacques said, "The master, he say that Toscanini plays the whole
thing."

Well, he had me there. What could I say? The conversation lan-
guished. I held out the record to Ravel to sign. (I had never asked
for an autograph before, have never asked for one since. It was pure
embarrassment.) Ravel looked surprised.

Jacques said: "The master say, he thought the record was for him."
Now *I* was surprised. Ravel had given every sign of loathing the
record and me. Then Ravel held up his hands, they were shaking.
He said that he had palsy, had written nothing in the past five years.
I apologized and we left. A few days later Jacques phoned me and
told me to get to his record shop at once; the master was there. Ravel
was bundled in a heavy coat and a scarf though it was a warm day.
He said that, by sitting in a dark room and concentrating, he had

been able to steady his hand long enough to write his signature and he had brought it to me. I was touched and honored by Ravel's gesture but felt guilty, as I hadn't really wanted the autograph.

In 1940 I was soloist with the Philadelphia Orchestra's Robin Hood Dell concerts. Saul Caston, the conductor, suggested an encore; when I chose *Bolero* the librarian objected. Performing fees for one performance were very high, not worth it for an encore. Elkan, Vogel, Ravel's publishers, were in Philadelphia; I went to their office and announced myself. Mr. Elkan came out and told me he knew about me. Ravel had left instructions that I was to have free rights to play the *Bolero* in whatever medium I pleased. That right is unique to me.

When I was performing at the Alhambra, I had a phone call from Felix Ferry, an impresario who produced the shows at the Monte Carlo Sporting Club. What was my fee for playing at a private party at Cap d'Antibes? I suggested 25,000. Ferry thought that rather high and said he'd get back to me. He came back with an offer of 15,000, which I didn't think was good but he said all expenses would be paid. I'd never been to the Côte d'Azur, so I agreed. I asked *how* I would be paid—he said that $200 in francs would be given to me on my arrival for expenses. The rest of the $15,000 would be given to me in a check. While I had been talking in francs, Ferry had been talking in dollars—no wonder 25,000 struck him as high.

When I was to fly from Paris to Nice all flights were full. Ferry tried to charter a plane but couldn't, so he persuaded the president of the Paris-Lyons-Méditerranée Railroad to put his private car on to the Blue Train for me. And that is how I traveled; a private railway carriage to myself.

At Nice a chauffeur was waiting with a Hispano-Suiza, one of the most beautiful automobiles ever made. We drove to Monte Carlo, to the Hotel de Paris, which is still one of my favorites. Later a pianist who would accompany me called, and we rehearsed. I knew nothing save that my employer was the Countess Constantini, who was paying out all this money, and it would probably be a grand occasion. I prepared some light classics.

Felix Ferry picked me up the next evening. It was a white tie affair and we drove to the Constantini villa. I would be playing to an audience of three; the Countess, King Gustav V of Sweden and ex-King Alfonso of Spain. That was $5000 per person.

The atmosphere wasn't right for music. My hostess made me feel one of the help; Alfonso seemed unaware of what was going on; only King Gustav seemed human; he smiled and made small talk. Dinner was over when I arrived and after coffee we went to the drawing room where there was a Bechstein concert grand. Countess Constantini signaled with a wave of the hand that I should begin. Damn her, I thought, she's making me *earn* my fifteen grand.

I played Kreisler's *Caprice Viennois,* and when I finished playing there was nothing. Perhaps applause would have sounded ridiculous from three people—but there was no reaction at all. I began the *Fire Dance* by de Falla. Damnit, Alfonso ought to like it, it was Spanish. No reaction. Well, I had prepared a program, I was being paid a fortune to play it, so gritting my teeth, which isn't easy when they're wrapped around a mouth-organ, I played an unaccompanied *Gavotte* by Bach. About halfway through I heard a slight buzzing sound. Gustav was snoring!

Now I was angry. Fifteen grand or no, I didn't like these people, and to express my feelings, I played the song I hated most, "The Music Goes Round and Round." *That* ought to show them! At once Gustav woke up, started slapping his knee in rhythm and sang along with my music: "Whoa-oh-oh-oh, oh-oh, and it come out here." When I finished the tune he got up, embraced me and said, "My boy, you are a genius!"

I couldn't top that. Liqueurs were brought in and Gustav asked if I played tennis? Yes, but I was leaving the next day at noon. What about eight A.M.? Fine; I didn't have my tennis gear but everything would be laid on, even shoes. Alfonso never said a word but Countess Constantini, delighted by Gustav's reaction, discussed having me play at another evening. (That never happened.)

At about six-thirty A.M. I had a phone call. It was the aide-de-camp to Gustav.

"Mr. Adler, you realize that His Majesty is no longer young." (King Gustav was nearly 80.) "Would you be so kind as to hit each shot directly to His Majesty?" Done.

"One more thing, Mr. Adler. If His Majesty hits a ball out, would you be good enough not to call it out?"

King Gustav looked splendid in a Bill Tilden–type sweater and long white flannels. He was tall and, despite his age, covered the court well. I don't want to keep you in suspense—he won.

I returned to Monte Carlo where I fell for one of Clifford Fischer's "Les Girls" who danced in the show at the Sporting Club. Her best friend was dating Prince Sirignano, Francesco di Caravita, and you got around that by calling him "Puppetto." Puppetto asked me to come with him to Ventimiglia to look at a new Alfa Romeo. He went, saw the car, but I wasn't allowed to reenter Monaco without my passport and, even with it, I'd need a visa. Puppetto said he'd go back to Monte Carlo, get my passport and all would be well. After several hours he hadn't returned and I was hungry. The border guard suggested I go to the casino in San Remo, where the food was good. The guard said he'd tell Puppetto where I'd gone. He also got me a lift.

At the casino restaurant I got a table despite my casual clothes— every man was in black tie—and ordered a meal. By ten still no sign of Puppetto and the waiter was looking anxious. I had a mouth-organ with me. When the band stopped, I began to play. People crowded around to listen. I did it again at the next intermission. Then a man came over and said he was the casino manager. He could tell that I was a professional musician; how would I like to play at the Casino? I told him I had to go to London. He offered me 5000 lira a day. I had to refuse. He raised the ante, getting to 15,000 lira a day. Nobody, he said, got more than that except Gigli. Well, *viva* Gigli. I couldn't accept the offer. I asked about my bill? He signed it himself, and took me to a club for a drink, telling the doorman where we'd be.

Puppetto didn't show up until about one-thirty. I should have known what delayed him. He had waited for Dolly and Ann to finish their shows so that they could come along. He'd found me; now we had to find an American consul. We drove to Genoa, sat up until office hours began, I got my visa and was allowed back in. "Wasn't it nice that I could bring Dolly and Ann along?" asked Puppetto.

I saw Puppetto again in 1938 in Capri in the lobby of the Quisisana Hotel, one of six escorts of Mussolini's daughter, Edda Ciano. He gave me a furtive smile of recognition but also a shrug as if to say: "Larry, I'm stuck with this. Please don't acknowledge me." I understood.

Once I stayed at the Pavilion Henry IV in St. Germain-en-Laye and heard from the adjoining suite a burst of piano playing, no more than eight bars, but what an eight bars! I went to the reception desk and asked who was in the adjoining suite. Why, was I being disturbed? No, not at all; but who was occupying the suite?

"I know he is a musician," said the clerk. "His name is strange—it is Or-row-weets."

"Is his first name Vladimir?"

Yes, it was. Did I know him? No. I told him Horowitz was considered by many to be the world's greatest pianist. Oh, said the clerk, bored.

Did he know, I asked, that Horowitz was married to Toscanini's daughter? That did it. "Toscanini's daughter!" And that's how Horowitz became a celebrity in St. Germain-en-Laye.

In 1936 I was on the *Queen Mary* for her maiden voyage. I was to broadcast *Rhapsody in Blue* with Henry Hall in mid-Atlantic to both the U.S. and Europe. The producer was Cesar Saerchinger; who could forget a name like that? We got the green light and we were on. When the number was over, Saerchinger came out. "Sorry, fellows, something went wrong and you weren't on the air."

"When did you find out?" I asked.

"Oh, a few seconds after you started."

"Well, damnit," I said, "why the hell didn't you stop us?"

"I *like Rhapsody in Blue.*"

I went to Hollywood where the William Morris Agency had booked me at Ciro's. I had arranged for my girl friend, Sylvia, to be there —she came from New York with her mother—and even persuaded George Raft to make a pass at mother to get her out of the way. Mario Braggiotti, from the piano team of Fray and Braggiotti, had made me an orchestration of "These Foolish Things" and it was a show-stopper. In the lobby, after my show, a man complimented me, using a Jewish accent put on for the occasion. I'm pretty good at that so I came back at him. We traded lines for a while, then he left.

Next morning I drove to Palm Springs. A message was waiting for me, to call Abe Lastfogel, who told me that the man putting on the accent had been Jack Warner, head of Warner Brothers Studios. ("Combining good pictures with good citizenship" was their slogan.) I was to return right away—Warner wanted me for a Busby Berkeley musical, *The Singing Marine* starring Dick Powell. Warner sprang me on Busby Berkeley but it didn't bother him. He put me into two scenes, one where I played "Night and Day" plus "Tiger Rag," the other in which, made up to look Chinese, I played "Night over Shanghai," by Harry Warren and Johnny Mercer. For the Chinese number Berkeley did some amazing improvisation; he had my hands painted one color, the mouth-organ another, and my face a third. The film was in black and white but Berkeley had a reason for using the different colors; each would show up under different lighting. The first light illuminated my hands, the second the mouth-organ, and the third my face. The camera was a long way away; you heard a sound, then saw something very small, writhing like snakes; these were my hands. As the camera came in closer, the second light was turned on and you saw that the hands held a mouth-organ. The third light lit up my (Chinese) face. The number ended with the close-up of my face, the camera now going away from me, the face disappearing, then the mouth-organ and finally the hands writhing; it was very effective and people still remember that scene.

Jack Warner took a liking to me, though it didn't include casting me in any other Warner Brothers films, and invited me to come with him and his wife Ann to the Academy Awards, in the ballroom of the Ambassador Hotel in Los Angeles. Bette Davis was at our table, confident that she would get the Best Actress award. It was not that she deserved it, she said, the film, *Dangerous,* was second rate.

"I should have won the award last year for *Of Human Bondage* and everybody knows it. So I'll get it this year, when I don't deserve it, because they feel guilty."

She did get it. Victor McLaglen, who seemed to be bursting out of his tails—he looked like a gorilla stuffed into a suit—made a tearful speech about the Oscar, which he kept calling "little pal." It was revolting. McLaglen had won the award the previous year for *The Informer* and deserved it. In one of his best scenes, while the IRA men are grilling him as to why he turned informer, he kept shaking his head dazedly and said, over and over: "I didn't know what I was doing, I didn't know what I was doing." It was very moving. Apparently, when sober, he couldn't handle the scene and John Ford got him drunk to do it.

During the making of *The Singing Marine* I met Simone Simon. She was at Fox making a film. She had made a hit in the German film *Mädchen in Uniform* and Hollywood was doing its best, if that's the word I want, to find out what made her unique, erase that quality and make her just like every other ingenue.

I wasn't the only one to find Simone delectable. Her romance with George Gershwin was the stuff gossip columns are made on. She liked me and I was pleased that when Ginger Rogers gave a roller-skating party at a Westwood rink, Simone invited me as her escort. I couldn't skate but what difference did that make? Kay Francis, Clark Gable, Fred Astaire, Franchot Tone, Joan Crawford, Fredric March, everybody except me skated.

Simone's picture was to be previewed and she asked me to take her to it. I was shooting on *The Singing Marine,* made up as a Chinese, and it took two hours for Wally Westmore, Hollywood's famous makeup man, to make me up, weighing down my eyes with what seemed like cement. It took another two hours to get the stuff off. On the night of Simone's preview there wouldn't be time to get out early to meet Simone. I left the makeup on. Simone couldn't stop laughing at my ridiculous appearance. In my cinema seat I couldn't watch the film because my eyes were weighed down with inscrutably Oriental makeup. I had to lie back with my head on the seat, my legs nearly in the air in order to see the screen. Simone made everybody come to look at me.

Oh well, it wasn't a good picture anyway.

Next day at the studio it was a four-hour job, taking yesterday's makeup off, putting the new makeup on. It was very close to real torture. Luckily Busby Berkeley didn't need me before noon. Had I been in the first shot, I'd have held up production, which could have been serious. After all, nobody *made* me go to the Simone Simon preview.

Simone invited George Gershwin and me to dinner, without tell-ing either that the other was coming. George and I glared at each other across the table, wondering what sadistic joy Simone was get-ting out of this. We soon found out. Two sound technicians arrived from Fox and set up a recording machine. Simone wanted George to play the piano, me, the mouth-organ, while she sang arias from *Porgy and Bess.* This was *chutzpah* but she knew her men and that we wouldn't refuse.

Simone went with George to the premiere of Berg's opera *Woz-zeck.* When the limousine in which Simone and Gershwin were riding arrived at the Academy of Music in Philadelphia, the crowds outside mobbed the car, shrieking Simone's name. (The publicity about her was: "Simone Simon; pronounced See-moan, See-moan.") No one knows what a composer looks like. When they finally got through the fans and into the foyer, Gershwin turned on her and shouted, "How dare you be more famous than me?" Simone was so upset, she didn't even correct his grammar.

In case you think I'm just being discreet about Simone and me, I never got anywhere. Simone liked me but not enough and used me mainly as bait, to make George Gershwin jealous.

When Gershwin died, aged thirty-nine, of a brain tumor, John O'Hara wrote: "George Gershwin is dead but I don't have to believe it if I don't want to."

Nineteen thirty-seven saw me crossing the Atlantic yet again for England. It was on this trip that I first saw Max Wall at the Penge Empire. Here was an original. Charles Tucker, my agent, had suggested a road show and we were looking for talent. This was talent, all right. Tucker also found Tommy Trinder. He was brash, had a machine-gun delivery, was a young Max Miller. But good as he was, he was no Max Wall.

Charlie Tucker, before he was an agent, did a comedy violin act. Once I was getting a haircut and a manicure. It was Saturday and the manicurist asked why I wasn't away for the weekend. I said it was because Kreisler was at the Albert Hall.

"Who's he fighting?" asked the manicurist.

"Kreisler," I said. "Fritz Kreisler."

"What does he do?"

"Kreisler," I said, "is one of the two or three greatest violinists in the world. There's Heifetz and there's Kreisler—then you have to think."

"Is he as good as Charlie Tucker?" she asked.

"Charlie Tucker is my agent. I know Charlie was a comedy violinist but, honey, I'm talking about real violinists."

"Mr. Adler," she said, "I don't know your Mr. Kreisler but I do know good old Charlie Tucker. Could your Mr. Kreisler play a violin standing on his head?"

She had me there.

With Wall, Trinder and me, a revue evolved. We formed sketches with each contributing lines. At one point the curtains parted to reveal Max asleep on the piano but wearing a tropical helmet. I shook him.

"Quick, quick," shouted Wall wildly, "your husband's coming!" Then he went into paroxysms of embarrassed apology. Later he came onstage carrying a guitar. He said: "I am going to play *this.*"

"How long have you been playing *this?*"

"*This*—will be the first time." Then, seeing the mouth-organ in my hand, he said, or groaned, "I suppose you're about to ask if you can join in?"

"Why, do you mind?"

"No," he sobbed brokenly, "no, no, it's nothing . . . I hoped . . . never mind . . . I'm all right now."

"What's the matter, Max, did you get out of bed the wrong side?"

He looked at me with both pity and rage.

"What did you expect me to do, jump over my father and mother?"

Max's life illustrated the truth of Macaulay's observation: "We know no spectacle so ridiculous as the British public in one of its periodical fits of morality." Max left his wife for another lady, a beauty-contest winner, whom he later married. You'd have thought he'd been caught practicing necrophilia on Queen Victoria. His life and his career were ruined and Max was out of work for years. In 1973 he was rediscovered, in a revue based on the life of C. B. Cochran. The show was a flop but the critics hailed Max as a new find. He became an actor and followed Laurence Olivier in the part of Archie Rice in John Osborne's play *The Entertainer.* I saw them both. With the first, it was Olivier being a second-rate music-hall comic. When Max played it, he *was* the part, he *was* Archie Rice. Of course you could never accept that he was second rate, but he was infinitely believable as the music-hall comedian, as Olivier never was. Max played in *Waiting for Godot* with Leo McKern. He has a regular spot in the TV show *Crossroads,* that soap opera that is more real to a lot of people than their own lives. Max gets older, his face more lined, his voice nearer to that of an old man, he seems to be chewing an invisible cud. But the timing remains impeccable, he is a trouper with class.

Our revue, *Tune Inn,* despite its title, was a good show, I've never seen a better one in music hall. Every act was solid, no dead weight. The Skating Whirlwinds were spectacular and I loved to watch them.

I was driving with one of them, Frank Wisner, when a car just in front of us stopped at a crossing. It stayed there for what seemed like minutes. Frank put his head out of the window: "The sign says *Stop* not *Stagnate*!"

Swan and Leigh did tricks on the bars and they let me try out on them. As they opened after the interval, the bars were set up well before time and I would practice swinging from bar to bar, to try, but never achieve, a full somersault (we called it a summerset in Baltimore).

Giovanni, the pickpocket, was a hit despite an aggressive manner that made me fear for his safety. He would get people to come on stage. If one tried a bit of banter, Giovanni would shut him up with, "I am the comedian," which wasn't true; a pickpocket he was, a comedian, not. He could take a belt, a wristwatch, braces, off a man without the man knowing he was doing it. He would hold the man's right hand, chattering rapidly to keep the man distracted and, with his free hand, remove whatever he was out to remove. Sailors bothered him because, with their tight uniforms, it was hard to get at anything. Sometimes, after taking a man's braces, watch and wallet, he would, while returning them, steal them again and still the man wouldn't realize what was going on. He never tried it onstage but I'll bet he could remove a lady's brassiere without her knowing.

He had practiced psychiatry, he said. He told a moving story of a woman whose illusion was that a bird was flying inside her head. Normal mental treatment wasn't working. "They had to come to me," said Giovanni. He hypnotized the woman, bandaged her head, then, when he woke her, showed her a dead bird on a glass slab. "You see," he said, "I have operated. The bird is here, it is no longer in your head." The lady was cured.

"But, what do you think?" he went on. "There was a doctor who had tried to treat this poor lady and he had failed. He was jealous of me because I had done what he, with all his fine degrees, could not do. This evil man, do you know what he did? He went to the woman, told her that Giovanni was just a cheap trickster, he told her that Giovanni hadn't operated, in fact he told her just what I had done. And that poor lady, she said: 'You are right. I can feel the bird flying in my head, it is still there.' I couldn't repeat the trick, it wouldn't have worked a second time, and shortly after, that poor lady died."

Later that week I bought the new *Esquire* magazine and noticed a short story called "A Birdie in Her Head." It contained exactly what Giovanni had told as a personal experience. That evening at the theater I gave him the magazine and asked him to read the story. He did so.

"My God," he said, "what a coincidence!" There is no counter to such *chutzpah*.

Max Wall and Tommy Trinder were not yet famous, so mine was the only name the public knew. Thus business was apt to start slow, with bad houses Monday and Tuesday, but by Wednesday word-of-mouth would have got around. From Wednesday on business was solid and both Friday and Saturday were sellouts. I was on a percentage and, theoretically, was doing very well except that I never saw the money. It went to my father, who was supposed to be taking care of it for me.

Sir Henry Wood introduced me to Rachmaninoff in Sheffield. I was overawed. The sins of omission in my life are grave. Why didn't I ask Rachmaninoff to consider writing for the mouth-organ?

During Coronation Week I had lunch with Arthur Christiansen, editor of the *Daily Express,* Frank Owen of the *Daily Mail* and Baron, the photographer. After the usual claret I had port and a liqueur. I didn't realize until I stood up that I was drunk. Chris spotted it and wanted me to go to an upstairs room and sleep it off. I couldn't; I was due on stage at the Holborn. I staggered out and, while my alarmed friends watched, lurched across Fleet Street and took a cab. I got to the theater so near time for my act that I had no chance to change. I grabbed a mouth-organ, went onstage and, holding on to the mike with one hand for support, played the mouth-organ with the other. At the end of my act, I was supposed to step back while the curtain came down, but I was afraid to let go the microphone, so I just stood there. The curtain came down, right on my head. I doubt if I even felt it.

CHAPTER

Six

*H*ANNEN SWAFFER ASKED ME if I would be watching the coronation procession of George VI. I muttered something about not liking parades. Swaffer disregarded my silliness and said: "You'd better see this coronation, probably the last we'll ever have." Swaff, as Britain's leading columnist, was going to Westminster Abbey but his wife would see the procession from a flat in Oxford Street. If I would escort Mrs. Swaffer, I could have a grandstand seat, the kind American tourists were paying hundreds for. Forcing myself to get up at four-thirty, I called for Mrs. Swaffer and took her to a flat owned by a family named Bloom. Within minutes I was aware of a beautiful girl, Eileen Walser, who modeled for the clothes designer Joseph Strassner in Grosvenor Square. As I wasn't interested in the coronation anyway, I concentrated on Miss Walser, telling her jokes, something I have always been good at and which I tend to use in lieu of conversation. Eileen Walser was a splendid audience; she reacted like an American, mine being mainly American jokes. A guest shouted that the gold coach with the royal couple was approaching. We paid no attention, I went on with my jokes and we missed the coronation procession.

When it was over we were served breakfast. Sir Louis Sterling, the head of EMI, said to Eileen: "Come and sit by me and be Lady Sterling." I said: "If she's going to be anybody, she'll be Mrs. Adler . . . Eileen, you sit with me."

We made a date for the following Saturday. Later I realized that I already had a date, with a girl whose address I didn't know; I couldn't reach her, to cancel the arrangement. I was knocked out by Eileen Walser and knew she was potentially important in my life. I phoned a friend and, explaining the situation, asked him to take the other girl off my hands, not realizing what a very awkward situation I was creating for all concerned. It made for a terrible evening. We were at the Ace of Spades, a roadhouse. Eileen left the table and went outside and I followed her. She knew what was going on, she thought it monstrous to subject her to such an evening. Our first date was our last, she never wanted to see me again.

"It's a great pity—I could have been very good for you."

This was an extraordinary comment to make. It hit me that what she said was true. She *could* be good for me. Despite her dismissal, I wouldn't accept it as final. I admitted my bad behavior and apologized, but said that I intended to get her to change her mind.

I phoned her the next morning. She told me that she had meant what she said. I was foolish, selfish, and she would waste no more time with me. When I made the first date with Eileen I had also made a second, to take her to the country cottage of Charles and Elsa Laughton the following Sunday. I told her that the Laughtons were expecting her, that I would hurt their feelings if I didn't come down and I certainly wouldn't go there without her. Perhaps she was moved by the desperation in my voice. She agreed to come with me, for that one occasion, but I mustn't think, etc. I phoned Charles and Elsa and begged them to make a big fuss over Eileen. They were good friends and did everything they could to help. Eileen had a good time and agreed to see me again. I was on the road with my show, *Tune Inn.* Sundays were free, getting from one date to the next, but that was now changed. No matter where I was I would drive to London to see Eileen. She had to be impressed, some of those drives were very long.

When I played in London I would see Eileen every day. I stopped dating anyone else. I was so impatient to see her that I would call

for her early at Strassner's. I forgot that I was a slob, in a sweater and
sneakers, hardly right for a West End couturier's. Eileen was embarrassed by me and usually got off early just to get me off the premises.

One evening we met Myrtle Farquharson, who said, "I think the
Kents would like you." First she introduced us to Colonel and Mrs.
Humphrey Butler. Humphrey was aide-de-camp to the Duke of
Kent and, between the Butlers and Myrtle Farquharson, we were
invited to a dinner party at the Kent home in Belgrave Square. The
Kents did like us; how could anyone not like Eileen? I knew all the
popular songs (don't confuse "popular" with "pop") and Kent was
a fan of such songs.

Once Eileen and I were having dinner at the 400 Club in Leicester
Square. The headwaiter said there was a phone call for me. I hadn't
told anyone where I'd be, we'd gone to the 400 by chance. It was
the Duke of Kent calling: Could I come over immediately, it was
urgent. He'd been calling all over town trying to find me. I warned
him that we weren't in evening dress—his parties were usually formal—but he said that didn't matter, could I please just come soon.

I couldn't believe the cause of it all. The Duke of Kent had asked
Richard Rodgers to play "Have You Met Miss Jones?" Rodgers,
who had composed the piece, couldn't remember the middle section.
This became important; someone had to play that bridge and the
Duke thought of me. I sat at the piano, embarrassed, playing Rodgers's song to Rodgers. He didn't look happy. It was humiliating for
a composer not to remember his own melody.

Although Eileen had come with me, in spite of knowing that it was
a white-tie party at the Kents', she was not always so lenient. Once,
when I called for her, me in tails, she said, icily, "Is that a ready-made
tie?"

"Yes . . . anything wrong?"

"I'm not going to the Kents or anywhere else with you wearing
a ready-made tie. We're going out to find a proper one."

"Eileen, it's eight-fifteen, we're already due there for dinner."

"Then go alone! I'm certainly not coming with you."

We drove around looking for a proper white tie. We found a shop
in the East End, bought the tie, Eileen tied it and we arrived an hour
late. But that was Eileen.

She modeled a mauve dress that I liked so much that I asked her
to sneak it out and wear it to the Kents'. We arrived to find the

Duchess of Kent wearing the identical gown. She'd bought it a few days before but Eileen hadn't known. I whispered to the Duchess what had happened. She grinned and said no more about it, a classy reaction. She could easily have had Eileen fired.

I have said Eileen was beautiful; she was also very witty and a good audience. It points up what is one of the most important elements in a relationship, shared laughter. The sex can be magnificent but you don't spend all that much time making love. Most of the time you talk—if you're lucky—and, with even more luck, you laugh as well.

To me laughter is the cement of a relationship. You can have many other things. Fine, but without shared humor and, if you're *very* lucky, shared wit, you're not going anywhere.

Dorothy Parker, in a short story, writes of a couple, the wife desperately trying to make conversation, the husband responding with an occasional grunt from behind his newspaper. The wife asks if he has noticed "my lovely daffy-down-dillies?" Then Parker inserts the stiletto: "To anyone else she would have called them 'daffodils.' " And in that one line you know that they are dead to each other, that the relationship is just stagnating.

Eileen and I were always able to laugh. We had the ability to see not only each other but ourselves as well as being ridiculous.

One way I could make Eileen laugh—and today I see it as a grave fault—was by putting on a little boy act. She was always amused when I reverted to being a backward child. I came to depend on it. I could laugh her out of the sulks by going into my pouting kid bit. But there came a time when Eileen found it less amusing.

I never proposed to Eileen. We were driving up to Scotland and I said that my tour would be over soon, that we could get married and out of the country that same day. Eileen said, yes, that was possible, and it was decided.

Eileen hated publicity. I asked Arthur Christiansen, editor of the *Daily Express,* what was the best way to have a nonpublicized marriage? Chris took us to a restaurant and explained to an unsympathetic Eileen that, if he could have the exclusive on our marriage, it would kill the story for the other papers. They wouldn't want, warmed up, what he'd served hot. Eileen gave Chris one of her looks. She couldn't see that our marriage was anybody else's business. Chris tried to show how a story breaks, what makes it die or keeps it going. Eileen was unmoved; she wasn't going along with Chris's plan, which might have worked. Chris didn't capitalize on the story, he even let other papers get it first, but once out, it was *paparazzi* time. (That word had yet to be coined.)

We decided that it might be easier if I disappeared. I did, to a hotel in Rottingdean, outside Brighton. There I used a phoney name. Bette Davis was also staying and we played table-tennis. She was the better player and usually beat me. However, in 1980, when I was playing at the Tango Club in Chicago, Miss Davis came to see my show. I announced that a friend was in the audience, a friend who used to beat me regularly at table-tennis.

"Not true," shouted Miss Davis, "you trounced me every time."

Another delay in getting married was my commitment to appear in the film *St. Martin's Lane,* which was being made by Charles Laughton's company, Mayflower Productions. Erich Pommer, in charge of production, wanted me to supervise the music and write the score as well. However Val Parnell, of General Theaters, wouldn't release me so I had to wait until the tour finished and by then I could only appear in one scene. Rex Harrison, David Burns and I tried to teach a number to Vivien Leigh. She was slow picking it up but finally Rex exclaimed, "I think she's got it!" Then we all did a celebration dance. I believe the "Rain in Spain" sequence in *My Fair Lady* derived from that number, but my only evidence is that Rex Harrison was in both.

In *St. Martin's Lane* Laughton played a street busker who recited Kipling's poem *If* to theater queues. Vivien Leigh played a street urchin taken as a protégée by Laughton. The two didn't get on, which made for tension on the set. Yet, when there were close-ups to be shot of Vivien Leigh on a Saturday, Laughton gave up his weekend in the country to stand behind the camera and feed her her lines. Laughton was the quintessential pro.

Another thing which didn't help was that Laurence Olivier was courting Vivien Leigh. He would visit the set, they would go to her dressing room and that was the end of shooting. Tim Whelan was the director and he lacked the authority to deal with Miss Leigh.

I had to provide a composer and got Arthur Johnston, who wrote "Pennies from Heaven" and "My Old Flame." He gave us a song, "Wear a Straw Hat in the Rain," another of the "Be glad you're miserable"–type songs, but that let him out. We could never find him to teach the number to the cast. *I* had to do it. Carroll Gibbons, the pianist-bandleader, was in the scene and he coped better than I did. I played about half a chorus.

Just before we shot the "Straw Hat" sequence, at the Latin quarter in Soho, Eileen and I took out a special license, enabling us to marry within three days. The ceremony was at the Marylebone Register Office. Eileen's mother, sister and uncle were there; I had my parents and my agent, Charlie Tucker. Tucker thoughtfully gave me a beautiful set of matching golf clubs, knowing I had never played in my life. We were to exit unseen by a side door but one photographer anticipated us and got a picture of Eileen, who wore a hat with a black veil. The press loved that veil.

My father had been against the marriage, even hiring a detective to check Eileen's past. He said that Eileen had had a lover. I said, "I know." Dad couldn't believe my reaction. "You don't mind that someone has been there before?" I tried to keep a straight face.

"Dad, I'm not marrying her past, I'm marrying Eileen. No matter how you feel, I love her. If you can't accept that, we can say good-bye because my future is with my wife."

Dad was upset though Mother was more lenient. It was against the tradition of the nice Jewish boy who listens to his parents. I had never had that kind of feeling; the fact that I wanted a civil marriage service proved that. I had lost my religious convictions, if I'd ever had any, and Eileen, though her mother was Jewish, had never seen the inside of a synagogue.

We drove to Dover and took the car ferry to Calais. Outside Clermont-Ferrand, we were rounding a curve when a motorcyclist shot across the road in front of us. His cycle hit the front of my car and he flew over the top, landing behind. I was sure that the impact must have killed him but, amazingly, only his wrist was injured.

Whenever an accident occurs, I assume it's my fault. (I was knocked down by a car in Beverly Hills and, getting up, assured the driver that I had carelessly walked in front of him.) So, I assumed that this was my fault too and predicted that my wedding night would be spent in jail.

The French police, when they arrived, would have none of this. I tried to plead guilty, they wouldn't let me. *M'sieu,* they pointed out, it was the fault of the cyclist for crossing the road without first making sure nothing was coming from the opposite direction. There was no need to delay me, the cyclist only had a broken wrist, they would take care of him and I was free to go.

We drove to the Hotel du Cap in Antibes. I had an engagement at the Juan les Pins casino. (Typical to book an engagement on my honeymoon.) Eileen and I rented a chalet near the water, to sunbathe and swim. I was taking a photo of Eileen when a tall, very dignified Indian asked, "Are you interested in cameras?" When I admitted that I was he said, "So am I." He clapped his hands and it was like a film sequence; several people appeared carrying cameras. He seemed to have every camera ever made.

He was Taley Mohammed Khan, the Nawab of Palanpur. We became friends and he gave Eileen, for a wedding present, some cloth of spun gold. I think of him as a man with more dignity than I have known in anyone else. He told me he was sure that I had Indian blood; well, why not? Though he had a son, Iqbal, he proposed that he adopt me. For India's sake it's just as well it never worked out. I'm not the Nawab type. Also, I had two serviceable parents but Taley didn't regard that as insurmountable.

As Nawab, Taley was the court of ultimate appeal in Palanpur and, in extreme cases, had to make a decision of life or death. A man had been found guilty of rape and murder, the death sentence was mandatory.

"I tried to find a way of commuting that sentence," Taley told me. "I consulted the best lawyers. There was no way out. I had to uphold the laws of my country. The day of his execution, I was ill. I hadn't had a night's sleep for weeks thinking about it. It was morally wrong to put a human being to death. It was dreadful that I, Nawab of Palanpur, had no real power. The man was hanged and it has been on my mind ever since."

Eileen and I had swimming lessons from the hotel lifeguard. Both Eileen and I could speak a fair bit of French but he wasn't having any. He would watch us swim and his comment never varied: "Ees no suffisant breeze in," which I felt was an improper comment to a mouth-organist.

Eileen, while swimming, said: "I think an octopus touched me." When I told this to the guard he bellowed with laughter, indicating with words and gestures that the mere sight of an octopus would produce drowning symptoms. Then he shouted, *"Merde!"* thrust his hand into the water and pulled out, not a plum, but an octopus.

They don't give medals out for the right things; Eileen deserved one.

The Duke and Duchess of Windsor were staying at the hotel. I sometimes had a drink with their bodyguard, who had been with the Duke since the days when he was Prince of Wales. Once I asked him for his opinion of the ex-Mrs. Simpson. He had another drink while he considered my question.

"Well," he said slowly, "if she were to ask me to light her cigarette for her . . . maybe I would . . . and then again . . . MAYBE I WOULDN'T!"

Print on paper cannot convey the venom in those words.

The death of Wallis, Duchess of Windsor, brought back the time when I was in cabaret at the Waldorf-Astoria. I got a call from someone at MCA, my agents. Lucius Boomer (one of my favorite names), president of the Waldorf corporation, was giving a dinner party for the Duke and Duchess of Windsor. After my show in the Empire Room, Boomer wanted me to do another show at his party. I asked what the fee would be.

"No fee. It's Boomer's party for the Windsors."

"Is it for a charity?"

"No. Why all the questions?"

"Well, if it isn't for a charity, why shouldn't I be paid?"

"Adler, you some kind of Red?"

If refusing to appear free at a private party for the Windsors was a Communistic trait, yup, I guess I was a Red.

I got other calls from as high an official as "Sonny" Werblin, vice president of MCA. By now I was dug in: no fee, no show.

Then I was phoned by Jules (The Octopus) Stein, president of MCA.

"Larry, what are you trying to do to 'Sonny' Werblin?"

I had a feeling that this time I was sunk.

"What am I supposed to be doing to Werblin?"

"You know perfectly well, everybody knows, 'Sonny' has a weak heart. Boomer has told us, if you don't do that show, he's going to cancel MCA's franchise to book the Waldorf. Do you want the responsibility of maybe giving Werblin a heart attack?"

"Oh, shit, all right, I'll do the goddam show."

I was really angry but I knew when I was licked. At the party itself, while I played, I stared fixedly at the Duchess's right ear. It's a useful trick for making someone uncomfortable. Try it sometime.

In fact, Windsor himself was friendly, he knew that I was a friend of his brother, the Duke of Kent. He made me feel a bit ashamed of my stubbornness.

Eileen and I then went on a tour of South Africa and Australia. In 1939 we returned to the United States because I wanted our first child to be born in America. We took a flat at the Chateau Marmont in Los Angeles. I only knew Charles and Elsa Laughton, living at the Garden of Allah, a sprawling collection of flats and villas on Sunset Boulevard. They gave a party at which a man said to me: "I don't know many people here; are you important?" "Mummy thinks so," I answered. At a London party Baroness Budberg's daughter had said: "Mummy never introduces me to anybody. Who are you and what do you do?"

"My name is Larry Adler, I play the mouth-organ."

"Ah, but what do you *really* do?"

In Los Angeles Paul Draper, nephew of Ruth Draper, was the attraction at the Coconut Grove. In his autobiography C. B. Cochran describes Paul at this period as "a dancer of individuality and distinction who had become one of the highest paid cabaret artists in the world. He had created an entirely original *genre* by embroidering the more or less static movements of the tap dance with the grace and flexibility of the ballet and a discriminating choice of good music." He was a big name. I, a name in the UK and the Empire, was unknown in my own country and it wasn't a nice feeling. Paul persuaded the Ambassador management to put me on with him but it wasn't good for my morale. Paul had star billing and my own name was in miniscule letters. I opened the show, hating it. *I* was used to being the star. I was grateful to Paul, he was a loyal friend, but I was jealous too.

One night, before my last number, someone called out, "Play 'Sonny Boy'!" I delivered a lecture on why I wouldn't be caught dead playing "Sonny Boy." When I finished my show, Paul was in the wings.

"Larry," he said, "if I had a baseball bat I would beat the bejeesus out of you. Know who called out for 'Sonny Boy'? Al Jolson, that's who."

I went back and said: "I've just heard that the best reason for playing 'Sonny Boy' is in the room. I would be honored to play it." And I played to my childhood hero.

I had the idea of giving a classical recital with Paul. We booked the Lobero Theater in Santa Barbara and my agent, Bill Stein, a vice-president of Music Corporation of America, came to the recital. He advised me to forget it.

"Larry," said Bill, "be practical. Who is going to pay good money to listen to a mouth-organist and watch a tap-dancer for two hours?"

Put like that, Bill had a case, yet I felt there was a future for the idea. Later we gave another recital, at the Civic Theater in Chicago. We got excellent publicity and good notices from all the critics except the one from the Chicago *Tribune.* He wrote that the mouth-organ was no instrument, tap-dancing was no art. We were a house of cards and would cave in. What really hurt was Eileen's reaction to the *Tribune* notice.

"Well," she said, "you must admit, he *has* a point."

Bill Stein told me that if I could change my name to something more WASP/Aryan he would find it easier to book me; for example, Henry Ford hated Jews, wrote against them in his paper, the Dearborn *Independent,* and tried never to hire one. However, without changing my name, I was booked as soloist with the Detroit Symphony on "The Ford Hour." Eugene Ormandy was to conduct and disapproved of me from the start. He barely acknowledged our introduction and, at the rehearsal, kept me waiting until the last minute so that I only had time to run through my piece, the Vivaldi Violin Concerto in A Minor, once. I was seething when I gave the concertmaster my "A." "What is this?" asked Ormandy.

I told him the mouth-organ was a fixed-reed instrument, I couldn't tune to the orchestra, it would have to tune to me. "This is ridiculous," said Ormandy.

I don't go in for temperament for its own sake. But this, before the whole orchestra, was too much.

"Mr. Ormandy," I said and I hoped my inflections matched his, "I played this work with this orchestra last year. If you feel that you can't conduct for me, we will play it without you."

Many in the orchestra gasped, some snickered. One did not talk that way to the chief conductor of a symphony orchestra.

There was a long pause. Then Ormandy tapped with his baton. "Let us begin the first movement."

We went through the three movements without stopping. He conducted an exemplary performance but didn't speak to me afterward.

I met him many years later at the Plaza Hotel. He had forgotten the incident and was quite cordial. I was told, after the broadcast, that he had at first refused to conduct for a mouth-organist. The orchestra manager had to point out that my contract was as valid as his; if he refused to conduct, the breach would be his. He conducted. I have never had difficulty with any other conductor and I have been soloist with Solti, Monteux, Ancerl, Sargent, Boult, Johnson, Bakaleinikoff, Gould, Cameron and others.

On a different level, Alec Templeton, the blind British pianist, wanted me to come with him when he played his composition "Bach Goes to Town" for Benny Goodman. Alec was nervous of Goodman. While we were in Goodman's suite at the St. Francis Hotel in San Francisco, Goodman ordered dinner from room service. He didn't ask us if we wanted anything. When dinner arrived, Goodman ate it, not offering us so much as a coffee. However, the evening wasn't wasted. Goodman was short on hospitality but fine on musical appreciation. He liked "Bach Goes to Town" enough to record it. So, much later, did I.

In 1940 Dinah Shore and I provided the cabaret at the White House correspondents' dinner to President Roosevelt. I was a strong Roosevelt man, this was an occasion—it was where Roosevelt made his "destroyers for bases" speech—and I played my guts out. A standing ovation, which I received, was a rarity, unlike today where they are given to the tea lady and the man who raises the piano lid. I came off, and a lady in the wings congratulated me and remarked that I seemed in great form.

"Thank you," I said, "and . . . I'm sure you will understand . . . I'm really quite excited about tonight. It's silly but . . . I do know your face but it's probably the state I'm in . . . I simply cannot remember your name."

She said, "Mrs. Roosevelt." Now, excitement or no, how could anybody forget Mrs. Roosevelt? It's like forgetting Gandhi.

Eileen's doctor told her that, because of his golf, he only delivered babies on Wednesdays and Saturdays, which I felt knocked the hell out of astrology. He induced labor. The night before the birth I was in a panic. The Laughtons coped with me and Charles fed me brandy. I was scared of becoming a father. I went back to the hospital and waited around until they let me into Eileen's room. She looked beautiful, the baby looked like a booking agent. Now I know that *all* babies look like booking agents.

I was in a daze when I left the hospital but exhilarated as well. I did something completely out of character. I raced another car up Santa Monica Boulevard and crashed into a parked car. I wasn't hurt. The driver I raced thumbed his nose at me and drove on looking gleeful.

When it was time for Eileen to leave I waited outside with the car. New mothers, clutching their babies, were coming out, looking wan and unprepossessing in dressing gowns and with disheveled air. They looked like Thurber drawings. Then Eileen made her exit, walking briskly in a gray tailored suit with, behind her, a nurse carrying the baby.

As a father I was a flop. Whatever a father is supposed to do, I didn't do it. I detested baby talk and couldn't have used it on my own baby. Why, when adults speak to a child, must their voices go up while they talk down? It makes them, I suppose, feel superior; I shrivel when I hear such goo.

I am twice a grandfather. My daughter Wendy has two children from her first marriage, to Ben Sonnenberg, Jr. They are Susannah and Emma and they call me "Larry." Carole and Wendy call me "PAF" which is an acronym for Poor Aged Father. (Peter calls me "Daddy.") Had I ever dared to call my grandfather by his first name, let alone a nickname, I doubt I'd have had enough teeth left to wrap around a mouth-organ.

Bill Stein, the MCA agent, was trying to get me work. We had met Bill in Juan-les-Pins and it was he who persuaded me to try coming back into U.S. show business. During my Australian tour Bill had written to me saying I was the "forgotten man," and how depressing *that* sounded! But I had done nothing for the American public to remember. Bill got me a date at the San Francisco Exposition, with Eddy Duchin and his orchestra. That kept me working but was bad for morale. The public was interested in Duchin, not me. The show was in the open, planes flew over and drowned me out. Leonard Lyons, the *New York Post* columnist, whom I had met in New York when I played at the Versailles in 1936, came and wrote about me. He sympathized with my position, a star overseas, an unknown at home. Herb Caen, the leading columnist of San Francisco, also helped to get my name known. Both journalists went out of their way to help my career.

I nearly lost Leonard Lyons as a friend with a joke. Leonard would show photos of his kids and retail their bright sayings. Once, at Toots Shor's restaurant in New York where the customers were a sporting crowd, showbiz and the Mob, I listened to another recital of cute remarks made by Leonard's kids. I told him this joke. A man says: "I must tell you about my nephew, he's *so* cute, the things he comes out with. Just the other day the doorbell rang and my nephew ran to the door to answer it. He came back in and said, 'Uncle, there's a policeman out there and he's going to arrest you!' I went to the door; know what it was, it was the mailman with a special-delivery letter. But wasn't it cute, the way my nephew immediately associated the uniform with the police."

His friend says: "Yeah, that is kinda cute; how old's your nephew?"

"Thirty-eight."

Leonard glared at me, left, and it was a year before he talked to me again.

In Lindy's (made famous by Damon Runyon as "Mindy's") I told Frances Lastfogel, who was married to the head of the William Morris Agency, that things weren't going well.

"Why don't you go see my Abe," said Frances. It was good advice. I went to see her Abe, who took me on and things did pick up. No artist can be his own agent, especially if he moves in different levels of the entertainment and musical world. Concerts require a concert manager; nightclubs and theaters, another. Films are a different world altogether and you need an agent who moves in that world.

I played at the New York Paramount. Bob Weitman was the manager and he offered me a deal to play there three times a year, a good offer. Before that I'd met a PR man, Hal Davis, who tried to get me some publicity. He told me that he would work a tie-in with the Thomas Hair Treatment advertising campaign. I would endorse the treatment, and Thomas would take full-page advertisements wherever I appeared. I disliked endorsements but told Davis I'd go along with it provided the copy was just some bland statement such as: "I believe that a man should take care of his hair." I didn't even like that. It took Davis a while to persuade me; after all, he argued, Artie Shaw, a lot bigger name than I, had given them a rave. Who the hell did I think *I* was? Finally Davis got an agreement and I signed it. The week I opened Paul Draper phoned me, asking if

I'd seen that morning's *Times*. There was a full-page ad publicizing my date at the New York Paramount. There was also some glutinous copy with quotes from me, declaring that my success, past, present and future, was due entirely to having my hair cared for by Thomas. It was revolting.

I phoned Hal Davis. Thomas had reneged on their agreement. Yes, said Davis, but there it was. Another advertisement was scheduled for the following week. And after all, it was a full-page and it was in the *Times*. I told Hal I didn't give a damn about the full-page. Thomas had lied. I had signed an agreement which stated clearly what would be in the advertisement and was certainly not accepting the nauseating crap that they'd come up with. I wanted to cancel the agreement and the coming advertisement, I didn't want my name used by Thomas again. If they refused to cancel, I'd sue for breach of contract. They canceled.

Hal discovered a new orchestra, the Bronx Symphony, looking for a way to get noticed. He arranged a concert with me to play the Vivaldi Concerto in A Minor. It was the first time a mouth-organist had appeared as a soloist with a symphony orchestra. The concert was held in the Bronx, no critic reviewed it, but it did get a lot of publicity and helped to get me known.

During the New York World's Fair in 1939, Hal persuaded the mayor to declare a "Larry Adler Day." The mayor probably wondered who Larry Adler was. I appeared at the Waldorf Astoria Starlight Roof. On opening night, one man at a ringside table was being noisy. I never know how to cope with a drunk, and just let him ruin my performance. During *Bolero* he hit the floor with a thud. I later found that he was rising and falling to the beat of *Bolero* and, on one rise, Ray Bolger had pulled out the man's chair.

Later, in the foyer, I saw the drunk. He turned out to be an old friend.

"Larry," he said, "have you been inside? There's a fellow doing your stuff, pinching your act—but he's *terrible!*"

I went to the showing of another friend's pictures. At the gallery a man with a walrus moustache and wearing an old-fashioned three-button jacket approached me, told me, "You are a much mismanaged young man," gave me his card and asked me to look him up. He was Benjamin Sonnenberg, the most famous PR man in New York.

I did look him up and he said it was time *The New Yorker* did a profile of me. He wanted me to meet E. J. Kahn, Jr., a writer on *The New Yorker.* Eileen and I went to Kahn's flat in Greenwich Village, as arranged by Sonnenberg. We were let in by a cleaning lady, no sign of Kahn. When he arrived he looked at us uneasily, wondering who we were. Sonnenberg had omitted to tell him we were coming. Kahn made stabs at hospitality but he looked like a man violated and the tension had the consistency of Blackpool rock. After as short an interval as seemed decent, Eileen and I got up to go. Kahn abruptly announced he would give us a lift uptown. Had he not done so I would have lost the chance to know a man who became one of my best friends. Jack Kahn introduced me to other staff members of *The New Yorker:* Bruce Bliven, Jr., whose father edited *The New Republic,* and William Shawn, who was to succeed Harold Ross as editor. They had a jazz group, Jack on drums, Bruce Bliven on bass and Bill Shawn on piano. I would play four-hand duets with Shawn, not knowing that he was claustrophobic and having me playing the treble register of the piano made him feel hemmed in. When I found out, I switched to the bass, leaving him the treble, and thus an escape line.

Kahn introduced me to Margaret Case Harriman, who was impressed because she found me funnier than her father, Frank Case, the manager of the Algonquin, host at the famous Round Table and a much quoted wit. I was impressed that Mrs. Harriman was impressed and our friendship blossomed; she went to Harold Ross, said she wanted to do a profile of me for *The New Yorker,* and Ross agreed.

When I first came to New York, I discovered *The New Yorker;* from it I'd learned about people like Hemingway, Fitzgerald, Wolfe, Faulkner, Dreiser. I admired their writing. I'd always loved reading and was a purist about language. A. J. Ayer told me that I had a good mind, what a pity I'd never had the benefit of a British education. I don't know if that's true, I do know my mind is unorganized. I've made little use of whatever potential it has.

The New Yorker was very organized. When it runs a profile, it doesn't kid around. Every fact is quadruple-checked, the spelling of proper names is measured against reference books and a typographical error is as rare as a clothed lady in *Playboy.* Just how tough Harold Ross was in questioning his profile writers is made clear in

Maggie Harriman's book *Take Them Up Tenderly,* where she also gives her outraged answers:

ROSS: What does she mean, "put a stop to"? Wording here doesn't make sense to me.
MCH: Nag, nag, nag.
ROSS: Courses in Enunciation are not new. A friend of mine took one in Lowell, Mass., because she was nasal.
MCH: Where the Nasals speak only to Lowells.
Oh, nasal Lowell, dat nasal Lowell
She don't do nuffin, she don't say nuffin
She just keep Lowelling, she keeps on Lowelling alo-oong. . . .
ROSS: How many servants? Just these two?
MCH: Just two and a werewolf.
ROSS: Does he know many of his women employees by name when he meets them outside?
MCH: Nope, calls them all Charlie.
ROSS: What became of his mother?
MCH: She afterward became his father.

It says much for Harold Ross that Mrs. Harriman kept her job. Robert Benchley, after receiving fifty-five queries from Ross on a profile he was writing, just scribbled in pencil: "You keep out of this."

Mrs. Harriman's "Profile" makes me out to be an uncured ham. She writes that, after my visit to Palestine, I told Eileen that in Jerusalem I visited the Wall in the Old City and, though nonreligious, I had actually prayed.

"What for?" asked Eileen. "Bigger billing?"

Maggie also observed that, "Adler is as used to being called the world's greatest harmonica player (or virtuoso) as, say, Hugo Zacchini was used to being called the world's greatest man-shot-out-of-a-cannon, and his eye automatically skips that phrase and gets down to the business angle."

What can I say? I *am* used to it and I *do* think it. If I heard a better one I would become that player's press agent. Mind you, there are players who top me. Sonny Terry is better on black blues, making a sound I couldn't equal, because Terry is playing about what he knows, and I don't. Jean (Toots) Thielemans plays better jazz. But for all around playing I nominate me. There are many players who are technically as good, perhaps better, but their playing lacks balls. They play the notes with accuracy and their sound is pedestrian, with the emotion of a bound copy of *Hansard.*

Maybe it's being Jewish. An Israeli violinist, Sascha Parnes, told me there was a practical reason why the leading violinists were Jews. They came from ghettoes and their parents wanted them to find a better life. A violin was portable, you could earn your living with it anywhere. Sounds reasonable.

CHAPTER

Seven

IN 1943 THE NATIONAL BROADCASTING COMPANY arranged to broadcast the first American performance of Dmitri Shostakovich's *Leningrad* Symphony with Arthur Rodzinski conducting the NBC Symphony. I was playing at the Paramount Theater and some friends of mine from *The New Yorker* were going to see my show, come backstage and then go to my flat to hear the broadcast. After my show, we got to the flat and turned on the radio. The concert was already on. I, as the only musician present, felt I should try to interpret the music to my friends.

"Listen to that," I said. "It's incredible, the way Shostakovich is able to draw on his experience as a firefighter on the roofs in Moscow during the siege . . . it's all there in the music." My friends nodded respectfully. The work ended and heavy applause was heard. The announcer came on:

"You have just heard the overture to *School for Scandal* by Samuel Barber." Collapse of emaciated musician.

Life was not going well. I was becoming self-destructive; I'd lost dates; I'd hurt myself, sometimes deliberately; I was a procrastinator.

I began to worry about this, so I spoke to my friend Dr. Samuel Fogelson when I was in Chicago and asked him if he thought I should be psychoanalyzed.

Fogelson arranged that I take a Rohrshach test, the ink-blots plus association test. It was given to me by a Swiss. I asked: "If I told you that what I saw were ink-blots, would I be normal?" He said: "Dis iss a very serious test, Herr Aidler." Fogelson found that Ernst Simmel, a pupil and friend of Freud, lived in Hollywood and was known to be good with creative people such as George Gershwin, Judy Garland and Artie Shaw, who had all been his patients. Simmel agreed to take me and so Eileen, our daughter Carole and I moved to California.

It wasn't as drastic as it sounds; we had no home in New York, just a rented apartment. In California, we also lived in rented homes: at first we had Norma Talmadge's house in Benedict Canyon, then a house in Beverly Hills. This was during the war, gas was rationed. Eileen found that if you rented a car no rationing applied, so we paid $100 a week, big money then, to rent a car. Eileen wasn't going to give up her mobility. Later she found a house on Linden Drive and we bought it. It was a fine house, plenty of rooms, its own garage with an apartment over it. No pool; I may well have been the only Beverly Hills resident without a pool. Big garden, though. We had a black couple as staff. I think they were reporting on me to the FBI but have no evidence. They were always congratulating me on my left-wing activities.

I committed a sin by buying a house without signing a non-Caucasian exclusion clause, meaning I wouldn't sell my house to a non-Caucasian, meaning black or yellow. I was visited by Chamber of Commerce people pressing me to sign; after all, my neighbors had. I wouldn't and didn't. Another sin was to walk, just walk, in Beverly Hills. A walker was automatically pulled up by cops in a police car. They were more suspicious of resident walkers than strangers. If you could afford to live in Beverly Hills, what the hell were you doing walking? There wasn't much crime in Beverly Hills.

I can't say that psychoanalysis *cured* me of anything. It did help me to know myself. One discovery I made was that, instead of being a good father as I imagined, I was more a policeman, pointing out right from wrong but showing no real love. One time I returned from a concert tour. Eileen asked me to pick up Carole from nursery school

—she was four. Eileen said that Carole had been withdrawn, unhappy. When Carole saw me, she ran with arms open to hug me. But
in the car she sat apart, saying nothing. I told her Eileen was worried
that she seemed unhappy. No, she wasn't, she said. Well, I said,
Mummy thinks you are; and if you're unhappy, so are we because
we love you very much. Carole turned around and looked at me.
"You don't show it," she said. It sounds dramatic but those four
words changed my life; from then on I showed it like crazy.

Simmel took no active part in the analysis, he insisted on me doing
the work, he would just keep me at it. Sometimes I would say
nothing for long stretches; he would then say: "I seenk zere is a
resistance at work." And I'd feel ashamed. How could I bore this
intelligent man with my babblings? Analysis, I found, was good at
keeping you from kidding yourself. Unfortunately, while it helped
you to see that your troubles were mainly your own fault, the method
was no good for keeping you out of trouble; but at least you would
know how you got there.

I didn't stick at it for long in any one year. At that time I went on
tour every winter with Paul Draper for three months. Also, starting
in 1943, I went overseas for the USO with Jack Benny every summer, and if a professional engagement came up in, say New York
or Chicago, I'd accept it. So, all in all, important (and expensive) as
analysis was to me, I was never deeply involved.

Once, however, after the war, Simmel did say something positive
which affected my life. Ingrid Bergman suggested we go off somewhere together, Honolulu perhaps. I seriously considered this,
though there was a risk that Eileen might find out. Simmel felt that,
while I was in analysis, I shouldn't take any drastic step like that. He
said it really wasn't his business to interfere but, as I was his patient,
he felt that he should say something. I accepted, and I didn't go with
Ingrid.

I sometimes regret I didn't marry Ingrid, but I couldn't face being
Mr. Ingrid Bergman. We talked about it. I was too much a coward
to break up my marriage, but also, my ego was such that I couldn't
see myself walking four paces behind Ingrid. I don't think it would
have worked; we might have been happy for a while but I would
always have been secondary to her, her fame was much greater than
mine. I don't think I could have stood that. But we always remained
friends. You had to respect her, she was a fine lady, dedicated to her

work. I don't think anyone could mean as much to her as her work, not her husband, nor even her daughter. She told me that once, after a tough day at the studio, her daughter Pia ran down the stairs to welcome her home. "And I slapped her face," said Ingrid. "I hated myself for it, I felt ashamed, I wanted to hug her, to say 'I'm sorry' . . . and I just couldn't."

Six months or so before she died I happened to phone her to invite her to a party. She wasn't well, she said, and she wasn't going out at all. I hadn't yet heard about the cancer.

"Larry, if you had called about three months ago I'd have asked you over and then, as you were coming through the door, I'd have hit you over the head with the hardest object I could find!"

I had no idea what she was talking about.

"Do you remember an interview with a Swedish journalist who wanted to talk to you about me?"

Yes, I remembered him. A sober, serious man, he seemed more like an accountant than a journalist.

"Well, *you* thought he was sober and serious. Larry, how could you be such a child? He wanted something sensational to write about *me* and he was just using you as an excuse. Do you know what the headline was on his story? It said, I WAS INGRID'S LOVER."

"Oh, my God!"

"That's when I was ready to kill you. If you had come anywhere near me I *would* have killed you. But everybody said: 'Larry would never say anything like that.' And I remembered, of course you wouldn't, you wrote two articles about me, I really liked them. So I felt better about it. But, Larry, really—to say *anything* to a journalist about me!"

"Oh, Ingrid. I am sorry!"

"You know who talked me out of wanting to kill you? It was Lars (Lars Schmidt, Ingrid's ex-husband). Lars said, 'Come on, Ingrid, you know Larry. And you know the Swedish press, what they're like.' He was right, I realized that. But, Larry, please don't ever do such a silly thing again."

Of course I promised I wouldn't. I still found it hard to believe that such a respectable sort of man would write a hack story like that. Ingrid and I were still friends, when we hung up it was on an affectionate note. I'm glad I can say that because it was the last conversation I ever had with her.

Once she gave a dinner party; Jean Renoir, son of the painter, and Alfred Hitchcock were the other guests. I said that I had a theory that the big budget was the enemy of the good picture, that a good director did his best work under pressure of economy. Renoir agreed, saying that a small budget challenged the director's imagination; with a big one, he was lost, didn't know how to spend it. Nonsense, said Hitchcock, the bigger the budget, the better picture he could make. I tried to argue the point, but Hitchcock had a surefire gambit—he fell asleep, right at the dinner table. It was a favorite device of his; he'd make his point, then drop off while you were trying to make yours. I took Ingrid to a party at Jack Benny's. She came to me in a panic. L. B. Mayer kept trying to paw her and she couldn't stand it. She wanted to leave but Jack's wife, Mary, made such a scene about it that we stayed.

Jack Benny had the idea of "love me, love my friends," and often tried to bring me together with his group, really Mary's, who were mainly right-wing. After a preview in Jack's projection room, showing *Double Indemnity,* I started to congratulate Barbara Stanwyck. She cut me short. "Jack's told me about you and your liberal bullshit; I hope we're not going to have to listen to that crap all evening." Another time, as Gary Cooper was taking my wife in to dinner, he said: "Tell me, Mrs. Adler, would your husband *really* not mind if your daughter married a Negro?"

Jack, Mary, Eileen and I went to a Jerome Kern concert at the Hollywood Bowl. Eileen drove in Jack's car, Mary with me. Mary asked: "Tell me, Larry, when you were with Jack on these tours, did he cheat?" I was appalled. "Oh, come on, it's just between us. I'd never say a word to Jack." I said the question was revolting, she should never have asked it and, were she not Jack's wife, I'd have asked her to get out of the car. Relations were distant after that. Some time before, she was in her car with the top down; I in mine, also with the top down. At a traffic stop, our cars side by side, she bellowed an intimate question about Ingrid to me. A lot of people must have heard her and I'm certain she did it deliberately. Not a nice lady.

Ernst Simmel had analyzed George Gershwin. Simmel told me that, when Gershwin first came to him, he was complaining of migraine headaches, which he thought might be neurotic. Simmel always asked new patients to have a complete medical checkup—and, in George's case, recommended a spinal tap. George, dreading the pain of it, refused to have one. Simmel said that, had Gershwin had the tap, it is possible that the fluid would have shown evidence of the brain tumor which killed him.

Gershwin had other warnings. I was in the audience when he played and conducted a program of his music with the Los Angeles Philharmonic. In the third movement of the Concerto in F Gershwin stopped playing for a few bars, looked out at the audience, then resumed. It was a weird moment. At an after-concert party at Ira's house on Roxbury Drive in Beverly Hills, I asked George what had happened that caused him to stop playing for a few moments.

"Well," he said, "suddenly, during the third movement of the concerto, I could have sworn I smelled burning rubber: I thought maybe the place was on fire. I stopped, looked around, but there was no panic anywhere, so I went on playing."

What we didn't know at the time was, if someone smells burning rubber when there is no burning rubber, that is another possible clue to a brain tumor. George collapsed one day outside Ira's home, sat on the curb holding his head in his hands. He was rushed to hospital. The best surgeon available happened to be on a yacht, sailing. They got Gershwin to hospital but, when he was opened up, it was already too late. Look what that man accomplished in his thirty-nine years, think what must have lain ahead. What a tragic useless waste.

There was a memorial broadcast and I was asked to play *Rhapsody in Blue.* Robert Russell Bennett, Gershwin's friend, who had orchestrated several Gershwin musicals and also arranged the *Porgy and Bess Suite,* had reorchestrated the *Rhapsody in Blue* for mouth-organ and orchestra, this with George Gershwin's permission. Oscar Levant, on the same program, came up to me during rehearsal in such a rage that I thought he'd hit me.

"What the hell are *you* doing playing the *Rhapsody in Blue,* goddamnit, that's *my* number!" I tried to explain, over Oscar's shouts, that the producer has asked me to play it, and after all, why the hell shouldn't I?

"You're a goddamn liar," yelled Levant. "There's something fishy going on here. You probably bribed your way."

How could you argue against that? Levant went to find the producer and gave him hell, but the number stayed in.

I was playing in St. Louis when Eileen phoned me from California to tell me Simmel had died. I had known people in Beverly Hills who collapsed if their analyst died. I felt sad, of course, but mainly at the loss of a good man, because I thought highly of him; he was always concerned about his patients. But I was not deeply moved nor upset. I resumed analysis with Judd Marmor, a much younger man than Simmel. Two patients tried a practical joke on him. At $50 an hour, that's a $100 joke. Abe Burrows, in the morning and Arthur Laurents in the afternoon, plotted each to tell Marmor the same dream. After Laurents had told it, Marmor said: "Isn't that odd? You're the third person to tell me that dream."

In England I tried therapy with Joseph Shorvon, who gave me methedrine to help me talk. It helped all right but it was impossible to sleep that night. It also had the side effect of making me want to work, although in general I don't think drugs help creativity. Once, however, I wrote a letter to James Thurber while high on methedrine. He not only told me that it was one of the six or seven best he'd ever received but he referred to it in a book of his own letters. Shorvon tried ether on me to get me to "abreact." It didn't work. I seem to fear losing control completely. Shorvon died while I was in the U.S. for a film score engagement. I then tried regular analysis with Dr. May. He died too. If I feel like trying again, it is probably only fair to warn the psychiatrist of my record. How many can say they've killed off three analysts? I don't think I will try again. Short term therapy for a specific problem, perhaps; but not the long analytical process.

It is a pity that, with all I have learned through experience, I am so bad at putting my knowledge to practical use. I am able to spot trouble coming but don't know how to head it off. I can see things clearly in retrospect but not in advance. While self-awareness was invaluable in helping me to start the most fulfilling relationship of my life, it was no use in preventing the collapse of that relationship after eight years. I now know what I did wrong; I may even have known at the time, but knowing my mistakes didn't stop me making them. Age hasn't withered me so far but custom doesn't seem to stale my infinite monotony. The most destructive fault of all, procrastination, the putting off doing things, is as bad as ever.

During my Hollywood psychoanalysis sessions I was engaged for a film, *Sensations of 1944,* with Andrew Stone producing and directing. I told Stone about the windfall Ravel had left me. Stone was delighted, we agreed that I would play *Bolero* in the film. I wired Elkan, Vogel to confirm my rights to the work and got confirmation by return. To understand the value, consider that Paramount paid the Ravel estate $20,000 to use *Bolero* in a film starring George Raft and Carole Lombard. They only wanted the title (though they did use the music) which they could have had free, since bolero is a type of jacket.

Stone showed me how he was staging my scene; it takes place in an agent's office, a lot of out-of-work performers are in the waiting room. The agent comes out of his office, I get to him first and blow *Bolero* into his face. I told Stone I couldn't do that, explained that I owed it to Ravel to treat his work with respect. I didn't mind doing the scene with some other number, a standard like "St. Louis Blues" or "Stardust." Stone said, "Don't tell me how to make pictures." One of the Nassauer Brothers, who backed the film, showed me an advertisement for the trade papers; along with Sophie Tucker, Eleanor Powell and Dan Duryea my name was above the title, meaning star billing. That was tempting but I couldn't give way; I can't compromise on a principle. I walked off the picture, which got me the only good notice I ever had from Hedda Hopper, the movie columnist.

That summer, at Guadalcanal, I saw *Sensations* scheduled for an afternoon showing for the troops. Jack Benny came with me to see what the film world had lost by my obstinacy. There was a circus scene that featured Pallenberg's Bears. At one point a bear kept riding a motorcycle around a ring.

"Look at that," I said to Jack, "that poor bear's in a rut."

"It's worse than you think," said Jack. "That animal, through no fault of his, is now typecast. In every picture, he'll have to be a bear."

We could see that bear going on strike and picketing the studio. Finally he wins script approval and, in a jungle film, gets to play a giraffe.

Henry Koster was going to direct *Music for Millions* at MGM. It was about an all-girl symphony orchestra; one male, José Iturbi, as the conductor. Koster had the idea of casting me in the film. His first choice had been Yehudi Menuhin; he was lucky he got me. Menuhin on the mouth-organ is a *mess.* Part of the shooting time was in July and I was scheduled to do a USO tour with Jack Benny. We had been in North Africa the year before; we didn't know where we would be going this time but we figured the South Pacific and we were right. I explained this to Koster. He was sympathetic, said he'd shorten the part but wanted me for one number, playing Debussy's *Clair de Lune.*

It was a cafe scene. I was to enter a cafe that had a string orchestra playing and be recognized by June Allyson and Margaret O'Brien. June—I don't think you're going to believe this—was a pregnant double-bass player in the film, Margaret was her niece, June's husband was in the Pacific. She calls me over, tells me that "their" song, meaning for her and her husband, was *Clair de Lune,* it was their wedding anniversary and would I play it for her? You can only do these things in the movies; not only would I play it, not only did I have my mouth-organ in my pocket, not only did the orchestra leader agree to accompany me, he even knew my *arrangement.* While I played it, June cried, Margaret cried and, from the reactions I got around the world, a lot of other people cried. June was an easy weeper, she would cry over seed catalogues, but Margaret O'Brien could match her, tear for tear. In fact Margaret said to Koster: "Uncle Bobby, when Uncle Larry plays and I cry, shall I let the tears run all the way down my face or shall I stop them halfway down?" Bet she could do it, too.

After the scene was shot Koster told me he'd had a hard time keeping me on the film. Joe Pasternak, the producer, wanted to fire me. Why? Well, Pasternak wanted to see how the scene would play so they brought in a mouth-organist to record *Clair de Lune.* After hearing it, Pasternak told Koster he'd have to get rid of me. Koster was appalled and asked the reason. Pasternak told him to listen again to that sound-track.

"But that's not Larry," said Koster.

"It's a mouth-organ," said Pasternak. "How much different can a mouth-organ sound? Get rid of him."

Koster refused and insisted that I be allowed to record the number. I did, without any idea of the goings-on behind the scenes. It stayed in.

On one shooting day Koster said, rather mysteriously, that I should go to the commissary (the studio restaurant) after we'd finished for the day. He wouldn't tell me why. I went, to find the commissary converted into an enormous banquet hall. It was Louis B. Mayer's birthday and he was the guest of honor. (He was also,

of course, one of the most feared and detested of men, with immense
power which he used against anyone he didn't like.) At the various
tables were the great MGM stars: Clark Gable, John, Lionel and
Ethel Barrymore, Robert Taylor, Ava Gardner, Charles Boyer,
Loretta Young, Doug Fairbanks, Jr., Garbo, Katharine Hepburn and
Spencer Tracy. One by one, each rose to say that all that they were,
all that they ever hoped to be, they owed to their beloved Louis B.
And when it came to crying, June Allyson was outclassed by Louis
B. Mayer, the best crier in show business. The more flowery the
speech, the more he cried. Then George Jessel got up to speak.
George was famous as an after-dinner speaker (President Truman
was later to designate him U.S. Toastmaster-General) but sentimen-
tality was not for him.

"Ladies and gentlemen," he said. "I have just one thing to say
about our guest of honor, Louis B. Mayer. Believe me, *he's* no
schmuck!"

Mr. Mayer stopped crying. Nor did he think that was funny. The
party ended shortly after.

Next day Mr. Jessel was fired from MGM and blacklisted at the
other studios as well. The court jester didn't know his place.

The next year Pasternak was making another musical film, again
with José Iturbi, to be called *The Birds and the Bees*. This title was
considered too sexy and changed to *Three Daring Daughters*. I was
to play Enesco's Roumanian Rhapsody in a Carnegie Hall setting,
with Iturbi conducting a symphony orchestra. Before shooting I flew
to Chicago for an engagement at the Chicago Theater. When I
returned I had a call from Abe Lastfogel. He told me that due to a
set designers' strike, they couldn't get the Carnegie Hall set built.
Would I let Pasternak out of our deal? He'd put me in another film
some other time. I could have insisted that I be paid—I had held the
time free and signed a contract—but it didn't seem important
enough to make it an issue, creating bad feeling and certainly ensur-
ing that I'd never work at MGM again. So I agreed, the deal was off.

That night Johnny Green rang me. Johnny, an old friend, was most
famous as the composer of "Body and Soul." He was in charge of
music at MGM.

"Larry," he said, "it means my job if word of this gets out." I
promised secrecy.

He told me that the set-designer story was phony. The set was up, they were shooting the number but without me. Instead of conducting the orchestra while I played, Iturbi would conduct from the piano while *he* played. And what would he be playing? Enesco's Roumanian Rhapsody. What a coincidence!

"And Larry," said Johnny, "he's using *your* arrangement!"

Even for Hollywood this seemed to be carrying *chutzpah* to extremes. I phoned Lastfogel and, keeping Johnny's name out of it, told him what I'd learned. I said find out if the set is up; if it is, then is Iturbi doing a number, and if so, what number?

Lastfogel called back.

"You're back on the picture," he said. "You don't know anything, you keep *schtumm.*"

Next day Pasternak phoned. He was delighted, he said, that all the difficulties were ironed out, that I would be in the film after all.

"Larry," he said, "I've got a script problem and I need your advice. Could you come out to the studio today?"

I'm in the picture as a mouth-organist and suddenly I'm advising the producer on script problems. I drove out to the MGM Studio.

"Larry," said Pasternak, "I've got to establish that José and Jeanette MacDonald are in love; there's only one logical place to establish it and that's during your number. Jeanette will be sitting in the audience and I want to show, with one look between them, that they're in love."

I had an idea what was coming.

"Now, Larry," said Pasternak, and this time I *could* have written the script, "if José is conducting the orchestra, his back is to the audience, right? And if his back is to the audience, he can't look at Jeanette. Ya with me?"

Joe, I was way ahead of you.

"And if he can't look at her, she can't look at him, right?"

Right.

"So, the way I worked it out, if José is at the piano, see, like he's playing a duet with you and conducting the orchestra at the same time, this way I can establish the look, the audience knows they love each other, you got it?"

I got it. I also know I'm screwed.

That's what we did, except that José had one more trick; he worked his *sister,* for God's sake, into the act. José Iturbi, Amparo Iturbi and Friend. I was the friend. The number was lousy.

Aged five. Success hasn't changed me. I'm still a jerk.

This photo is heretical. It goes against my religion, the Church of the Orthodox Coward.

*My parents, my brother and me.
My brother thinks this looks
like a still from an old
Cagney movie.*

*Baron's first photograph of
me, taken in 1935.*

*The scrutable Oriental. With
Dick Powell in* The Singing
Marine.

*In music hall with Max Wall,
photographed by Baron in 1936.
A rare photo—it shows me
listening.* (BBC HULTON
PICTURE LIBRARY)

*Stuttgart is the location,
1935 the date. Could I have
been so naive that I didn't
know what the emblem in the
background stood for?*

*Leaving for South Africa with
my wife Eileen in 1938.* (BBC
HULTON PICTURE LIBRARY)

*Playing bedtime music to my
children, Peter and Wendy.*
(POPPERFOTO)

With Jack Benny in the Pacific in 1944. "What do you mean, 'Give me an A'? I've just given you one."

Entertaining injured servicemen in Korea.

Playing to the troops in Berlin from the balcony of Hitler's Reichskanzlerei with Ingrid Bergman photographing me on the right and Martha Tilton standing below. Inset is the photograph that Ingrid took.

A duet with Malcolm Sargent. "No, no, no, Malcolm, you're supposed to inhale." (BBC COPYRIGHT)

With Paul Draper shortly after the war. (KRONGOLD, LONDON)

With Ralph Vaughan Williams after the Promenade Concert in September 1959 at which the Romance for Harmonica and Orchestra *was first played.* (BBC COPYRIGHT)

Sheik Suleiman holding the dagger which he subsequently presented to my son, Peter. Shortly after this picture was taken Sheik Suleiman proposed to Mrs. Roosevelt.

Taken on set of Music for Millions, *directed by Henry Koster, 1944. From left to right: Frank Sinatra, Larry Adler, June Allyson and Gene Kelly.*

A duet with Lord Mountbatten. If you look carefully, you'll see Mountbatten is hogging the mike.
(SOUTH LONDON PHOTO SERVICES)

*With Sally Cline, my
second wife, on our wedding
day in 1969.* (POPPERFOTO)

*Entertaining a group of
Chinese children at a school
in Tsingtao.*

*Practicing for the Edinburgh
Festival in 1963.* (ALAN
DAICHES, EDINBURGH)

*Rehearsing with Solti and the
Chicago Symphony Orchestra.*

A.C.
AMER
CHILD
CITIZ
RIGHTS

*Subverting American youth. A
group of demonstrators outside the
American embassy in protest against
new laws that could cause them to
lose their citizenship.*
(POPPERFOTO)

The personality most likely to split.
A photograph by the late Bern Schwartz.

Part of a national cycling campaign: from left to right,
Kenneth Horne, Muriel Young, Joe
Loss, Miss World, myself and the
doorman of the Talk of the Town.
(S & G PRESS AGENCY LTD.)

Henri Temianka, conductor of the California Chamber Orchestra, told me that after Amparo died, José came to him and said he wanted to give a fund-raising concert, to establish a chair of music at UCA in Amparo's name. What would such a concert cost to put on?

Temianka drew up a budget, so much for advertisements, publicity, printing, programs, the orchestra. Temianka told Iturbi that he, Temianka, would be happy to give his services free as conductor. Iturbi as soloist. He figured the concert could be put on for, say, $12,000.

"Add another $7500 on to that," said Iturbi.

"Seventy-five hundred dollars? What for?"

"My fee," said the great man. The concert never happened.

Iturbi was weird. He flew his own plane and told me that on every flight, he had an urge to power dive into the ground. He once arranged to kidnap his grandson from the child's father, the violinist, Stephen Hero. Hero was poor, Iturbi was rich; he got away with it.

Hollywood had a hierarchy, a morality, a code of ethics all its own. In the censorship days of the Hays Office, later called the Breen Office, morality was spelled out; in a bedroom scene the man had to keep one foot on the floor, which wouldn't have stopped Errol Flynn. Cleavage, the gap between the breasts, meant a constant battle as to just how low, in every sense of the word, cleavage could get. (Sam Goldwyn spent a fortune trying to make a star out of Anna Sten. When her contract ran out, Goldwyn wanted her false breasts back. They were studio property.)

Guest lists for parties were ticklish affairs. You didn't invite a $500-a-week writer to the same party as a $1500-a-week one. I once made an error trying to be a good fellow. For one dinner party we gave there were three directors on the list: William Wyler, Mervyn LeRoy and Henry Koster. I knew a young actor with talent but who hadn't had a break. I invited him.

After dinner Wyler took me aside. "Larry," he said, "I know what you were trying to do. It doesn't work that way. This kid shouldn't meet us at a dinner party; if anything, it makes things tougher for him."

Well, okay, he taught me a lesson and I learned it.

A friend of mine, Armand Deutsch, who was very rich but who didn't appear to do much of anything, bought the novel *This Side of*

Innocence by Taylor Caldwell, rented offices, took space in *Variety* and *The Hollywood Reporter,* and he was in business. Deutsch lived near me in Beverly Hills and I knew his wife, Benay Venuta, a Broadway musical comedy singer. We went to their parties and they came to ours. The day that Artie Deutsch took the trade-paper space he asked me to come over to his house. He showed me a list of names and said he was about to give his first big party. Who qualified as eligible? I was surprised. Surely he knew who his friends were, he'd never had trouble choosing his guests.

"But, Larry," said Artie, "I can't invite just anybody. I'm a *producer* now!"

I left his house wondering if I were important enough to make Artie Deutsch's guest-list. The picture was never made.

When Louis B. Mayer was deposed as head of MGM, his place was taken by Doré Schary. (Doré was both short and fancy for "Isidore"!) Doré Schary was a successful playwright who had come up fast at MGM. Schary appointed Artie Deutsch as his assistant vice-president, an odd appointment, since Deutsch had no showbiz or film experience, but as noted, he was rich. Shortly after Artie joined MGM he phoned and invited me to play singles with him at the Beverly Hills Tennis Club. This surprised me. Artie had been a college champion and was far better than I. I didn't get it.

I did later. Artie beat me 6–0, 6–0, and in the locker room he clarified things.

"Larry," he said, "Doré wanted me to ask you why you haven't sent in your United Jewish Appeal contribution?"

Now why the hell couldn't he have asked me that on the phone? Why go through the rigmarole of a tennis match? But that's Hollywood.

In the forties, during the war, you couldn't get a new car. A dealer offered a shipment of Standards, a tiny British car, and Artie and I each decided to buy one. Then, after Artie's new job at MGM, he phoned me, saying he hoped I wouldn't think he was letting me down, but an MGM vice-president really couldn't run around in a midget car.

Autres temps, autres whatever the hell they are.

One day Charles Chaplin phoned me.

"Larry, can you get up here right away to make a fourth at tennis

—Bill Tilden's dropped out." William T. Tilden was, in many an expert's opinion, the greatest tennis player ever. When Tilden drops out whom do you call? Larry Adler. It figures.

I drove up to Chaplin's house and went down to the tennis court. Chaplin was hitting against a lady and a man and, when he saw me, motioned to me to get on court. He didn't introduce me. The lady had badly combed hair lying flat, blue shorts, no socks and black sneakers. The man wore a black shirt, slacks, had a weird moustache and couldn't hit a ball. Chaplin was the best player, with incredible anticipation. He never seemed to run for the ball but was always there where it landed. After hitting for a while, the lady suggested that we start a set. The minute she spoke I realized it was Garbo. The man was Salvador Dali.

I once won a name-dropping contest with Walter Cronkite. His top story involved dining with John and Jackie Kennedy, shortly after Kennedy's election. But that was only two names; my story involved Chaplin, Tilden, Dali and Garbo. I won on points.

We had iced tea between sets and Chaplin told us about a biography of him, unauthorized, that had been published. He had never met the author and wanted us to promise that we would not read that book. As this was the first we'd heard of it, I couldn't see Charles's news stimulating a stampede to the nearest Beverly Hills bookshop.

I left first, walking up the path to the driveway. I started the car and, at the same time, heard the patter of not-so-little feet. It was Chaplin, who had run up the driveway from the tennis court.

He came up to my car window, winded from the run.

"Now remember, Larry, you gave me your word—you will *not* read that book!"

I was playing at the Palmer House in Chicago in '44, and had arranged to take time off from my show to go to New York where Eileen was ready to give birth to our second child. I had arranged for Paul Draper to sub for me; he was playing at the Congress Hotel but it was okay with both managements. I flew to New York but there was a heavy snowstorm, my plane was grounded at Pittsburgh. I went on by train but got there too late. I don't think Eileen ever forgave me.

My best friend, Jack Kahn, was there when Eileen opened her eyes, and Jack told her it was a boy. Peter was born five years after

Carole and then four years later, Wendy. I had Mike Romanoff send caviar and garlic toast to the hospital.

Once when we gave a birthday party for Carole, Peter made friends with another boy at the party and asked me if he could invite this boy to his party. Sure. The boy said he would ask his Nanny when she called for him. The Nanny said after checking, "I'm afraid not. Loretta Young is giving a children's party that day and Gavin's mother *never* lets him miss a film-star's party."

That, too, is Hollywood.

CHAPTER

Eight

I N 1943 MY MANAGER, Abe Lastfogel, had been made head
of the USO, which sent shows to military bases in the U.S. and
overseas. Abe said that he could arrange for me to go overseas on
a really exciting tour. He knew that I was at the Palmer House in
Chicago for ten weeks—he ought to know, he'd booked it—but left
it to me to get out of the engagement if I wanted the USO tour. I
went to Merriel Abbot, who staged the shows at the Palmer House,
and said that the Army had drafted me for an overseas tour. Pure
bullshit, of course, but it worked. I went to New York, where Abe
told me I was to go to Africa with Jack Benny, Wini Shaw (famous
for "Lullaby of Broadway" and "Lady in Red," which she sang in
Warner Brothers musicals) and Anna Lee, an English actress.

When the USO tour was announced, Marshall Field, who had
founded the Chicago *Sun* in 1941, suggested that I do weekly dis-
patches for the *Sun*. The idea delighted me. I'd always wanted to
write. It was agreed that my fees would go to the Red Cross.

I told Samuel Grafton, the political columnist for the New York
Post, that having accepted Marshall Field's offer, I was now nervous
about it. "How do you write a dispatch?"

"Simple," said Grafton. "You write down what happens each day, then you write at the top, 'This is a Dispatch,' and it is."

I bought a light Hermès typewriter at Macy's, which, as I'd seen photos of Ernie Pyle with a similar machine, made me feel a real war correspondent. When I returned to the U.S., the *Sun's* foreign editor, Von Hartz, told me he'd submitted my pieces for a Pulitzer Prize. The committee wouldn't consider it. I couldn't have written the articles, I was a mouth-organist. How in hell did they think I could find a ghostwriter in Africa? And doing daily pieces, because I was sending not one a week, but seven. Von Hartz ran every one.

Each piece had to be submitted to Army censorship and I wish I'd kept the copies the Army returned to me. One piece had so many lines scissored out it looked like a lace curtain. It was about an incident where a military car in which I was a passenger struck a man outside Cairo. The officer with me said, "I hope we've killed him."

This seemed callous. The officer explained.

"If he's wounded we have to take care of him for life. If he's killed we make a payment to his family and bingo, that's it."

The censors didn't say I'd written lies; they just cut out the truth.

In general Jack Benny was mild mannered, anything for peace and quiet. I saw him angry just once, after we had done an open-air show in Benghazi. Halfway through, a sand storm started, blowing directly into our faces and completely ruining one of my few good mouth-organs. (They were made in Germany and, once the war began, the supply of mouth-organs stopped.) After the show we had coffee and doughnuts in a Red Cross canteen. After such an unpleasant experience, coffee and doughnuts lacked something. A lieutenant came over and, without invitation, sat at our table. When he opened his mouth his heavy Southern accent made Stepin Fetchit sound like Abe Lincoln.

"Hiya, Jack," he said, pronouncing it "jay-yuck."

"Hi," said Jack, wearily.

"Hey, Jay-yuck, how come y'all didn't bring Rochestah?" (The black man who was Jack's butler on his radio show.)

Jack said that Rochester had commitments at home.

"Thay-yuts a goddamn shame, pahdon mah French," he said. "Y'know, back home in Tallahassee, m'wife and me, we listen in evah Sunday night, wouldn't miss it foh the world. But shee-*yit,* man, that Rochestah, whah, he's ninety percent of yoah show."

"Wish we'd brought Rochester, eh?"

"Sure do! Not to say y'all ain't veh funny, Miz Benny, but shee-*yit* man, m'wife and me, we just crazy 'bout that Rochestah."

"Okay," said Jack, "now let's suppose we had brought him. He'd be sitting at this table with us. How would you like that?"

"Now just you hold on one minute," said the lieutenant. "Ah'm from the South!"

"That," said Jack, "is why I didn't bring Rochester."

That evening, after doing the show in the sandstorm, I felt awful and, wandering down to the beach, lay down and fell asleep. What I didn't know was this was a military area; it was also mined.

Suddenly someone pulled me to my feet, thrust a light into my face and bellowed, "Who the fuckin' hell are *you?*"

I was still half-asleep. I mumbled that I was an entertainer, that I was on tour for the USO. My interrogator—captor, really—was British and USO meant nothing to him.

"You got an ID card?" No, I hadn't.

"Okay, you're in an area where you shouldn't be, you haven't got any identification. Now, before I take you to the guardhouse, suppose you tell me your fuckin' name?"

"Larry Adler."

He stood back, shone the light into my face again.

"Yes," he said, "and I'm the fuckin' Duke of Windsor!"

I did a show at dawn for a group of airmen, about to go on a bombing mission. We were not supposed to know where they were bound but it was an open secret that the U.S. air force was sending bombing missions against the Ploesti oil fields in Roumania. It was a dangerous assignment, the casualty rate was high. On the airstrip, at dawn, I played for the airmen, knowing that many of them wouldn't be coming back.

In Cairo you could feel the hatred from the Egyptians. They were pro-German and hoped for a Nazi victory. One night with Frank Gervasi, war correspondent for *Collier's* magazine, we hailed a horse-drawn gharry (taxi). It was dark—the city was blacked out—but when the gharry-driver got close enough to see our U.S. uniforms he raised his whip and aimed across our faces—he missed—then whipped his horse and got away.

NBC wanted a forty-five-minute shortwave broadcast from Jack and the rest of us, from Cairo to the U.S. I thought it would be easy to find, among the GI's, men with radio-writing experience. We found several but they were scared, more of Jack's mighty reputation than of Jack himself. No one who knew him could be scared of him. The GI stuff was impossible to use. I told Jack that I knew his style and thought I could write the program. Jack said okay. I thought it an idea to have a war hero on as a guest and we got an airman who had shot down a record number of German and Italian planes. The airman told me of his war philosophy: to kill as many of the enemy as possible. If an enemy pilot bailed out, he said, he would follow the pilot in his own plane and machine-gun him. He was amused at my shock.

"Look, he's been trying to kill me, right? Just like I've been trying to kill him. And if he bales out do I just sit by and let him land? What for? To give him a chance to try to kill me again? No, sir, I say you kill the enemy and stuff the rules of war."

For technical reasons the broadcast didn't reach the U.S. and we had to repeat it. The airman was no longer available and I got Frank Gervasi. It ran too long and we were cut off before my writing credit, so nobody knew I wrote the show. "You see," said Jack, "what you get being Mr. Nice Guy?" NBC cabled Jack to sign the anonymous writer and Jack wanted to do it but I felt that, much as I liked and respected him, I didn't want to be another of his writers. Jack returned after our African tour in 1943 and told everyone from his own writers to George Burns that I was the world's funniest man. This annoyed the writers, especially since Jack, at a script conference, would say that he wished Larry Adler was there, *he* would know how to make that joke work. George Burns, who knew me, found the whole thing unbelievable. He asked Jack for an example of this lightning humor, something to demonstrate that I was the funniest man in the world. Jack told Burns about the time we were received by the Sultan of Morocco, in Marrakesh. To enter the palace we had to wait while two huge iron gates, each looking as if they weighed several tons, were drawn back by guards. When we left the same thing had to happen. As we went through the gates, I whispered: "Mind your manners, Jack, don't slam the door." This convulsed Jack, who leaned against the wall, shaking with laughter, and it may well have been funny as an off-the-cuff remark. But I doubt if reading about it has caused you to drop the book while you doubled up laughing, and when Jack told it to George Burns it was received deadpan.

" 'Mind your manners, Jack, don't slam the door,' " repeated Burns, slowly. "That's all he said? That was it, the whole thing? Wasn't there a payoff somewhere? Something extra thrown in?"

"No, George," said Jack. "That's the whole thing. Mind you, you had to be there at the time, you had to see those doors. And it was the way he delivered the line."

"Yeah, I can see that," said George. "I knew there had to be something. He'd have to have some delivery to make that line funny. Let me go over it once more. 'Mind your manners, Jack, don't slam the door.' Well, well. And that line, together with his absolutely terrific delivery, makes Larry Adler the funniest man in the *world!* Tell me, Jack, do you have any other examples? Maybe not as sma-sheroo as that, but he must have said some other funny things?"

By now, of course, Jack was sorry he'd ever brought the subject up. But Burns wasn't going to let it go. At the Hillcrest Country Club with Groucho Marx, George Jessel, Sid Caesar, Danny Kaye and Phil Silvers sitting at the round table, Burns would bring it up again, begging Jack to tell the others the fantastic ad-lib that proved Larry Adler to be the funniest man in the *world.* Jack, sick of the whole thing, would refuse, whereupon George Burns would tell it himself, timing it so that it would be received in dead silence. He made it sound even grimmer than the original. Burns told that story on the Johnny Carson Show, the Dinah Shore show, he told it every chance he got. In 1980, when I played an engagement at the Cookery in Greenwich Village, George Burns came downtown, with Henny Youngman, to see my act. He came to the microphone and told the story all over again. By now he'd worked it into a seven-minute monologue.

(It reminds me of James Thurber, when someone told him that he'd read a French translation of Thurber's *My Life and Hard Times.* "And, do you know," said the friend, "it reads even better in French." "Yes, I know," said Thurber, "my work tends to lose something in the original.")

When we returned from the African trip in 1943 Jack Benny told John Royal, a vice-president of NBC, that I should write and star in my own comedy program. Because it was Jack who said it, Royal had to take it seriously. He phoned me, I met him at his office in Radio City, and when he told me what he proposed, in line with Jack's suggestion, I panicked.

"My God," I said, "I can't do that! It's one thing to write a

program around Jack. Hell, anybody could do it, with all his stereo-
types, the stinginess, the bear, Rochester, and stuff. But I couldn't
write for me—I haven't any personality."

John Royal didn't press the idea. I may well have been an idiot but
I do not think I could have done it.

In Omdurman, during the African trip, Jack and I visited the best
PX (Post Exchange) I've ever come across. Julie Horowitz, an Army
captain, who was in charge of it, had ivory, African wood carvings,
Egyptian sandals, all sorts of things such as I've never seen in any
other PX. We bought things for our wives and Julie arranged to have
them shipped back.

At the Stork Club in New York, several months later, Mary Benny
asked Eileen, "Tell me, honey, did Larry send you back the same lot
of shit that Jack sent me?"

Jack had promised Horowitz he'd phone his fiancée who worked
at Macy's in New York. I was with Jack when he phoned her.

"Miss Cohen? This is Jack Benny."

"Oh yes," she said.

"I've just returned from the Middle East. I ran into your fiancé,
Julie, in Omdurman."

"Oh, did you?" said Miss Cohen. She was making it tough going.

"Julie's looking fine," said Jack, "and he sends you his love."

"That's nice," said Miss Cohen. "Was there anything else?"

"Well—uh—no, I don't think so."

"Thank you," said Miss Cohen. "Nice of you to call. Good-bye."

Jack just looked at me after he hung up.

As I have noted, on the war tours we weren't paid although for
a lot of entertainers war work was their main source of income. It
is nothing against them that they accepted a fee; many couldn't have
afforded to make these trips as volunteers. Jack was in a different
category and I was doing well enough not to take the salary. However, USO had a strict rule that applied to everyone from Jack Benny
to the accompanist: $25 a week was paid for out-of-pocket expenses.
These were given out in travelers' checks and, over my strenuous
objections, I was elected to hand out the checks and keep a record
of them. When anyone needed money I'd give them a check, and
wouldn't record it. When we returned to the USA I was asked for
the expense list and I had none. I had paid out about $1000 and had
no receipt. The accountant stared at me grimly and said nothing.

"Look," I said, "I didn't want to do this in the first place. You're acting as if you expect me to pay you this money out of my own pocket."

He smiled. That was what he expected. And, like a *schmuck*, that's what I did.

On the war tours we were given our transport, usually by military plane or, if a short haul, by bus or jeep. We were fed in the Army posts—I got to loathe Spam—and we were put up in military quarters, which might be barracks, might be a tent and occasionally, as in Cairo, might be a hotel. When we flew from Washington to Africa we went via South America and Ascension Island, where we did our first show. I played the accordion behind Wini Shaw's songs but had no accompanist for myself. When we reached Accra, on the coast of Africa, we met a nightclub act, the Yacht Club Boys, who had just finished an African USO tour; they had an accordionist, Jack Snyder, who was making a good salary and who was delighted to join our troupe.

We did a show in Accra and I played the Liszt Second Hungarian Rhapsody. In the finale, which is a fast 2/4 rhythm, I was getting laughs, and Liszt isn't all that funny. The first thing a performer thinks when he gets an unwanted laugh, is that his fly is open. I looked down but *alles was in ordnung.* Then I happened to get a look at Jack Snyder. He was chewing gum while he played and the rhythm of his chewing matched his playing. Coming up the home stretch into the finale, Snyder was chomping with mighty 2/4 chomps. I persuaded him to eliminate the gum for future shows.

We got a break in Accra. A general had a C-47 cargo plane for which he had no immediate use. He offered it to us. (This is one of the perks of having a star name in the show.) It made the rest of our trip a joy. There was a film called *Five Graves to Cairo.* It was natural to name our plane *Five Jerks to Cairo.* We had this painted on the nose of the plane. We had our own crew. The pilot later married one of our troupe, Anna Lee.

Flying from Kano to Lagos we flew over a military base and got an urgent signal to land. We felt we couldn't disregard it. The airstrip was too small to take our plane. We overshot, landed on our nose and were considerably banged about but, by luck, there were no injuries. We found that the signal had been an idea of the men on that base; they knew Jack Benny was on that plane and they wanted to see the show. I was angry; these jerks had risked our lives. Jack, good-natured slob that he always was, gave the show. I, seething with rage, refused, which shows what a bastard I am.

Then, from Cairo to Teheran, we ran into a sandstorm. I got worried, went forward and asked the pilot what was wrong. "We're lost," he said. "I can't pick up anything on the radio. And we're running low on fuel."

When I went back into the cabin the look on my face made everyone begin to be airsick. I fastened my seat belt, feeling that this might be my last act, and found myself praying. Almost immediately I stopped. I was not religious, had given it up long since. I was ashamed of myself for, in effect, trying to take out a last-minute insurance policy.

"Take it back, you sonofabitch," I said to myself. "If you're going to die, do it honestly." I got a prayer refund.

A bit later a hole opened up in the sandstorm, we were near an airfield, though not the one we were heading for, and we landed. I'm glad I took back that prayer.

The following year, 1944, I wrote a piece for *Collier's* magazine called "They Must Have Loved You Over There," because that was the stock remark to any overseas entertainer. I showed that the love could vary; that if the GI's thought you were patronizing them, they could *loathe* you over there. I described our rules for our show: no segregation, no color discrimination, no preferential seating for officers.

I received a letter signed by four officers in the South Pacific. They pointed out that the officer was responsible for the safety and comfort of his men, that he had work to do that lasted beyond working hours, and only after that could he see a show. That was why seats were reserved for officers. I didn't agree; I'd seen officers drinking in the club while the GI's sat outside in bad weather, waiting for the show. The officers came in when they liked, their seats were reserved up front. It was unfair, and that was why we had made our rules. However I wrote to the four officers, and I apologized for any offense. The commander of the base replied; all four officers had been killed before my letter arrived.

When I was a kid Charles Augustus Lindbergh was driven through downtown Baltimore. He sat in an open car while confetti and ticker tape were hurled from office windows. Lindbergh was *the* American hero, he had flown the Atlantic in a single-engine plane, *The Spirit of St. Louis.* He seemed shy, modest, tousle haired, Tom Sawyer become a man. The image of him, sitting in an open car, grinning at the crowd, is still in my mind.

He wrote a book, *We,* and he married Anne Morrow, daughter of a U.S. Senator. Then came the tragedy, his son kidnapped, later found dead. (The press was at its worst, blowing up headlines over an obscure priest who was a go-between. He never made contact with anyone.) Even the gang world offered to help. A man was arrested, tried and convicted by the press before his case got to court, and Bruno Richard Hauptmann was hanged on what still seems like circumstantial evidence.

Lindbergh became a spokesman for "America First," an isolation-ist group headed by General Wood, chairman of Sears, Roebuck, the mail-order house. General Wood and Lindbergh called Roosevelt a warmonger. Lindbergh, who had been awarded the Iron Cross by Goering, said that the Germans were invincible, England was deca-dent and that Germany was our natural ally. (Even when the U.S. was at war Lindbergh never returned his German decoration.) He made speeches about the arms trade controlled by "our international Jewish brethren." When I hear the word "brethren" I react as Goeb-bels did to the word "culture." Odd how "brethren" is almost always a pejorative.

I bring all this up—"What's Lindbergh to me or me to Lind-bergh?"—because of an occasion in 1944 when our USO troupe, Jack Benny, Martha Tilton, Carole Landis and I, landed at Christmas Island in the South Pacific. The landing itself was memorable. Sev-eral thousand GI's on the airstrip waited to see the bigshots. Jack Benny came out first, then Martha Tilton, followed by Carole Landis, who wore a halter that was more a flimsy brassiere. I was behind her. At the sight of those tits a roar went up from the GI's. Carole bowed and smiled, the roars increasing as the bows got lower. I waited for quiet, then shouted: "Anyone would think you fellows had never seen a mouth-organ player before!"

A public relations officer had a message for us. The commander was giving a cocktail party. Now he knew we'd had a tough flight from our last island but could we possibly shower, change and join the CO at his quarters? Wearily, we agreed.

At the party there was a tall officer to whom I was introduced and who looked familiar. While we were talking, he remarked: "People think that I was responsible for this 'short snorter' business but it wasn't me at all." (Short snorters were dollar bills on which you collected autographs. When one bill was full of signatures, you added another bill and so on. Some GI's had rolls of, maybe, $100 in pasted-together "short snorters.")

I suddenly realized that this was Lindbergh. My childhood hero. My recent villain. Mixed emotions are what you feel when your mother-in-law drives off a cliff in your new Cadillac. No mother-in-law, no Cadillac, but mixed emotions are what I felt. I started to giggle. Lindbergh looked at me in surprise, he hadn't said anything funny.

I tried to apologize. "I'm sorry," I said, "I don't know what . . ." and I was off again. This time it became hysteria. Everyone was looking at me. I had to get to hell out. Jack came out after me. "Kid, what's come over you? You drunk or something?"

"Jack I haven't had one drink." I explained it to Jack who said I was being silly; I must pull myself together and go back in. After a while I did so, but one look at Lindbergh and I was off again, crying with laughter. I could do nothing about it. I'd try not to look at Lindbergh but, fatally, I *would* look at him and it was hysteria time again. The only thing to do was not only to get out but to stay out. Jack apologized for me, saying that long flights affected me badly.

Jack and I amused each other with basically childish jokes and our self-congratulatory glee over them exasperated Wini Shaw, who said that we were children, not grown up at all. "You laugh at such silly things," she said.

And so we did. In Iran, where we did shows in 110-degree heat, we parodied the score of *Oklahoma:*

> Oh, what a hell of a morning
> Hundred and ten in the shade
> Oh, what a hell of a mor—ning
> Even too hot to get
> Oh much too hot to get
> It's much too hot to get . . .

Then we'd launch into the chorus of *Oklahoma,* breaking ourselves up at our own wit. "People will say we're in love" became "People will say you're a *schmuck.*"

At one base in New Guinea it was so hot that we slept naked. Jack and I shared a tent and at night I read by the light of an open lightbulb, not realizing I might be keeping Jack awake. One night, along with the heat, there was a heavy rain that beat upon our tent like a demented snare drummer. Jack said, "What's that you're reading, kid?"

"It's a textbook," I said. "I'm studying Spanish."

"Read me some of it."

"It's technical stuff," I said, "just grammar. Nothing interesting."

"Let's hear it anyway."

"Well," I said, "there are the various ways of saying 'I want.' You can say *yo quiero* or you can say *tengo ganas de* . . ."

Jack got out of his cot and, stark naked, marched out into the storm, pausing just long enough to say: "I'll be glad when this fucking trip is over."

We went to Brisbane at the request of General MacArthur, who said he'd like to thank us personally for our troop work. (I think he just wanted Jack Benny's autograph.) We had an audience with the great man and "audience" is the word. We were seated in his office, Jack Benny, Martha Tilton, Carole Landis and I. MacArthur didn't talk, he orated, every word carefully enunciated. I think if he asked for a light he'd have made it sound like something to be sealed in a time capsule. He would intone a sentence, reading it off some invisible cue card, and then drop a first name at the end of it, thus proving him one of the boys, a regular fellow. Yuck! An example of the MacArthur style: "I have-uh killed-uh the uh-Jap, hunder-reds and-uh thousands of-uh him-uh . . . Larry." You see how it worked? The "Larry" at the end made him just your home-grown, down-to-earth Supreme Allied Commander in the South Pacific.

He asked us to visit his wife and small son. Afterward Jack and I were invited to tea with MacArthur's general staff in a suite at the Brisbane Hotel. Jack and I visited Mrs. MacArthur and the boy, who was very tense, in fear of something, he didn't seem like a kid. In his playroom there were photos, posters, plates, plaques, all of Daddy, one with a large legend, "Our Hero." It was no way to bring up a kid, having daddy practically canonized at home. Mrs. MacArthur tried to be friendly and hospitable, but it was obviously a strain and we left with relief.

Having met the General, I didn't want to meet his staff. Jack felt

the same way. We tossed a coin, the loser would have to go. I lost.
I went to the suite at teatime and found no tea but three drunk
generals and one sober colonel. A fourth general was expected. He
arrived, a loud Texan, my least favorite type. I often thought Texans
fought on the wrong side. He'd just heard what he called a limerick,
funniest goddamn thing he'd ever heard. Here it is:

> Roses are red, violets are blue
> Said Eleanor to Franklin, "How long must I stay in the White
>   House with you?"
> Said Franklin to Eleanor,
> "You kiss the niggers, I'll kiss the Jews,
> We'll stay in the White House as long as we choose."

This cheap joke was made against their Commander-in-Chief; not
only that, it got belly laughs from these louts. I was outraged and was
about to let go with a blast when I got a look from the colonel who
put a warning finger to his lips. The signal was: "Shut up!"

He came over and said, over the guffaws of the generals, "Look,
Larry, I know how you feel and I feel the same way. But I have to
live with these bastards. Another thing, any one of them could send
you back to the U.S. under arrest." I shut up, and I still regret having
done so.

As well as touring the troops in their camps, we often visited them
in hospitals. For reasons I've been afraid to go into, I was always the
one sent into the psychoneurotic wards. In one ward I was playing
when a soldier, a patient, said, "Hey, Mac!"

I stopped playing. "Yes?"

"Why d'ya keep tappin' ya foot like that when ya play?"

"Sorry, I didn't realize I was doing it."

A bit later: "Hey, Mac!"

"Yes?"

"Ya hafta sway from side to side like that? A guy could get drunk
just watchin' ya." I tried to control my sidesway. A nurse said:
"Don't keep interrupting Mr. Adler . . . he's trying to entertain
you."

"Look, lady," said the soldier. "I'm nuts, ain't I? I'll tell 'im what
I think!" When I finished the number he gave one perfunctory clap,
signifying applause. Then, "Didja hear what I said to the broad?"

"Yes."

"You think I'm nuts?"

"I think you're the first intelligent man I've met here."

He put out a hand. "Shake, Mac, we unnastan' each other. What's your rank?"

"No rank. I'm a civilian."

"C'mahn, don't bullshit me. Ya got officer's tabs on ya shirt. So, what's your rank?"

I explained that we were given the "assimilated" rank of captain so that, if captured by the enemy, we would have officer status.

"Nobody made ya come here?"

"No."

He shook his head. "I got very bad news for you, Mac. You belong in this ward."

An experience I wish I could forget was playing in veterans' mental hospitals. My audiences were mainly casualties of the First World War. They would sit, staring straight ahead of them. Sometimes one would move his mouth but there would be no sound. There was never a reaction to my music. I would go back to my hotel and stare at the walls, dreading the next time I would have to do more such shows. Did I do any good? I doubt it; these men seemed unaware of anything, as if lobotomized.

In Boston, I was sent into a psychoneurotic ward alone. One veteran pinned me against a wall. The Germans, he said, were outside, in the harbor. They were in submarines and he was the only one who knew it, that's why he was confined there. I had to warn everybody. I was scared, I thought he might decide I was a German and choke me. I didn't dare to yell and also, I didn't want him to think I didn't believe him. So I stayed put, nodded seriously at everything he said. Finally a nurse came into the ward and rescued me.

In 1945 Jack Benny, Martha Tilton and I were on another tour, this time in Europe. We arrived in Augsburg in June to await one more "name" performer. We were told that an actress was coming to join our troupe. Nobody knew her name. We were in a private house and that evening I was playing the piano. A lady came in and sat down to listen. I thought she looked familiar, but wasn't sure. When I finished playing she said, "That was nice, what is it?"

I told her it was something of my own.

"Is it published? Have you written it down?"

No, I hadn't written it down because I couldn't write music. The lady looked disapproving.

"You're very smug, aren't you," she said, and I was now aware of her accent—Scandinavian, it sounded. "You seem to be proud of your ignorance."

And that was how I came to meet Ingrid Bergman, whom I was later to get to know so well in Hollywood. She had come to join us but was uncertain about what she was expected to perform. She had the script with her of a play, *Joan of Lorraine,* which had been written for her by Maxwell Anderson and she knew she was to do a sketch with Jack Benny.

I liked her immediately, she was simple and direct, there was no coyness, no coquetry. I felt a great rapport with her and was soon apologizing for my smugness and promising to study musical composition when we returned to the U.S. I suggested she sing a Swedish folksong, with me to accompany her. Jack and I then worked out a sketch, a send-up of *Casablanca,* which she could do with him.

Ingrid Bergman wasn't really right for the troops. She didn't have the showmanship of Martha Tilton, who was perfect for the GI's with songs they knew from her recordings with Benny Goodman. Ingrid Bergman was something else. *Joan of Lorraine* meant nothing to the GI's, whose main reading was comic books. Once, in Kassel, Ingrid stopped in the middle of the *Lorraine* speech and came off, crying. I looked out and saw that some goons were waving inflated condoms. I said to them: "What a pity you haven't a better use for those."

I added some lines to the *Casablanca* sketch. In it Ingrid was trying to get Jack to leave his wife and run away with her.

"You fool," she cries, shaking Jack like a bunch of old laundry, "can't you see, this is bigger than we are."

"You're bigger than *I* am!" was supposed to be his answer. Jack was a sucker for the literal meaning of a line. He'd look at Ingrid who *was* bigger than he was, and he would break up. The line only got read when Jack, with a cold, couldn't do the scene and I took over. Ingrid was bigger than I was but I didn't mind.

I mentioned that the GI's reading was confined mainly to comics. The intelligence level was a lot higher in the medical corps and also in signals, but even there I noticed that those men, who read newspapers, *Time* and *Newsweek* or even an occasional *New Yorker* magazine, were careful not to appear too intelligent or, worse still, intellectual. They would lard their speech with the same predictable obscenities, where a verb became an adjective. It was depressing.

Someone had showed up with a print of *Saratoga Trunk,* a film with Ingrid and Gary Cooper. Ingrid played a flighty New Orleans Creole courtesan. It is hard to imagine a greater miscasting. Ingrid had it run at a preview room in Nuremberg, just for the two of us, and asked me what I thought of it. "Ingrid," I said, "I'm sorry but I don't think that's a very good part for you." Ingrid, so direct, so honest, so free of any kind of affectation, was blind to the faults of that film, in fact she thought it was the best work she'd ever done. She froze when I criticized it—I was less than diplomatic, saying she looked too healthy and Swedish for such a role. It was almost a week before she was her normal friendly self again.

She told me that, almost without exception, her leading men fell in love with her. When she made *Gaslight* with Charles Boyer, he had to stand on a box for their love scenes and, if they walked together, a ditch would be dug for Ingrid, because Boyer only came to Ingrid's breast level.

In Pilsen a Czech civilian, Jacques Schwarzwald, said we ought to see Prague. It was in Russian-occupied territory but Jacques thought we could get a pass. (Jacques couldn't get to Prague on his own and he wanted to get there to see his family.) Neither Jack Benny, Ingrid Bergman nor Martha Tilton would go; there were stories about the Russians; they'd cut your hand off to get your wristwatch. I have a built-in immunity to propaganda, I want to see for myself. I got a pass for Jacques and me and we went to Prague. There was a tower at one end of a bridge across the river that runs through Prague and Jacques took me there, promising me a superb view of the city. Two Russian soldiers were occupying the lookout point. One of them saw me in U.S. uniform, nudged his friend and they both stepped down, gesturing that we were to take their places. When we had seen the view, there were the two soldiers beaming at us—the friendliness was almost tangible. By gestures they invited us to walk around the city with them; they took us to where the black market operated. You could trade a pistol for a piano. The Russians wanted to barter their things to get gifts for us. I refused, but invited them to have a drink. Leaving them was like leaving friends. When we got back to Pilsen,

Jack, Ingrid and Martha, seeing both my hand and my watch intact, refused to believe I'd been to Prague at all!

At an officers' club in Frankfurt we had to join in the dread game of chugalug. "Dread" because it was what barroom drunks dream up. Some doggerel was recited, you were handed a full mug of beer and everyone chanted, "Then *drink,* chugalug, chugalug" and you had to drink without pause until you had drained the glass. I found it revolting, but then, I dislike all jolly-good-fellow games (including singing "For he's a jolly good fellow"), and dislike pub bonhomie.

I talked with an attractive lady who said she was Eisenhower's chauffeur. I told her we were anxious to get to Berlin but civilians were not yet being allowed in. She thought it could be done, the thing was to see Ike.

"Eisenhower? How in hell do we get to see Eisenhower?"

"Through me," she said placidly. Excusing herself she went to the telephone. She returned to say we had an appointment with the general the following morning, at eleven. The attractive lady was Kay Summersby. Everyone knew of the affair she was having with Eisenhower but while it was talked about, nothing got into print.

Ingrid, Jack and I had breakfast together. A GI came in to say our car was outside to take us to our appointment with Eisenhower. Jack and I got up. Ingrid remained at the table.

"Ingrid, come on, the car's here," I said.

"No," said Ingrid, "I've changed my mind. You two go, you don't really need me."

"For God's sake, Ingrid, you may never get a chance like this again. Don't you want to meet Eisenhower?"

She shrugged. "I have nothing to say to him." She meant it.

Jack and I were driven to the Allied Command HQ in the I. G. Farben building. The building was intact, though the city seemed almost totally destroyed. One heard of a deal between Farben and the U.S. government, and to look at that building was virtually to verify the rumor.

Eisenhower didn't keep us waiting, we were shown into his office. He greeted us cordially, though he looked distressed when he saw that Ingrid wasn't with us. I think he had only given us the appointment to meet her.

When we told him why we were there the general phoned General Parks and told him to get a plane to take Mr. Benny and his party to Berlin. Well, that was that; we saw no need to waste Eisenhower's time so we got up.

"You fellows busy?" he asked. "Why not stay and have some coffee."

We sat down. Eisenhower was a friendly man, he seemed to enjoy talking to us. He said he didn't like the mounting anti-Russian press. (I had already met one general who toasted, "Here's to the next war against the Russkies," and it was said that General Patton, now that the Germans were defeated, wanted to move immediately against the Soviet Army.)

"Take General Zhukov," he said. Zhukov was Eisenhower's Russian counterpart. "He comes to a meeting looking stiff and formal. I offer him a drink, crack a joke and in no time he's a human being. They're not all that difficult, the Russians. You just have to know how to approach them."

I asked how he felt about the campaign to run him for president. Truman had even offered him the Democratic nomination. For the first time Eisenhower looked serious.

"Bad business," he said. "Of course I'm aware of it but why don't people read their history? It's never worked, that a military man has made a good president. I'm a graduate of West Point and I'm trained to take my orders from a civilian commander-in-chief. I know they're talking about me running but I'll have nothing to do with it."

Now, I may be a gullible fellow, probably am, but he seemed to mean every word. However, when the head of General Motors tells you that you are indispensable and that your country needs you, that kind of pressure is probably impossible to resist.

Jack, Ingrid and I were driven to Nuremberg in a Mercedes that had belonged to Hermann Goering. This was said of every car we sat in and I didn't take it too seriously. Suddenly I felt a hard blow to my back and heard a shot. I figured that I'd been hit by a bullet and that the wound was fatal. (Remember, I had Ingrid and Jack for an audience.) I began slowly and dramatically to die; all we needed was *The Swan* by Saint-Säens. I forgot that Ingrid was a practical Swede. She saw no hole in the backrest of the car, therefore there was none in me. My dying scene was going badly and it was all Ingrid's fault; I really hated that girl. She told me to sit up and stop moaning, I wasn't shot at all. I am too shot I said (or snarled between clenched teeth) and tried to resume dying but it was no good; I'd lost my audience.

The car had stopped and a soldier came up, carrying a pistol. He had signaled to us to stop and, as we hadn't stopped, he'd fired at us. The bullet had hit a car spring, the spring had hit me. It was my luck that he had only a pistol; a rifle bullet would have done serious damage. The soldier seemed hysterical. I said I thought it dangerous just to fire at a car like that.

"Them's my orders," he shouted at me. "Them orders was given by Uncle Sam and I'm *proud* of them orders." His voice had risen to a shriek and we were alarmed since he still had the pistol. The soldier wanted to take us to the guardhouse. Fortunately a colonel arrived who managed to pacify the soldier and we were allowed to proceed. I found that I had quite a large bruise on my back.

The next morning the colonel came to see me. I could, he said, bring a charge against the soldier who had exceeded his authority by firing at our car. (A symphony conductor had been shot and killed in a similar incident around that time, in Berlin.) I felt it was bad for a civilian to bring charges against a soldier. I said that the soldier seemed to me a very neurotic young man who shouldn't be allowed to carry guns. A psychiatric examination might not be a bad idea.

Oh no, said the colonel, no need for that, nothing wrong with the kid. "I know him," said the colonel, "he's a good boy."

A fine boy. Well, if I didn't bring a charge, the army wouldn't (though I thought they should) and the matter was dropped. A week later, when we gave an outdoor show to U.S. troops at Nuremberg, a soldier came to our tent.

"Hey, Larry," he said, "howsabout signing my short snorter?"

"You remember me?" asked the soldier. I said no, I didn't. He whooped derisively.

"Hoddia like that, he don't remember me! Jeez crize, Larry, I'm da guy that shot ya!"

I was outraged. He might have killed me, and he asked me for my autograph. But he seemed to think it a hilarious incident and, as I am a coward, I did sign his short snorter.

The incident was picked up by AP. A few months later I got a letter, mailed from Buffalo, with each word made of letters cut from a newspaper and pasted together. One sentence read: "Too bad the bullet missed your lousy yellow Jew spine." From then on I had a

letter a year from this charmer. He had an obsession about Jewish
performers including such Hebraic types as Bob Hope, Red Skelton
and Desi Arnaz.

During the war, but before the U.S. entered, I couldn't get mouth-
organs. They were made by M. Hohner in Germany and the supply,
not surprisingly, was cut off. When I had met the minister of supply
in Churchill's government, I'd asked if he knew how I could get hold
of some German mouth-organs. No, he said, he didn't know. "But
if you find a way, do tell us so we can put a stop to it." We were based
in Stuttgart, not far from the Hohner harmonica factory at Trossingen in the Black Forest. I went to the U.S. commanding officer to
see if I could go there. He said Trossingen was in French-occupied
territory and it took a fortnight to get clearance. When I left his office
there was an airman waiting. He said he knew I'd be turned down.
If I could find the place from the air he'd give me a lift there in a
Piper Cub plane, and the hell with clearance.

We set off at noon using two guides: a Baedeker and a piece of
waxed paper, used to wrap the mouth-organs, that had an illustration
of the Hohner factory. We flew low, following the motor road.

"There it is," I told the pilot, and we landed in a field. In no time
we were surrounded by French soldiers.

"Je suis Lah-ree Ahd-laire et je suis joueur de l'harmonica à bouche."

By luck one soldier played the mouth-organ. He knew of me and
escorted me into Trossingen and to the Hohner factory. The first
person I met was Kurt Burgbacher, an old friend, who hugged me
and then burst into tears. Karl and Ernst Hohner also were quite
emotional at sight of me. I was the first friendly face in a long time.
They loaded me down with mouth-organs.

Karl Hohner wanted to talk privately. He felt that I should know
that he, Karl, was a Nazi party member. (He was the only German
to admit that to me.)

"Karl," I said, "I've known you since 1934. You're no Nazi."

He was glad, he said, that I had reacted in that way. An officer
from Dr. Goebbels's Ministry of Information had come to Trossingen to say that if one token Hohner joined the party, the factory
would be left to make mouth-organs, which were held to be good
for Army morale, and the working staff would be left intact. I told
Karl that I might have done the same thing. How do we know how
we will behave when the pressure is on?

We visited Bad Nauheim in Czechoslovakia. I made a little joke
in my show saying I'd be grateful if some GI could "liberate" a
few mouth-organs for me. After one show Sgt. Coletti told me he'd
seen mouth-organs with my name on them in Graslitz, forty kilometers away, and he could take me there. We went by jeep. However, the road to Graslitz was now Russian occupied. We were
stopped by a guard whom Coletti bribed with cigarettes to let us
through. A few more kilometers and another Russian sentry;
Coletti gave a scream, clapped his hand to his heart and pretended
to fall dead. The Russian thought this was very funny. *He* let us
through. Then, outside Graslitz, a *third* sentry. Nobody was going
to bribe *him* nor did pantomine work. I took out a mouth-organ
and began to play "Meadowland" a Russian song. The Russian
beamed with delight. I played a Red Army song called "Tachanka"
(little tank) and he was amazed that I knew it. (Both tunes were
popular in the U.S.) He waved us on. In Graslitz we found an
army post and I spoke to the commander, Konstantin Vrbacki (pronounced "ver-batz-ky"), in French. He invited me to lunch and
sent a soldier out to look for mouth-organs. The soldier returned
with a sackful, all Larry Adler models. On the black market they'd
be worth several thousand dollars. I asked Vrbacki how much they
would cost. He drew himself up.

"Compliments of the Czech army," he said.

On the way back, our third Russian sentry was waiting for us. He'd
rounded up several hundred Red Army soldiers and wanted me to
play to them. I repeated the two tunes I'd played before, then "Otchi
Chornia," "Dvyai Gittary," Tchaikowsky, Borodin, everything Russian I could think of. That was some audience! They took off their
medals and pinned them on me. They seemed intensely musical.
Some of them cried when I played the sentimental songs.

I had played for Russian soldiers two years before, when Jack
Benny and I were in Iran. We gave a show to an audience of U.S.,
British, French and Russian troops. After the show we met the
Russian commander, Karlov, and his wife. We stood in a reception
line and Karlov and an interpreter, Mme. Karlov with *her* inter-
preter, talked to the performers. Mme. Karlov talked to Wini Shaw.
As Mme. Karlov spoke in Russian Wini nodded, smiled, kept saying,
"Thank you, thank you very much, you're very kind." Then the
interpreter took over.

"Miss Shaw," he said, "Mme. Karlov says you are strong husky girl—why you are not in the field fighting with the guerrillas?"

Karlov told me he was flying next day to Moscow, then to the Russian front. He could take me along to play for Russian troops. I'd have loved it. But I couldn't. Oh boy, don't I wish I had!

CHAPTER
Nine

A LARGE, TOO LARGE, part of my life revolves around the question: Was I or was I not a Communist. In the days when there was a penalty if you were, I wouldn't answer the question. I had friends, I still have friends, who were or are Communists. It is their right and I would do nothing to damage that right.

I was never attracted to the Communist party. Often I agreed with them, often I worked with them, often I found that the Communists were the only ones saying anything worth saying. As a group, they were by far the most intelligent people in Hollywood. They were sometimes the most highly principled.

I never felt like joining them. The Communists, often intellectuals individually, were willing to put their intellect in blinkers if the party told them to. They followed the party line. And that is where they lost me. I cannot follow *any* party line.

I believe I can pinpoint the start of my political troubles to three events: a dinner in San Francisco in 1946; a visit to Washington with Bogart and other members of the First Amendment Committee; and playing the Roxy Theater in New York in 1948 with Paul Draper.

At the Mark Hopkins Hotel in San Francisco in 1946, I played, but I also spoke. The chairman was the head of an advertising agency and I attacked advertising; I said it created a false demand for things that were neither wanted nor needed. I knocked the campaigns to get people to smoke (this was well before the information that linked lung cancer to smoking), to drink alcohol, to use some product because it promised you sexual allure, would help you land a husband, etc. The chairman didn't like it and later I was sent a magazine called *Aware.* I was reported as parroting the Communist party line and described as being either a dupe or a fellow-traveller. I should have followed it up but it seemed like hate mail, uncomfortable but harmless.

Then I met Humphrey Bogart. He had many friends who seemed to adore him but we started off wrong and I never liked him after that. Lewis Milestone, who directed *All Quiet on the Western Front,* gave a party. One guest was Jeff Cassells, a French screenwriter who had a party trick; he ate glass. He would eat light bulbs or wine-glasses—he always asked permission first. I noticed that, as we admired Cassells's trick, Bogart was glowering. He was jealous of the fuss made over Cassells.

After dinner, Desi Arnaz and Eddie Albert were singing Mexican folk songs together, very soft, subtle close harmony. There was a crash and Bogart appeared in a doorway, blood running down his chin. He staggered over to Cassells and pointed a bloody finger into Cassells's face as he shouted, "You sonofabitch, I can eat more glass than you can!" Bogart had smashed his fist into Mrs. Milestone's full-length mirror in the hall, taken pieces of glass and tried to eat them. He succeeded in cutting his mouth to bits. I told Bogart that he should apologize to Mrs. Milestone and perhaps replace her mirror. He didn't like that.

A few months later I was entertaining some friends at Chasen's Restaurant when Bogart suddenly appeared. He was drunk.

"Fellas," he said, "I'm giving a birthday party for Phil Baker in the private dining room. He knows you're out here and he wants you to come in and have some booze. Come on, huh?"

Phil Baker was a famous stage and radio comedian.

"Bogey," I said, "we're just in the middle of dinner. . . ."

"Fuck that!" said the great actor. "Who gives a shit? Skip the goddamn dinner, come on, fa crissake, it's Phil's birthday!"

"We can't leave in the middle of dinner. Look, we won't have dessert or coffee and we'll come in for a drink then, okay?"

He agreed and went back to the private dining room. About twenty minutes later he appeared at the far end of the restaurant.

"What the hell kind of fair-weather friends *are* you guys? Your pal's in there—it's his *birthday,* for Christ's sake—and just look at you —just sittin' there guzzling. You oughta be *ashamed!* What am I supposed to say to Phil?"

Like idiots we got up from the table and filed into the private dining room. Bogart offered me a drink, which I refused. He peered at me and put an arm on each side of me so that I was pinned against the bar.

"Adler, you're a pain in the ass . . . anybody ever tell you that? Cos that's what you are, a pain in the ass. Wanna know why?"

I didn't want to know why.

"I'll tell you why," he said, his face almost against mine. "It's because you call yourself a liberal. That's a lot of horseshit. Cos you're not a liberal at all, you're a fuckin' phony!"

I tried to get away but he had me pinned.

"Nah, you stay right where you are, you listen to me. I said you're a phony. Know why? I hate niggers. So do you, you hate 'em just as much as I do, but you won't admit it, cos you're a phony. I hate 'em but I'll admit it. So who's a real liberal, you or me, hah?

"And I'll tell you something else. I hate Jews." I looked over at Lauren Bacall. "Aaah, I know you're one. And sure I married one. That don't made no goddamn difference, I hate 'em. And so do you. But you won't admit it cos you're a phoney. I'll admit it. So who's the real liberal, hah? You or me?"

He peered at me as if he couldn't believe what he saw.

"What kind a guy *are* you, anyway? Ya come crashin' into my party, ya drink up all my liquor. . . ."

This time I did break away. I told Eileen we were leaving. While we were waiting outside for the attendant to bring our car, there was Bogart again. He took my hand in a crushing grip.

"Jesus, Adler," he said, "what are we fighting about? We're both on the same side!"

What can you say?

Not long after that there was a meeting at Ira Gershwin's house on Roxbury Drive and we formed the Committee for the First

Amendment. Nineteen writers had been subpoenaed to appear before the House Committee on Un-American Activities in Washington. The question they would be asked was, "Are you now or have you ever been a member of the Communist party?" We thought the First Amendment to the Constitution, part of the Bill of Rights, guaranteed freedom of speech and specifically forbade any such question being asked by any congressional committee, hence our name. We decided to go to Washington as a group to protest and to lend support to the writers. We met again at Romanoff's restaurant. Charlie Einfeld, publicity chief at Warner Brothers, said that we should charter a plane to make the trip. It would be expensive and he suggested we canvass our friends to raise money. Humphrey Bogart was there.

Looking straight at me, Bogart said, "I haven't got any friends. I meet people but I get nasty with them and I get into fights. So I'm no good to you." This was pure self-pity. Bogart had plenty of friends, in fact he only joined our group because one of them, John Huston, had helped found the committee. I don't think Bogart had any convictions.

However, he was on the plane when we flew to Washington. A photograph of our group appears in the autobiography of his wife, Lauren Bacall. I'm surprised it's there, because Bogart was the first to cave in. We were attacked as Commie sympathizers by the Hearst press, the McCormick-Patterson and the Scripps-Howard papers. Without telling any of us in advance, Bogart made a public statement. It was a belly-crawl. He apologized for having gone to Washington, said he was neither a Communist nor a sympathizer, he detested Communism "just as any other decent American does." He called himself "a foolish and impetuous American." The letter was widely reprinted and George Sokolsky, Hearst's main Red-baiter, reproduced it together with a few comments of his own.

"Somebody was using you," wrote Sokolsky. "Who is that somebody? . . . Tell us who suggested and organized that trip?" Bogart didn't do that but there was no need; our trip was no secret, it was reported in the press and the newsreels.

Bogart's cop-out defeated the whole purpose of our trip. Others, such as Gene Kelly, Frank Sinatra, Danny Kaye, followed Bogart in disavowing the group they had joined. Those of us who didn't stood out like carbuncles.

The third event which aggravated my political problems occurred in 1948 when I was playing the Roxy Theater in New York with Paul Draper. Paul had a dance called "Political Speech," in which he kissed imaginary babies, walked a tightrope, all the politician's clichés. We were on the bill with an anti-Communist film, *I Led Three Lives,* a story of an ex-Communist turned FBI informer. Left and Communist groups picketed the theater outside, with Paul and me performing inside. Once, during the "Political Speech," someone booed and it was taken up by others. I, never able to keep my big mouth shut, came on and said that if the audience saw anything in Paul's number to boo, they might as well boo me too. So they did. Two days later, in the gossip column in the Hearst *Journal-American,* written by Igor Cassini, Paul and I were criticized for selling Red propaganda from the stage. This column prompted Hester McCullough, a lady who lived in Greenwich, Connecticut, to write to Cassini. She also wrote to the Greenwich *Times.* Draper and I were booked to give a recital in Greenwich. We were, she wrote, pro-Communist, money paid to us would go to Moscow to be used against the American way of life. From that time on, Cassini made Draper and Adler his main whipping boys.

Mrs. McCullough did not call us Communists, which would have implied membership in the Communist party, but pro-Communists, a vaguer accusation, much harder to disprove.

I was never called before the Un-American Activities Committee, nor was I grilled by Senator McCarthy, but I was told by the William Morris Agency that if we did not sign a non-Communist affidavit or sue Mrs. McCullough for libel, we would be blacklisted. We sued.

Here is the background.

I supported the Progressive party, formed by Henry Wallace to run against Truman and Dewey in 1948. I had met Wallace in Washington when he was vice-president, but the Democratic party had turned against him. I had been told by Mrs. Roosevelt that she had been sent by her husband to the Democratic Convention in 1944 to work for Wallace's renomination. There she had been told by James Farley, the postmaster-general, that the party would not accept Wallace. There would be revolt that could harm Roosevelt, running for an unprecedented fourth term. The compromise candidate was Truman, regarded as a party hack, hardly more than a gofer for Boss

party rally at Madison Square Garden. I knew, because I had seen an advance copy of Wallace's speech, that it contained a strong criticism of Stalin. When he delivered the speech the criticism had been deleted. It wasn't hard to guess why. There were hard-line Communists on Wallace's staff. Wallace was a weaker man than I had first thought.

Then there was a press conference. At the time Westbrook Pegler had been hammering away in his column at Wallace on the issue of the "guru" letters. These were letters that Pegler got hold of which Wallace was supposed to have written to his "guru." They seemed pretty silly and of no great importance.

At the press conference Westbrook Pegler asked Wallace if he was the author of the "guru" letters. Wallace replied, "I will not answer questions from Westbrook Pegler." Then John O'Donnell from the New York *Daily News* asked Wallace the same question. Wallace replied, "I will not answer questions from any stooge of Westbrook Pegler." (I began to grow cold at this point—the conference was broadcast.) Then Doris Fleeson of the *News* said, "Mr. Wallace, no one can accuse me of being a stooge of Westbrook Pegler. I would like to know, did you write the 'guru' letters?" Wallace declined to answer and I knew I was backing the wrong man. What difference did it make whether or not he had written those letters? He had only to say either way, and that would have been that.

So why did I stick with Wallace after that? The reasons are so silly as to be embarrassing. You don't desert a man when he's down. Wallace was being hammered by almost all the press. I reasoned like a Boy Scout. I had chosen to support Wallace because I thought he was a better man than Dewey or Truman. The Communist party supported him. Did I change my mind just because my opinion coincided with that of the Communists? An editorial in the Cleveland *Plain Dealer* had said: "What should our foreign policy be? The answer is simple; find out what the Communist party would like us to do and then do the opposite." By that logic the Communists could control political thinking in the U.S. On the masthead of the *Daily Worker* it said that today was Tuesday. Was I, in order to prove I was no fellow-traveller, to say today was Wednesday? Wallace was my man for *my* reasons and I would not be pressured out of them.

The nearer it got to election day in 1948, the worse it looked for Truman, but he was sure he was going to win. He said so to Bartley

Crum, publisher of *PM;* had Crum believed him and switched his
support his would have been the only paper to have predicted correctly the election result; it might have saved the paper which didn't
last much longer. Crum told me that he asked Truman what made
him so cocky, so sure against all the polls, all the papers, all the odds.
"Because," said Truman, "they don't shoot Santa Claus."

On one thing I was adamant. I never put political content into my
professional performance. I felt it wrong to work politically in any
city where I gave a concert. The concert committee had brought me
to their city; it wasn't right to use them to finance my politics. I once
had an argument with Paul Robeson about this. Paul loaded his
recitals with politics; it was his right to do so, I said, but he should
play fair. Advertise that Paul Robeson will sing and will also speak.
Robeson smiled, that wonderful grin of his, and said, "You do it
your way, Larry, I'll do it mine."

I slipped up once and paid for it. Paul Draper and I were giving
a recital in Birmingham, Alabama. After the recital Paul told me that
there was a meeting of Wallace supporters. Common sense told me
to stay away but I did not listen to my instincts and went along. Why?
I didn't want to appear a coward in front of Draper. Well, I never
said I was bright.

We got to the hotel and there was the local press. That should have
made me turn around and go the other way. For a nice Jewish boy
I can be incredibly pigheaded. I stayed. I played a number. There
was a political story about us in the paper the next day that dwarfed
the excellent notice for our recital; the notice was on the arts page,
the political story on the front page. I insisted to Paul that we go to
the committee and apologize. They accepted, but coolly. They never
invited either of us to Birmingham again.

The plane next day stopped at Atlanta, where I read a wire service
story headed, "Two mix art and politics." I phoned the editor and
explained that there was no politics in our concert. In New York the
Scripps-Howard paper, the *World-Telegram,* had an editorial which
stated flatly that we had lured an audience into a concert hall and
then fed them pro-Wallace propaganda. That was a lie, but I'd never
get a retraction from the *World-Telegram* and it wasn't worth suing.
I didn't realize that there was bad publicity building up and it was
already damaging our careers.

After I'd been to Washington with the Committee for the First
Amendment, I had an engagement at the Chase Hotel in St. Louis.

I had recently lectured several times for the National Conference of Christians and Jews. This had begun in Chicago; at a high school, white students had gone on strike, refusing to sit in the same classroom as black students. This could have spread; someone from the mayor's office asked me to play at the high school; a show might help. I went to the school, found a hundred percent white audience. Instead of playing I talked about race prejudice, trying to keep it funny. It worked and the strike was called off. But the idea had spread to other schools. The mayor sent me to these and again I was able to joke them out of their strike. The National Conference of Christians and Jews asked me to speak. I agreed. Now in St. Louis, for the first time I faced a hostile audience; they were out to get me.

These kids had been primed. My jokes, usually sure-fire, were flops. I finished my speech and asked for questions. It seemed that there were more hands raised than there were people. I selected a girl, about fifteen.

"What do you think of the Communists?" she asked and a kind of giggle went through the hall. (She pronounced the word "Commanists.")

It wouldn't have been hard to evade the question, but my big mouth is ever open and probably always will be. I said that what I thought of the Communists was not important; what was important was the rights of the Communists. They were a legal party, they could put up candidates in an election, they could vote, they had the same rights as any other party. This didn't go down well, there were boos and walkouts. The next day the St. Louis *Globe-Democrat* had a headline on an inside page: "Communists have rights, says Adler." A lady wrote that the showbiz group, the Committee for the First Amendment, were fools, Communist dupes or sympathizers and that they had no idea of why they went to Washington. I wrote to the *Globe-Democrat* saying that I, as a founding member of that committee, knew damned well why I'd gone to Washington and I needed no political party to advise me on how I should feel about anything. I also explained what I had said at the school lecture and why I had said it. My letter was neither printed nor acknowledged.

In New York Rabbi Schultz had an organization called Jews against Communism. He complained to the NCCJ (National Conference of Christians and Jews) that they were sponsoring a known Red (me). His complaint was taken seriously and I was dropped.

In 1949 I played in Chicago, at a time when I was blacklisted all

over the country. I had talked to A. J. Balaban, of the Balaban and
Katz Theaters, and told him that the blacklist was total. "Not in my
theaters," said Balaban and kept his word by booking me. While
there I received a letter from an old friend, Bishop Bernard J. Sheil;
he was glad that I had returned to fight the blacklist and he wished
me well, pledged friendship and signed it "Yours in Christ." That
same week I had a call from his secretary. The bishop was away, in
a religious retreat, but, said the secretary, she knew that he would
want to make a gesture of friendship toward me. Therefore she
invited me to address a meeting of Catholic youth. I accepted and
showed up on the day. There were about one hundred and fifty
young people to hear me speak. There were also a priest, Father
Cardinal, and a lawyer from the Catholic Youth. I knew the priest
didn't like me ever since I'd made a joke about him; I'd said that,
with a name like Father Cardinal, he could go only so far before it
became ridiculous. He and the lawyer were there to try to keep me
from speaking. The lawyer said that it would be an embarrassment
to the bishop if he were seen sponsoring an alleged Communist.
Finally I gave in. Very well, I would cancel my talk. It must have
appeared odd, there I was and yet the talk was canceled. I don't know
about Bishop Sheil, it certainly embarrassed me.

When I next saw Bishop Sheil, he seemed uncomfortable, ill at
ease, not at all his normal self. He apologized to me for the incident
when I was talked into canceling my talk. Had he been there, he said,
it would have been different.

But now something far worse happened. Bishop Sheil told me that
he had been told "by my superiors" that if his friendship with me
were to be publicized in any way, dire things would occur.

"I am told," he said, "that if my name appears alongside yours I
will be transferred out of the country. Larry, my life's work is here."

I couldn't believe that Bernard J. Sheil, a bishop of the Catholic
church, was humiliating himself in this way.

"Larry," he said, "I must ask you to give me your word, to promise me that in your libel case I will not be mentioned. I remember
what I wrote to you. I meant every word of it. But I have to do what
I am now doing, Larry, it isn't any decision of mine. I have no other
choice."

Hadn't he? Didn't his religious beliefs demand that he stand up
for his friend? He had written a letter to me pledging his support and

his friendship. What kind of religion was it that forced one of its high officials to renege on his own word? The incident was, by comparison, trivial, but I thought of Galileo and his recantation under threats of torture, threats authorized by Galileo's friend, Cardinal Bellarmine. I thought of Martin Luther, with his famous words, *"Hier stehe ich; ich kann nicht anders."*

I, Larry Adler, a musician of no political power whatsoever, was being asked to get a Catholic bishop off the hook. I felt immense sorrow for this man. He was being made to go against his own principles; he knew it and I knew it.

"Bernard," I said, "you have my word. Our friendship will not be mentioned. I know how hard this must be for you. I don't want to make it any harder." We said good-bye and I never saw him again.

I was finding it hard to get any work, when my agent, Abe Lastfogel, told me that George Jessel had talked to Walter Winchell about me and Winchell had agreed to meet me at the Roney-Plaza Hotel in Miami. I saw no point in this. Winchell wouldn't help me unless I agreed to give names. Lastfogel said I mustn't pass up a chance to talk to a man who could restore my position in show business. Winchell's influence was enormous—press agents could get clients merely by claiming to have an "in" with him. A line in his column was better than a feature elsewhere. His Sunday night radio broadcasts were required listening for journalists, politicians, show people. At first Winchell had been a Roosevelt liberal but he was right-wing by Roosevelt's third term; he was in favor of the Un-American Activities Committee, was a friend of J. Edgar Hoover, and wrote against anyone on the left.

I flew to Miami. At the hotel I called Winchell, who was unfriendly.

"I don't know why Lastfogel wants me to see you," he said on the phone. "You can't do me any good, you can only drag me down to your level." I said in that case I saw no need to waste his time. He softened after that and we arranged to meet in the Roney-Plaza coffee shop at six. There were three men with Winchell, one of whom was Marshall Rothe, of the Miami *Daily News*. Winchell opened by saying he had them there as witnesses, "I want to make sure you don't misquote me," a remark I found odd from a man with nationwide syndication.

Then he did a switch, acting as my advocate. He said that I'd had a bad deal from people who used me as a dupe, that I had done war work, touring with Jack Benny. He knew about my friendship with Bishop Sheil. A lot of good people, such as Lastfogel and Jessel, were on my side, which proved that I must be all right. I listened, bemused, to this panegyric from a man who had written nothing but damaging things about me. What was he getting at?

I found out. He said he would put me on the air on his Sunday night broadcast, to present me as a man who had been wronged. He would talk about me on his TV broadcast and write about me in his column. This was quite an offer; the Winchell Seal of Respectability would have had the same effect as the Good Housekeeping Seal of Approval. Naturally there was a trade-off involved. He didn't want a lot, he wasn't even proposing that I go before the committee. No, he just wanted me, on the air, to denounce as Communists Henry Wallace and Paul Draper.

I was seething with anger but said only that it wasn't very patriotic to denounce a former vice-president and surely Winchell knew that Draper and I were jointly waiting for our case to come up against Mrs. McCullough.

"But we all know about Draper's mother. She's either a Commie or a fellow-traveller." I said I wasn't there to discuss Muriel Draper. Paul was my close friend, my concert partner, and I refused to consider Winchell's suggestion.

"Look," he said, "don't make any quick decisions you might regret later."

He dictated a statement for me to sign. He walked up and down the coffee shop (we had the place to ourselves) ad-libbing my statement while Marshall Rothe wrote it down.

"Now look, kid, you don't have to say it the way I do; think about it, sleep on it, put it in your own words. This could put you right back on top."

The awful thing was, he was right, such a statement from me plus nationwide coverage by Winchell, really could have put me back in business. I agreed to take the statement and think about it. That night Marshall Rothe phoned me.

"You going to give Winchell what he wants?"

"Oh, come on, Rothe, you know better than that."

"Yeah. I figured. Well, you know what that means, don't you? From now on, boy, he's going to beat your brains out."

I left Miami next morning. A few days later an item appeared in his column, not mentioning my name but saying that a certain mouth-organ-playing leftie had been to see him. "I don't know if he's a Commie or not," wrote Winchell, "but he spouts the party-line." That was the end of that. It had cost me a trip to Miami that I couldn't afford and no good had come of it; harm, if anything. Still, I had showed Lastfogel I was at least willing to make an effort to clear my name.

A friend of mine, Albert Kahn, put out a liberal newspaper called *In Fact*. Kahn asked me to appear at a rally to honor two Soviet artists, the writer Solomon Mikhoels and the poet Itzik Feffer. I told Kahn I'd do it but I wanted one assurance.

"Ordinarily I wouldn't even mention this, Albert, but you know I have a libel suit pending. Therefore I just want to be sure that the rally isn't being organized by the Communist party."

Kahn guaranteed that it was just for U.S. artists to honor two colleagues from the USSR as an anti–Cold War gesture. The Communist party had nothing to do with it. Albert Kahn was my friend, I took his word and, unable to be present on the night, I recorded some music to be played and said something on the recording as well.

The day after the rally was held at Yankee Stadium a piece appeared in the Scripps-Howard paper, the *World-Telegram*. Written by Frederick Woltman, a right-wing journalist, it listed the names of those who appeared at the rally. Woltman stated that the rally was organized by the Communist party and that Albert Kahn was an official of it.

I was hurt by this dirty trick. Kahn knew the trouble I was in, that I had a case coming up. To play at something sponsored by the Communist party could damage me severely. Yet Kahn was willing to put me on the spot in this way. I still find it incredible, but then, as I've said, I am naive.

I hope all these details help to explain attitudes during the McCarthy era, as well as the background of our libel action against Mrs. McCullough who wanted to cancel our concert in Greenwich because of our pro-Communist activities. Her concert committee then asked us for a non-Communist affidavit, which we refused to give.

If I was not a Communist, why should I object to saying so? Because one should not ever have to state one's political beliefs.

Charles Wilson, then head of General Electric, said of the Hollywood Ten, the writers being questioned by the Un-American Activities Committee: "I don't know if those guys are Communists or not, but if anybody asked me to state, under oath, whether I was Republican or Democrat, I'd say it was none of his goddamn business."

Eileen had realized that it was going to be difficult for me to get work in America after I had been blacklisted. She brought the whole family over to England in 1949. I was in England when the case finally came up in 1950 and asked Paul Draper to find a lawyer. He choose O. John Rogge, a former attorney general, but Rogge, if anything, was more left-wing than we were. Paul switched to a law firm in Connecticut, Baldwin and Baldwin, who, with a month to go, withdrew from the case, leaving us without a lawyer. I heard that a vice-president of Pan American Airways had told one of the lawyers that, if he wanted to get anywhere in Connecticut politics, he'd better drop Draper and Adler.

A firm in New Haven, Wiggin and Dana, agreed to represent us, but wanted to meet us first. I came back from London to meet them and also to give preliminary depositions. Fred Wiggin was a typical New England lawyer. (In retrospect I think we'd have done better with a villain.) At the time I was pleased, even moved, that he agreed to take our case. I'm sure that had he suspected anything shady about either of us he'd have turned us down.

Wiggin and Dana represented Yale University. William Buckley, already famous as the author of *God and Man at Yale,* now wrote an article in the Yale paper, saying that a lawyer who would defend Paul Draper and Larry Adler wasn't fit to represent Yale University and should be dismissed by the college. This suggests a whole new concept of justice. I've never met Mr. Buckley, who, unusual for a right-winger, has wit, but I'd love to know if he still stands by his anti-Voltaire opinion.

Fred Wiggin told me that, in order to file the suit at all, I must swear that I was not and had never been a Communist. I would have thought that it was up to Mrs. McCullough, having called us pro-Communist, to prove her point, but again, that shows my naiveté. I knew Fred Wiggin to be a man who would not give specious advice, so Paul and I did, in preliminary affidavit, swear that oath. I still think it shocking that in the United States, with its Declaration of Independence, its constitutional guarantees of free speech and protection against self-incrimination, a citizen should be made to act as if these guarantees did not exist.

Three more cancellations occurred before the case actually began. A Detroit club manager wanted to cancel me. I was put on the line and his first words were: "Is this conversation being recorded?" This manager said that, if I would come to Detroit and go on the air to declare that I was not a Communist, he would honor the booking. I didn't play the date.

There was a division of Columbia Concerts (they handled our concert engagements) called Community Concerts, that operated in about 1500 small communities. Established artists played the Community dates for a reduced fee (bringing culture to the masses) and paid 15 percent commission instead of 20 percent. Ward French, the head of Community Concerts, sent a letter to all 1500 subscribers telling them that he had had no idea of the political leanings of Draper and Adler and that had he known he would never have allowed our name on his books. He added, for good measure, that he, Ward French, had voted Republican all his life. This outraged even George Sokolsky, the Hearst columnist. Sokolsky wrote that, if French was willing to take our commissions, he shouldn't run out on us now. That's the nearest I ever got to a good notice from either Sokolsky or Westbrook Pegler.

In 1945, the New York City Center had got started through Paul Draper and me. A revue was to have opened the theater, which had been taken over by the City of New York. The revue had been a flop in Philadelphia and it looked as if the City Center would die before birth. Newbold Morris, who was acting mayor of New York, approached us with an idea; if we would go in to the theater, which otherwise would remain dark, perhaps permanently, he would publicize us on every bus and subway, we would be plugged several times a day on WNYC, the city-owned radio station, and most tempting of all, we would get a special mention from Mayor Fiorello LaGuardia on his Sunday morning broadcast, after he finished reading comics to the children. This was too good to miss and we agreed.

I tuned in on Sunday morning to hear the mayoral plug.

"Next week," said the mayor, in that famous high-pitched voice, "the new City Center will present Paul Draper and Larry Adler. A tap-dancer and a harmonica player." Now his voice rose to a near-scream: "AND WHY NOT?"

From then on, every year, Draper and Adler were fixtures of the Christmas season at the City Center. We did children's shows in the afternoons—these proved so popular that we had to do morning shows as well—and our regular recitals at night. In our last engagement at the Center, in 1948, playing the Christmas to New Year season, we took in the highest gross on Broadway, not bad for a hoofer and a mouth-organist. But the Center, too, caved in after the Red publicity. In a recent resumé of the theater's history Draper and I are not even mentioned. Like Trotsky in Russian history books, we had become nonpersons.

Thinking about Westbrook Pegler, George Sokolsky, Fulton Lewis, Jr., and other such journalists, I am impressed by their righteousness. They don't doubt, they *know*. I don't think I'd like to be that sure of anything. Igor Cassini was so sure that Paul Draper and I were villains that he even suggested that we be deported . . . to where? In some columns he had us as moral lepers; in others we were physical cowards whom he challenged to a fistfight. He, like Pegler, depicted us as mincing queens. Other Hearst journalists invited us to go back where we came from (in my case, Baltimore) or, more simplistically, why didn't we go to Moscow where we belonged? (I doubt that Moscow would have welcomed us.)

Yet a curious thing happened. When the case came to court, in Hartford, Connecticut, some of the journalists, who had started off loading their stories against us, gradually altered their tone, so that by the time the case was nearing its end, after five weeks, some were actually writing in our favor. One writer, on the *World-Telegram* (a Scripps-Howard paper with the same slant as the Hearst press), seemed so much on our side that I warned him he could lose his job.

"Fuck 'em," he said. "From where I sit, you guys are being railroaded. And if that's how I see it, that's the way I write it."

I wish the jury had been equally open-minded. There were eight men, four women. As I learned later, in a letter from the foreman of the jury (who thought the case should never have come to court), the jury stood eight to four against us when they first sat down. And when it ended that's where they stood; eight to four against us. The evidence had changed nobody's mind.

A man and his wife came, apparently at their own expense, from Kansas City to say that, while dining at their home, Draper and I had expressed Communist sympathies. These were obviously nice people; what made them do such a thing? Well, we never denied we were left in our sympathies and to many a mid-Westerner at that time, anything left was Communist or worse. No, there was nothing worse.

On the other hand Colonel Stevens, who had been in British intelligence, MI5 during the war, wrote to me from Montreal. He had had to investigate me for clearance before I could play in the Middle East, which was his territory. He offered to come and testify on my behalf. He did, and his apparent goodwill and honesty should have been impressive. Well, it wasn't. (A sad aftermath: Colonel Stevens was working on a history of the Bronfman Distilleries in Canada. After his action in testifying for me hit the papers he was fired from the project. This is one of my bitterest regrets in the whole affair.)

Sir John Foster QC, deposed on my behalf. He said that I had volunteered to play for the British army at Tobruk. This was during the Nazi-Soviet pact; no self-respecting Communist would have been caught dead playing for the British. His testimony produced a note from John T. McCullough, husband of the lady we were suing. It was handed to his lawyer and our lawyer got a glimpse of it; it read, "What about Klaus Fuchs?"

Mack Kriendler, of "21," the famous restaurant on 52nd Street insisted that he testify for me. I asked him not to, not that I didn't value the prestige of his name but, as I pointed out, "Mack, all of your customers are right-wing Republicans. You'll lose business."

"Stuff them and stuff their business," said Kriendler, "you're my friend."

But Jack Benny called me to his house to tell me that he had been advised by his business manager—who was also his brother-in-law— that he must not appear. He was commercially sponsored and could lose that, were he seen to be lending support to a leftie—a pinko— a Red, or whatever. Jack seemed distressed as he said this; I think he would rather not have said it and, on his own, I don't think he *would* have said it. But I had never intended to call Jack, I knew how vulnerable he was. Sponsors don't like knocking letters and just a few can cause a performer to be taken off the air. I doubt whether that would have happened to Jack Benny, but I wouldn't put him on the spot.

Despite having had to swear an affidavit that I was not, nor ever had been a Communist, in order to file the suit in the first place; despite the sworn testimony of friends; despite the evidence presented; the jury remained eight to four against us. It was as though there had never been a case. If I wanted a verdict I would have to initiate a new trial, have all the evidence re-presented and pay more lawyer's fees.

With nothing proved either way, I returned to England.

CHAPTER

Ten

*M*Y BLACKLISTING PROBLEMS were not over. In 1952 I decided to return to America to give a first performance in New York of a work which Ralph Vaughan Williams had composed for me. While trying to raise money for this, I dined with Meyer Davis, *the* society bandleader. I'd heard, on the news, that Elia Kazan had testified before the House Un-American Activities Committee and had named many people, including the playwright Clifford Odets. When I arrived at the Davis apartment there was Odets. I said how awful he must feel to be named as a Communist by a close friend.

Odets said, "I think you're being hard on him, Larry. After all, who are we to judge?"

"My God, Clifford, who do we *have* to be to judge? This man has betrayed his friends, including you. Do you condone that?"

"Larry," said Odets, "we don't know what kind of pressure he was under. You have to be in that spot yourself before you can pass judgment on someone else."

"Clifford, I'm sorry. I find your tolerance extraordinary. To be an informer, to give away the names of your friends, is a lousy thing to do. I know goddamned well I wouldn't do it, pressure or no pressure."

Clifford smiled and I thought the man must be a saint. I felt guilty at my outburst and dropped the subject, feeling somewhat of a heel.

A week later all became clear. Odets went before the committee and named names, including Elia Kazan. They had made a deal; you name me and I'll name you.

Kazan's giving testimony had been particularly painful. I had sat at Sardi's with him and a group of friends. Kazan had received a subpoena to appear before the House Un-American Activities Committee. (I always wondered how you defined an un-American activity. Joining Bundles for Britain?) Gadget—Kazan's nickname, due, it was said, to his fondness for all kinds of gadgets—was militant in his contempt for the whole business of informing.

"I've got two million bucks in the bank," he said, "and nobody can make *me* talk!"

Good old Gadge, he'd show 'em.

But Gadge didn't show *them,* he showed *us.* On April 10, 1952, not long after his tough statement at Sardi's, he appeared in secret session before the House committee. The day after that his testimony was released. Somebody *could* make him talk, in fact they could make him sing, because that is what he did; he sang like Caruso, he did what he had previously said he abhorred, he named the names. And from then on his former friend Zero Mostel always referred to Kazan as "Looselips."

My own theory is that Spyros Skouras, head of 20th Century–Fox, talked to him. I think he pointed out that his company had a fortune tied up in as yet unreleased Kazan films and that they simply couldn't afford his principled stand.

The day following the release of Kazan's testimony, he took a quarter-page advertisement in the *New York Times,* which not only defended his decision to name names but advised others to do the same.

Lillian Hellman, in her book *Scoundrel Time,* writes: "Clifford Odets had testified as a friendly witness, throwing in the names of old friends and associates. His old friend Elia Kazan had done the same thing a month before and followed it up with an advertisement in the *New York Times* that is hard to believe for its pious shit."

Miss Hellman was a remarkable lady who contributed a notable phrase to the language; in her letter to John Wood, the chairman of the House committee, she wrote that she was willing to testify about herself but would refuse to incriminate others. "I cannot and will not cut my conscience to fit this year's fashions. . . ."

I admire Lillian Hellman. However, I disagree with her on one important point. She was willing to talk about herself to the committee but would not implicate others. I would go farther; I would not talk about *myself* to the committee. If I were subpoenaed I would have to appear, of course, but I like to think that I would give that committee, for which I have real contempt, no information of any kind. This is brave talk; I've never been summoned before any committee, maybe I'd cave in completely, but I like to think that I would not.

A few days after Kazan testified I had to go to see my agent, Abe Lastfogel. As I approached his office, Kazan came out of it. It was about noon and Kazan looked awful; unshaven and red-eyed. It looked to me as if he had been drinking all morning. We stopped when we saw each other and neither of us knew what to say. We must both have remembered that evening in Sardi's.

I finally managed to speak. "Hello, Gadge."

"Hello, kid. Uh—Abe tells me you're giving a recital at Town Hall—that's great news. I told Abe, put me down for twelve tickets, I'm bringing my whole family. You're gonna kill 'em, kid, you're gonna knock 'em dead."

"Thanks, Gadge. Glad you're coming to the concert."

Again, we stood there, the silence painful.

"Well, don't forget, kid, I'll be there in the front row. Bye now." He walked away, down the hall. I went into Abe's office, feeling guiltily that I should have tried to be a bit nicer. I despised Kazan for what he had done but anyone could see that he was in real distress. Would it have killed me to say something comforting?

"I just saw Gadge," I said to Lastfogel. "He looks a mess."

"Yeah. Well, he's had a rough time. They gave him quite a going-over in Washington."

At that moment Kazan burst into the office, came up to me, grabbed my hand in both of his.

"Larry—it's up to you. You gotta lick those bastards. It's up to you, kid, you gotta *lick* those bastards!"

He started to cry, made a great effort, stopped crying, grabbed my hand again, shook it, and ran out of Abe's office.

I was so shaken by what had happened that I forgot what I'd come to see Abe Lastfogel about.

Kazan's defection was crucial. Had he stood out against the black-listers it might have helped to break the blacklist itself. He could have continued to direct plays on Broadway—the blacklist never extended to the legitimate theater—and only in films would the blacklist have hit him. He has for the most part refused to talk about his appearance before the committee, his naming names. He has said he's saving it for his own book, but he has never written that book. In one interview, with the French critic Michel Ciment, he both condemns naming names and justifies it. In another interview on NBC he expresses regret for what he did but says he would do it again. A complicated man.

A few days after this a party was given for me by Howard Lindsay, co-author with Russell Crouse of the play *Life with Father.* At one point Howard Lindsay called for silence; he said how glad everyone was that I was to play once again in my own country, he talked about the iniquity of the blacklist. Then he said how wonderful it would be if Larry made a public anti-Communist statement and were seen to be signing a non-Communist affidavit. It caught me off balance, as I had expected nothing like that. Everyone looked at me expec-tantly. I said that I considered everyone in the room to be a friend, that I had known many of them for years. I wanted to ask them a question: Was it so important to them that, if I didn't make this public gesture, they would feel that they couldn't come to my recital? If that were the case I would take notice because I had respect for everyone in the room. But is that what Howard Lindsay meant? I went around the room; almost all agreed that they would need no preconditions before they could come to my concert. But Abe Burrows said he felt I ought to make it easier for myself by making such a statement— it would clear the air.

The toughest reaction was from James Wechsler, the liberal editor of the New York *Post.*

"Larry," he said, "I have to agree with Howard. I'd like to know from your own mouth that you weren't a Communist before I plunked down my $5.50 at the box office."

"Well, Jimmy," I said, "you're outnumbered. If you all were unanimous I'd certainly have to consider it. But that isn't the case. I've fought the Loyalty Oath, and as you know, I wouldn't tell a congressional committee what my politics were. I'll tell any of you —you're my friends—but no public statement."

After that not a line of publicity about my concert appeared in the *Post,* nor did the *Post* review it. The Hearst, Scripps-Howard and Patterson papers gave me good advance plugs and good notices as well.

Abe Burrows asked me to lunch. He said he knew I was disappointed with him for standing with Wechsler in asking for a non-Communist statement from me.

"But, Larry," he said, "you make it tough for your friends. Your name comes up, I don't know what to say about you. I can't defend you because I don't really know where you stand."

"Oh yes you do, Abe," I said. "You know exactly where I stand. Still, I don't want to embarrass you. Look, when my name comes up, why not say you don't know me?"

Abe protested, that wasn't what he meant at all.

"Well, that's the way it sounds, Abe."

As I didn't have any money, Mack Kriendler introduced me to a textile manufacturer, who offered to back my concert. With that pledged, I booked Town Hall, hired a PR firm, took space in the papers, engaged a piano accompanist and the Little Symphony Orchestra. Even a sell-out wouldn't break even, but a New York recital is a showcase.

I got a call from Town Hall. There had been an objection from a director—the mouth-organ was too frivolous an instrument for Town Hall, the booking was off. I was in a panic. Helen Morgan, my PR lady, who had connections at Town Hall (it's not what you know, it's *who* you know), found out that a pro-McCarthy, anti-anything to the left of Goebbels's priest, had vetoed me. The "frivolous" angle was a phony. In the same week as my recital, Town Hall was rented to a comedian/magician, George Givot. When I discovered this I was with Dan Golenpaul, who produced the quiz program "Information Please" on which I had been a guest in the forties. Golenpaul was outraged and phoned Norman Thomas, the perennial socialist candidate for president. Thomas spoke to me and said, "I'll get on to this tomorrow, and if what you say is true, you'll have

Town Hall." And I did get it back. Thomas had told the board that Town Hall was founded on the principle of free speech; if the booking were not restored, he, Thomas, would resign from the board. That did it.

About ten days before the recital I got a call from the textile man backing my concert, asking me to come to lunch. When I got there I found a very nervous textile man; he was sweating. He should have told me, he said, that his personal lawyer was Roy Cohn. (Roy Cohn, for God's sake—McCarthy's chief assistant.) Cohn had told the textile man Senator McCarthy wanted to see him in Miami. He had flown down there and McCarthy had told him that if he backed Larry Adler he would order a Senate investigation of the man's textile business.

"Larry," he said, near to tears, "nobody's business can take that kind of publicity."

I understood, I told him not to worry, he was off the hook. So there I was, with several thousand dollars worth of commitments and no money. I told my friend, Herman Liebman, also a textile man.

"I've got money," said Liebman and my financial troubles were over. The PR man, Benjamin Sonnenberg, took $1000 worth of tickets, Abe Lastfogel gave me an office with secretary and telephone, and I was back in business.

There was a constant factor in certain areas of blacklisting. Anyone who had gone through the motions, either through having been subpoenaed or having voluntarily appeared before the House Un-American Activities Committee, wanted people like me to do the same. They proselytized like Catholics seeking converts.

On Broadway, I met Edward G. Robinson. Robinson hadn't been called by the Washington committee; yet, because he was known as a supporter of left-wing causes, he found himself blacklisted. He asked to appear before the committee; they were not interested. He wrote to J. Edgar Hoover, seeking his help in getting cleared. Hoover ignored him. Finally he got Sam Yorty, mayor of Los Angeles, to intervene, and through Yorty he appeared before the committee. He appeared twice, and it was after the second occasion that I met him on Broadway. He looked and seemed shattered. He asked if I'd read his testimony. He had it with him and took me into a nearby hotel lobby to read it. It was harrowing. Robinson was a good man, the antithesis of his gangster image. The committee had made him crawl on his belly, abase himself, denounce and insult himself. The testimony, the entire hearing, could have come from the Moscow trials or from Koestler's *Darkness at Noon.* It was sickening to read. Eddie, seeing how moved I was, broke down and wept.

"Larry, you see what they did to me. It was dreadful, but I'm working again. You must do the same thing."

"Eddie, I can't," I said. "I'm not condemning you—it's just not for me."

"Larry, get back to work. You're an artist, people should hear you. Say whatever they want you to say. Fuck 'em. The main thing is, get back to work. What do you care what you say to those shitheels? Don't let those bastards keep you from working. You've got to do it, Larry."

But I couldn't do it. And though it served its purpose, though it got him back to work, Eddie was ashamed at having kissed the asses of little men unworthy to be in the same room with him.

Mind you, had it been a question of physical torture I wouldn't have held out. Lenny Bruce has a monologue in which he at first talks about high principles, he's not going to rat. Then he sees that his inquisitors are heating hot lead which they intend to pour through a funnel into his ass. His principles dissolve at once, he babbles that he'll tell them anything they want to know. "I'll betray my grandmother, for God's sake, just don't pour that hot lead in my ass."

I'm sure that, faced with the hot lead, I'd have betrayed my grandmother, my country, anything and anybody. So long as the pressure is mental, moral or whatever, I know I can hold out. Physical torture? That, friends, is something else.

In innumerable interviews I get asked the same question, "Are you bitter?" No, I don't think I am. Those days have left a mark, how could they not, but I don't think bitterness is part of it. I played at the Hungry i nightclub in San Francisco in 1960 and Enrico Banducci, the owner, told me that the spotlight operator was Alvah Bessie. Alvah Bessie! One of the original Hollywood Ten, a scriptwriter who earned $3500 a week in the good days. And now he was operating a spotlight. I invited him to dinner and then I knew what bitterness was; Alvah Bessie hated the informers, he hated the committee and it seemed to me that he lived for revenge. He told me that one of the Ten, who had served a jail term for contempt, as had Bessie himself, but who, after coming out of prison and finding

himself still blacklisted, chose to recant, on seeing Bessie, had put out
his hand in greeting. Said Bessie, "I knocked the bastard down. And
nothing gave me more satisfaction." Well, all right, I can understand
Bessie. At the same time I feel it is dreadful to live your life hating,
hoping for revenge. Lillian Hellman can hate like that too. In her
book, *Scoundrel Time,* she hates the people who informed in the
forties as if those days were still here. I can't do that. I have no
respect for informers, I could never trust them, I wouldn't want to
make friends of them, but hate them? No, that is too much, it eats
away at you and is, I think, self-defeating. I met one such person, a
man who had been a good friend in the days when I lived in Beverly
Hills. Then he not only turned informer but gave one of the biggest
list of names ever. I met him in a New York drawing room years
later. I was actually glad to see him. I didn't want to see him again
but I had no feelings of hate for him. Damn it, he had once been a
friend, I had dined at his house, he at mine.

Through Hugh Johnston, former secretary of the navy (whom I met
through Ben Sonnenberg), I went to the office of a high official of
the American Legion, and talked with him. He was cordial, and
surprised me by saying that there was no evidence that I was a Red.
Then what was all the fuss about? Well, he said, it was that libel suit;
a lot of people thought I shouldn't have sued Hester McCullough;
they thought I was unfairly picking on a lady who was only trying
to do her duty as an American patriot. But if there was nothing to
link me with subversion, why was the Legion picking on me? Ah,
that had been unfortunate, but it was all in the past.

"Let me get this straight," I said. "I do understand from you that,
setting aside what has happened, there will be no more trouble from
the Legion?"

"Of course not," he said. "From our point of view, you're clean."

That was good news and I told it to Art Buchwald, who made a
column out of it. That produced a wire from the official saying, so
help me, that there had been no meeting with him and that he
couldn't have said I was clear with the Legion because I was still on
their blacklist.

In 1955 I flew from London to New Orleans for a booking at the
Monteleone Hotel. On opening day the local American Legion came
in and told Mr. Monteleone that if I opened, they would picket.

Monteleone couldn't risk that and I didn't open. (They paid me the contracted salary, more than had happened when the Legion managed to cancel my engagement at the Sands in Las Vegas.)

That night, in my hotel room, I knew real depression. I felt this was the end of my career, that I would never work again. The phone rang.

"Adler? This is a friend o' yourn." I asked his name.

"Nemmine mah name. Ah'm jes a friend o' yourn."

"Well, you know my name but I don't know yours. Who is this?"

"Lissen, you lousy Jew-bastard, y'all better git on outa town before we ride you out on a rail!"

Well, it may sound silly but that cleared the air enormously. That Ku Klux Klan–type language made the whole thing a farce.

I suggested he meet me in the hotel lobby and we'd see who rode whom out on a rail.

"You wouldn't show up, you yellow kike." I said I'd be at the cigar counter in half an hour. No one showed up. I think I recognized the caller. It was the most militant of the Legion group, the chairman of which, to my shame, was a Jew. He too phoned me and we met. He was apologetic, explained that it was unusual for a Jew to have elected office in the Legion—I could understand that—and he hadn't gone along with the threat to picket. He'd done nothing to stop it either.

Ben Sonnenberg then arranged for me to go to Washington to see Arnold, Porter and Fortas, one of the most important legal firms in Washington. Thurman Arnold, Paul Porter and Abe Fortas were all well-known liberals. They agreed to take my case free if I would sue the Legion. It was a wonderful opportunity and, with hindsight, I see that I might even have broken the blacklist. I couldn't do it; I lacked courage. Having been through a five-week suit against Mrs. McCullough, I couldn't face the publicity of another court case. Today it is one of my great regrets that I backed out. I think Sonnenberg lost interest in my plight after that and who could blame him?

There were professional informers at work during the McCarthy era. Harvey Matusow, in his book, *False Witness*, describes how he would phone an executive of a radio network to complain about the left-wing activities of the comedian Jack Gilford. He made several calls, one after the other, in different voices, and was able to get Jack Gilford taken off the air. Matusow relates this with pride. He worked for Senator McCarthy and sometimes, when he ran out of names to inform on, would pick them at random from the phone book. Later Matusow said that he was a double agent the whole time, really working to expose the witch-hunters, but I don't think anyone ever bought that story.

Three years after my libel case, I was booked in a nightclub in Pittsburgh. The owner told me he'd been pressured on many sides about booking me. One night three huge men sat at a ringside table and, during my first number, made audible remarks about the Red, the commie. I spoke to these men from the floor. I said if they wanted to say something about me, don't say it while I was playing; come up and use my microphone. They didn't, of course, but they kept quiet for the rest of the show.

In 1956, after I returned from the Jewish National Fund tour of South Africa and the Rhodesias I had a message to report to the U.S. embassy in London with my passport. I was told by Thomas Walsh, whom I knew personally, that he had received word from Washington that I must hand in my passport. I asked why? Walsh looked distressed.

"It doesn't say why in the message but you know why as well as I do. They must have information that you're a Communist party member."

"Oh, come on, Tom," I said. "You know about my libel case. I'm on oath that I've never been a CP member."

"Larry, I'm just doing my job. This is the word from Washington and I can't do anything about it. You'll just have to turn in your passport; we'll hold it until you're ready to return to the U.S. Meanwhile, you can't travel anyplace else."

"Tom, I don't give a damn what they think in Washington. I'm not handing over my passport just because they say so, without them giving any reason. That's police-state stuff."

"Larry, you don't have any choice."

"Like hell. I'll go to Washington with a lawyer, they'll damned well *have* to tell me."

Walsh looked really unhappy.

"Larry, *please* don't do that. If you try to get tough you'll never get your passport back. You're talking about the State Department now."

"Well, the hell with them. They want my passport, they've got to have a damned good reason and they've got to say it to my face. No, Tom, I'm sorry, but I'm not handing it in. I'm not trying to make things tough for you. You've done your job, you've asked me to hand in my passport. I've refused; that's not your fault. See you, Tom." And I left.

I did as I said. I returned to the U.S. and called Fred Wiggin, of the firm who had handled my libel suit. He put me in touch with Sturgis Warner, in Washington. Warner set an appointment at the State Department. We met with two men, Mr. Nicholas and Mr. Franzmathes, I never knew their first names. Both were bland, both very smooth. They just sat there smiling at me, saying nothing.

"I've been told," I said, the first to speak, "that you want my passport. Why?"

Mr. Nicholas looked almost avuncular.

"Well, Mr. Adler, why do you *think* the government might want it?"

"Look, this was your idea, not mine. I haven't volunteered to hand it in. Why do you want it?" My lawyer was looking nervous.

"Come now, Mr. Adler, surely you can think of *some* reason why we might require you to hand in your passport."

I was angry.

"Damnit," I said, "you're just talking baby talk. I've asked you a specific question, why do you want my passport? You just answer with another question."

"Search your heart, Mr. Adler. We're sure that, if you do, you'll come up with the reason. . . ."

"Look, I've had enough." Sturgis Warner was kicking my leg under the table and trying to be discreet about it, which takes doing. "You want my passport. I want to know why you want it. I ask you, you won't tell me but you keep making with the cute questions. Okay, you won't tell me? Then I'll tell *you* something. I'm going to sue the State Department. In court you'll damned well *have* to tell me." I got up from the table. "Come on, Mr. Warner, this isn't getting us anywhere."

"Mr. Adler, just a moment," said Franzmathes. I sat down. He whispered for a while to Nicholas.

"Mr. Adler, let's not be hasty. We can tell you this much. We have information that you were a CP member. Our informant tells us he was with you in a Communist group, a cell of three members, for about twelve years."

"Well, bring him around. Let him say that to me. One of us is lying and it shouldn't take long to find out which one."

"I'm afraid we can't do that," said Nicholas, or was it Franzmathes —they both looked and sounded alike. "I'm sure you understand, we have to preserve the anonymity of our informant."

"No," I said, "I don't understand. Why are you protecting some faceless *schmuck* who won't come out in the open? I'm not anonymous, I'm right here and I'm laying it on the line."

More whispering between The Smiling Twain. Warner was looking at me in despair.

"Well, Mr. Adler, there is an obvious discrepancy somewhere, we can see that. We will investigate this matter here in the department."

Replying to a question from Sturgis Warner, Nicholas said it should take about five weeks to clear this up. Warner told them I had a concert to do in England, with the Hallé Orchestra in Manchester. The meeting ended there.

Warner told me next day they wanted to see the Hallé contract, also to know when it was signed, was it before or after I knew that they wanted my passport? Warner advised me to hand in the passport, in any case the government could put out a stop order on me so I couldn't leave the country. Reluctantly I did this.

Finally they gave me back my passport but a much restricted one. It was valid for a visit to England for sixty days. I couldn't go anywhere else. Warner said that this was a good sign.

"It means they're not sure of their case. If they were, they'd never let you out of the country, because what's to prevent you staying out? No, believe me, I know how you must feel, holding a restricted passport. It's awful and frankly it makes me ashamed of my own government. But this is good news. You just wait, you're going to win this one."

Entering the UK with a temporary passport good for sixty days made me feel as if I was guilty of something. That is one of the worst things about being on the receiving end of the blacklist, you begin to feel that perhaps something *is* wrong with you.

While in the UK my Paris agent offered me two weeks at the Moulin Rouge. I had to cable Sturgis Warner to ask the State Department, might I please cross the Channel? He replied, take my passport to the U.S. embassy, it would be extended another sixty days and valid for France.

During the Moulin Rouge engagement Warner cabled me to ask if I had ever been a reporter for the Brooklyn *Daily Eagle*? No, I hadn't. It turned out to be a case of mistaken identity.

When it turned out that "Larry" Adler was not the same Larry Adler, did I get an apology from the State Department? Did I even get my passport back? The questions are rhetorical. Although the department now *knew* that they had made a mistake, my passport was still restricted, I still had to ask permission to visit any country. I would still have liked to sue them for full passport restoration but Warner advised me not to do it.

"Your passport expires early next year. When it does I know you'll get a new one, clean, and with no restrictions."

And that is what happened. But if you want to know why I continue to live in England, that whole passport business says it all.

Sam Spiegel took me to see Nate Spingold, the New York head of Columbia Pictures. Spingold, Sam told me, had been useful in getting blacklisted performers back to work. Spingold said he'd like to see some background material, on my political past. I'd already had my libel case against Mrs. McCullough, so there was plenty to show him. I came back a week later. Spingold said: "I've helped a lot of people get back to work. I have to tell you that you're the only one I've come across for whom I can do absolutely nothing."

"Well, that's that," I said, getting up to go, "but thank you for trying."

"Wouldn't you like to know the reasons why?"

"Only if you feel like telling me."

"Well, people in your kind of trouble generally fall into one of two categories. Either they were card-carrying Communists who will admit it, will give names, or else they were duped into doing things. They're willing to say they were duped and, again, they'll give names. Now in your case you're already on oath, from your court case, so okay you weren't a Communist. But neither can anyone say you were duped. You knew what you were doing, nobody was kidding you. Also you're against giving names. So you're a hopeless case. I'd help you if I could; this time I can't." We said good-bye.

Ben Sonnenberg told me that Roy Cohn owed him a favor and thus Cohn agreed to see me, the idea being that he could help to get me off the blacklist. I doubted this, but went to Cohn's office in Foley Square. Cohn told me first thing that he was seeing me only because of his friendship with Ben. He said that he had arranged that I appear as a friendly witness before Senator McCarthy's Internal Security Committee. It would be a secret session, nobody would know I'd been there.

"Now I already know, you don't want to give names. That's okay, you don't have to. We've worked out a special deal for you. I've prepared a list, these are people who have been named before, we already know them. You just read these names out to us, remember, you're not giving us any information, therefore, you're not hurting anybody."

"Mr. Cohn, what is the sense of me reading you a list of names that you already have?"

Cohn went to the window, looked out, then turned back to me.

"Go fight City Hall," he said, spreading his hands. "We're all trying to get you back to work and you won't help us."

Obviously, I have neither liking nor respect for Mr. Cohn. Yet, during an engagement at The Ballroom in New York, when a TV journalist told me that Cohn was dying and would I, at Cohn's death, join in a celebration party, I was shocked. The details of Mr. Cohn's illness were grisly, I would not wish such a fate on anyone. I suppose, when it comes to death, I'm with John Donne.

While revising the final proofs of this book I learned that Roy Cohn had died. But I was not happy over his death. Roy Cohn ruined the careers of many brave, good, and valuable people. I hope his like does not appear again, though I think it probably will. It is sad that experience seems to make us only older, not wiser. Cohn and McCarthy exemplified Samuel Johnson's dictum that patriotism is the last refuge of a scoundrel.

Eleven

THE HASIDIM, the ultrareligious Jews, scare me, but I am always repelled by dogmatism. Once you say that your faith is superior to my faith, any excess can be justified. The Hasidim stone those who ride on the Sabbath. They already exercise an influence in Israel well beyond what their numbers entitle them to; I think they are likely to ruin Israel as a place to visit. They insisted that El Al, the Israeli airline, stop flying on the Sabbath and got away with it. The airline had other problems, labor ones, but the religious group, I believe, started the trouble.

The first time I visited Israel, it was Palestine. I was on a USO tour with Jack Benny playing to Allied troops. It was 1943 and they flew us from Cairo to Lod airport (now called Ben Gurion) outside Tel Aviv. I long ago stopped being a religious Jew. I was a Jew, because that's the group I came from and also, the non-Jewish world never let me forget it. It is possible that, had there been no Nazi movement the whole idea of being Jewish might have slipped. However, once I knew that there was a place where there was a death penalty for being Jewish, I no longer had the option: it sounds silly, but

Hitler, more than any other factor, made me a confirmed Jew.

I had an immense spiritual feeling when I landed at Lod. It wasn't a sense of coming home, but I was not just visiting another country in the Middle East, there was a special tie.

I met Israel Rokach, mayor of Tel Aviv, a gentle philosopher, and compared him with Fiorello LaGuardia, the mayor of New York, whose greatest joy was to chase fire engines in a police car. I couldn't imagine Rokach doing that. Then there was Henrietta Szold, the founder of Youth Aliyah, whose purpose was to bring young people to Palestine. She came from my hometown and while I was eager to hear about her work, all she wanted to talk about was Baltimore.

I picked up two hitchhikers in British uniform. They were Palestine Jews, speaking only Hebrew—I didn't know that they had units in the British army. I could only make contact in pidgin English. I went to Hebrew school as a kid but remember little of the language; my classroom achievement was to translate "Yes, We Have No Bananas" into Hebrew and I can't even remember *that.*

In Jerusalem, Jack Benny and I visited the Old City and went inside a church on the Via Dolorosa. A nun—she seemed to be played by Maria Ouspenskaya—showed a party of tourists around and we joined them. At one point the nun surprised us by dropping to her knees.

"I am going to say a prayer," she said, in an accent that convinced me she *was* Maria Ouspenskaya, "that you all return safely to your loved ones, who must miss you so much—as I know you miss them. And it may interest you to know that where my knees touch the stone is where our good Lord, Jesus Christ, paused on his way to be killed . . . by the *Jews*!" This with such venom that Jack and I fled: we were sure that, had she known about us, she'd have beaten hell out of us.

I was proud when Palestine became Israel; for the first time there existed a country which welcomed Jews. I'd even met the founding father. Eileen and I were once invited for a weekend at Grossinger's, the famous Jewish hotel in the Catskills in New York state. It wasn't the first Jewish hotel, just the first famous one. When we arrived we were told there had been a booking mixup; our room had been given away. However, there was other accommodation provided we wouldn't mind sharing a chalet with Chaim Weizmann. I was honored. Chaim Weizmann as much as any man was responsible for the state of Israel. I didn't see much of Weizmann, but we made a few amiable social noises at each other. About a year later I received a letter and a bill sent from Jerusalem. The letter was from Weizmann, who wrote that he had enjoyed meeting me and sharing the chalet, "but I don't think it right that I should be asked to pay your laundry bill."

In subsequent visits I have come to dislike the growing chauvinism of Israel; it is understandable but not endearing. I feel, illogically, that the Jews *do* have a special code of morality. A Jew should be able to be a sonofabitch without it singling him out as a Jewish sonofabitch. Yet when something hideous, like the massacre in Lebanon, happens, I, as a Jew, am ashamed; we—and yes, *I* find myself saying *we* were responsible and *we* let it happen. There have been other, far greater, massacres that went virtually unnoticed. I know that, I know the illogic of my thinking, but I cannot ignore my instincts; we are Jews, we know persecution from the inside, and we should not permit atrocities in our name. A Jew should not create refugees.

After my political troubles in the United States, I'd lived in England. British justice isn't flawless but I reckoned I'd get a squarer deal in England than anywhere else. I was in London when I read that Jack Benny was to make a tour of U.S. troops in South Korea. I wrote to my agent, volunteering to go with Jack. Lastfogel wrote back: not a hope, I was still blacklisted and the U.S. army would turn me down. Woodrow Wyatt, then under-secretary for war in Clement Attlee's Labor cabinet, dined with me that night and I showed him the letter.

"Good God," he said, "won't your chaps take you? Come for us!"

I was moved by this very British response but pointed out that, if I got to Korea via Woodrow's intervention, he himself might get in bad with the U.S. government.

Nonsense, said Wyatt briskly, he could take care of himself. Ten days later I left for Korea, by way of Japan, by invitation of the British Commonwealth Division.

Stephen Barber of the *News Chronicle* was on the same plane and, in Tokyo, took me to the Press Club. A man came over and introduced himself as a representative of an American newspaper. He asked me for a story for the hometown paper. I said that I had agreed to tour the wards at the military hospital next morning. Why not come with me, we were certain to find someone from his hometown and there was the angle. He agreed. Next morning I did the rounds but he didn't show. The VD ward at the hospital had barbed wire around it. The doctors didn't like it when I wanted to play for the men in that ward but I got temperamental about it and they gave in. I was told later that, as the army gave the GI's prophylactics and instructions, any man who caught a venereal disease was considered a criminal and punished accordingly, hence the barbed wire. After the ward shows a Red Cross nurse gave me a message. I was to go to the Dai Ichi Building where the U.S. command was located, with my passport. Sounded ominous.

At the Dai Ichi building I was sent to an office where a captain and a lieutenant examined my passport. The captain said: "It looks perfectly okay to me." The lieutenant looked angry and said: "I don't know, Captain, there's something fishy about this." Nothing else was said, my passport was handed back and I left. Outside the office a captain was waiting who invited me to the canteen for coffee. He was PR to General Ridgeway and told me that he knew I was a friend of E. J. Kahn of *The New Yorker* and so was he; because of that, he was going to give me some information. Two newspapermen, one of them the man I had already met, had visited the Dai Ichi Building to ask how come this Commie, Larry Adler, was being allowed into Korea. Their complaint had delayed my trip by one day, I should have flown to Seoul right after the hospital show.

In Tokyo, on my return from Korea, the journalist was at the airport. He held out his hand and said: "Welcome back, Larry, I hear you did a great job."

I ignored the hand. "Listen, you sonofabitch," I said, "I know how you damned near stopped my trip. So don't give me that 'welcome back, Larry' bullshit."

"Larry, I was only trying to help you."

"I've heard of *chutzpah* but this is the tops—*you* were helping *me*?"

"Don't you see? If the brass had actually kept you out, I could have done a story about what horse's asses they were and you'd have come up smelling like roses."

"Okay, that's how you were helping me. Don't ever speak to me again, you bastard!"

I later heard that he was a rabid right-winger. But even so!

In Tokyo I stayed at the Imperial Hotel. My phone rang soon after I'd checked in.

"Larry, baby? This is Charlie."

"Charlie who?"

"Charlie Hasegawa, kiddo. I work for *Yomiuri,* biggest paper in Japan. I wanna talk to you about something very big, very important." He came to the hotel. He wore a checked sports jacket, a bow tie, and looked like a Japanese Flash Harry.

"Larry, baby," said Charlie, "I've heard a lot about you, you play your thingummybob with symphony orchestras, classical music and all that crap, am I right or am I right?" He was right.

"Well, here's what we're gonna do. We're gonna put on a concert with the Tokyo Symphony, you as the soloist, playing something that'll knock 'em right on their ass, right?"

We made a deal, I would give the concert on my return from Korea. I chose the Vivaldi Violin Concerto in A Minor. Charlie was euphoric about it and he left, with my confirmation.

When I got back, he met me with a glum face.

"Larry, baby," he said—he never said the name without the "baby" follow-up, so that I wondered if he thought that was my name? Larrybaby Adler.

"Ya know, we got a great research department at *Yomiuri*, they can find out anything about anything. I checked that tune you gave me, what was it, that Eyetalian thing?"

"The Vivaldi concerto."

"Yeah, sure, that. Well, Larry baby, the research department searched all over the place and you wanna know something? That Eyetalian thing is zilch. But nowhere! It ain't in any of the charts and, believe me, we checked it out real good."

I said I regretted Vivaldi's standing in the charts. But a concert wasn't based on "Top of the Pops."

"Oh, sure, I yunnastan that and I admire you for it, ya don't wanna lower your standards, sure, I see that. But we're both out for the same thing; I want the concert to be a big success, right?" Right. "And you, you want it to be a big success, right?" Right.

"So okay, we're both after the same thing. Now get a load of this; our research department, they found out just what the public wants and we wanna give 'em what they want, right?" Wrong, though I didn't say so.

"Okay, so you know what's biggest, top on the Hit Parade? 'You Are My Sunshine,' 'Home on the Range' and 'Buttons and Bows.'

So I've chucked the Vivaldi in the ashcan, we'll stick in these hit tunes and we got a sellout, right?"

"Charlie, baby," I said—I was becoming fond of this spiv, "I've nothing against those tunes. They're good tunes and if we were doing a club date, say, with a rhythm group, I'd play them. But this is a symphony concert with your best orchestra, you're holding it at Hibiya Hall, which is like Carnegie Hall. It's no place for a pop concert."

Charlie kept trying to get me to change my mind but I wouldn't. Then he brought up the big guns.

"Larry, baby," he said, in a voice right out of *East Lynne* and managing to look like a wounded Japanese spaniel, "if I ast ya a personal favor, you'd do it for me, wouldn't ya?"

This was a tear-jerking scene. I hardened my heart.

"No, Charlie," I said, "I don't want to hurt your feelings, but no, I can't play 'You Are My Sunshine,' 'Home on the Range' and 'Buttons and Bows' with the Tokyo Symphony."

"Larry, baby," he said brokenly, "wouldn't you at least do it for the Japanese people?"

I was ready to cry myself by now. But, like Simon Legree faced with the plight of Eliza, I maintained my hardened heart. Charlie left me like a man contemplating suicide.

When I rehearsed with the orchestra I heard one violinist who seemed to be pitched a half tone above the rest of the string section. Between movements I went over to the violinist and mentioned this. He gave me a black look. Later, at a break, the conductor asked me to come to his room. He told me the orchestra had been ready to walk out on me.

"You mean for correcting the violinist. But he was playing a half tone above the others."

"Yes, I know that. I can hear as well as you, Mr. Adler. But this is Japan. You don't correct a musician in front of the others; that is a humiliation."

"Well, how the hell do you get anything corrected?"

"You wait until later. I intended to call the violinist in here, tell him privately—that's the important thing, privately—what was wrong. The orchestra only put up with it because you're American and don't know our ways. But please, if anything else goes wrong, say nothing. Wait and tell me later, in private."

Well, that's Japan for you.

*   *   *

From Japan I went on a concert tour of Israel with my partner Paul Draper. This created an ironic situation. When it was publicized in Israel that I'd just come from South Korea, the Israeli Communist party picketed my concerts. Now why wasn't *that* publicized in the United States?

Paul and I were asked to perform at a village, Ben Shemem, populated mainly by orphan children. There were a few adults as executives, but the kids ran things. They had a string quartet led by a twelve-year-old violinist and I was asked to play something with them. I suggested the Mozart Oboe Quartet. We played it without rehearsal, in the mess hall, to an audience of about two hundred. Everything went well until the third movement, which had some very rapid passages. I missed a few notes. I doubt if anyone in the audience was aware of it but that twelve-year-old violinist, *he* knew. Still playing, he said out of the side of his mouth, *"Schmuck."*

After the last recital I was booked to fly Tel Aviv–New York, the plane stopping to refuel at Heathrow Airport. We flew El Al and the plane developed engine trouble. We were told at Heathrow that the cause of the engine trouble was unknown. It looked as if we'd be sitting in the airport lounge overnight.

A man approached me and said he was from BOAC. Would I please come with him outside. He said that BOAC could put me on their flight leaving in an hour for New York. The secrecy was because he didn't want the other passengers to know; he didn't have room for them.

I said I appreciated the offer and would like to accept, but as I'd been sitting with an extremely nice lady with whom I'd chatted all the way from Tel Aviv to London, I wondered if it would be possible to accommodate her as well? I'd really feel guilty getting this unexpected perk and leaving her to wonder why I'd disappeared. The BOAC man looked glum, said he had to discuss it with head office, then disappeared. When he returned he was smiling again, all was in order, he sneaked the lady and me out of the lounge, arranged for the transfer of our luggage from El Al to BOAC and that's how I gave a lift to Golda Meir.

In 1954 I was back in Israel again to find that my Israeli impresario had booked a concert in Beersheba on Friday night, the Jewish Sabbath. Israel is a country of religious contrasts. In Tel Aviv you could give a concert on Friday night provided no money changed hands at the box office, which meant the tickets were sold in advance. In Haifa you could give a concert on Friday for the military, but you couldn't do a professional concert. Jerusalem shut down on the Sabbath. Beersheba was more or less like Las Vegas, an "anything goes" place.

About a fortnight before the Beersheba concert I received two telegrams on the same day. One, signed Society for the Protection of the Sabbath, was quite rudely worded, ordering me to cancel my concert with implications of violence if I refused. The other was from Chief Rabbi Herzog of Jerusalem. He was sure I would not wish to give offense to religious Jews by appearing in a concert on the Sabbath. He signed himself with cordial good wishes. I ignored the first wire and sent my impresario to see the Chief Rabbi; my message was, I obey the laws. I wouldn't try to give a concert in Jerusalem on the Sabbath. Beersheba was different. I felt the religious lobby was trying to make an issue over my concert, to get control in Beersheba. I respected the office of Chief Rabbi but I intended to honor my contract. The rabbi said: "Obviously I cannot give official approval to this concert but please tell Mr. Adler I send him my *brochas* (blessings)."

The concert did take place, the hall surrounded by armed police, because bomb threats against me and the concert hall had been received. In fact there was no trouble, it was bluff, and my main memory is that the Beersheba concert was the first where I saw Arabs in the audience.

In Beersheba I visited a friend. The previous year, with my son Peter, then eight years old, I had dined with about fifteen Arab sheikhs on the Jordan–Israel border. An Israeli colonel had invited me to this event. I, as the guest of honor, had to go through with eating a sheep's eye. I did, too, wrapping the eye in a kind of chapatti; despite this precaution, and trying to swallow it in one gulp, I half strangled and saw sheikhs before my eyes. The Arabs thought this very funny. One sheikh had a dagger in a jeweled scabbard and Peter was eyeing this with interest. He must have known his Arab; the sheikh unbuckled the dagger and, with a bow, presented it to Peter. Peter immediately removed a TWA badge from his lapel and presented it to the sheikh. The Arabs roared with delight; apparently it is a tradition, metal for metal, and Peter was a hero. The sheikh was Suleiman, famous throughout Israel for having proposed marriage to Mrs. Franklin D. Roosevelt. He invited Peter and me to visit him in Beersheba the following day, which we did.

Now, a year later, I was going to Israel again. Peter insisted that I bring Sheikh Suleiman a present from him; I had a special case made at Hill's in Bond Street to hold a mouth-organ, with a silver plaque fixed on which read, in English, Arabic and Hebrew: "Peace and friendship to Sheikh Suleiman from his friend Peter Adler." Suleiman was delighted with the gift and gave me his best *nargileh* (hookah pipe), which had been in his family for generations. Trouble with Arabs? They should send for Peter; *he'd* fix things.

Suleiman had advertised in Germany, in *Die Stern,* for a bride. He already had thirty-nine but felt deprived. He showed me a reply from a German girl, written in English and enclosing her photo; she was pretty. From the letter she obviously imagined Suleiman as a Valentino-style sheikh. Suleiman told me the government wouldn't give the girl an entry permit. Had I any influence with Ben-Gurion? I hadn't, though I had met Paula Ben-Gurion several times, but even if I had, I told Suleiman, I wouldn't try to help. I pointed out that his thirty-nine wives were all Arab; the German girl, who didn't even know Suleiman was married, was expecting a romantic life. Those thirty-nine wives would make that girl's life hell if she survived at all. Suleiman looked pained but didn't press it.

In 1955 I returned to Japan to tour for the Kokusai theaters. In Tokyo, at the Kokusai Gekijo, it was like Radio City Music Hall with a ballet of about two hundred girls. Each one on seeing me, would bow; I would bow. The back trouble that sometimes bothers me may date from that time, because I never learned the trick of when to stop bowing. I'd come up, only to see the girl bobbing down again.

After Tokyo I played Kobe, Kure, Yokohama and Kyoto. A stage manager was sent around with me who spoke English and who was impressed, as I was, at the numbers of Japanese mouth-organ players in each town. They would come backstage and stare at me adoringly. I would try, through my stage manager, to make contact with them, at least to get them to ask me technical questions about the mouth-organ. No, they preferred to stare and say nothing.

One day Sessue said, "You know, to Japanese harmonica player, you not just Larry Adler, you not just human being, you *God*!" It figures.

In Kyoto, one of the most beautiful of cities, I was invited to watch the Japanese film master Kurosawa, who was shooting about twenty miles away. I had to be there by six A.M. The set was a seventeenth-century samurai village. There were several hundred extras. By noon not a single foot of film had been shot. I told Kurosawa that I was honored to be invited to see him at work; however, my first show in town was at two P.M. and therefore with great regret, I had to leave. But why, I asked him, in six hours, had there been no action?

"Ah," said the master, beaming, "must wait for crowd."

Yeah, sure, I saw that. But surely, as the producer/director, he shouldn't have to wait for his crowd—didn't he tell them what time to be on the set.

"Ah," Kurosawa said, beaming even more, "you not understand. Must wait for crowd to pass across sun."

There are moments when I have wanted to kill myself. That was one of them.

Before the provincial tour I was entertained by, so help me, the Romanian Jewish Club of Tokyo. After the dinner I, in black tie, was walking down the Ginza. A prostitute, looking about forty-five, wearing a mannish double-breasted jacket and with several gold teeth, stepped in front of me, blocking my way.

"Hello," she said, displaying all the gold teeth, "you like come to my house?"

"No, thank you very much." I made to pass her. She put out an arm.

"Wait. You got nice manners. You artist?"

Well, uh, no.

"You musician, maybe?"

I was astonished. "Yes, in fact I am."

"Ah!" she cried in triumph. She said, "I know, you with Toscanini orchestra."

I found this extraordinary. When Toscanini resigned, the NBC orchestra that he had created was just given its notice, crudely, harshly, a crass gesture to a first-class group of musicians. They had kept themselves together, first touring without a conductor and now, in Japan, with a guest conductor, Thor Johnson. They were giving four concerts in Tokyo.

"No," I said, "I *am* a musician. But I'm not with the NBC orchestra."

"What you do?" she asked.

"I play the harmonica."

"Please?"

I made motions of brushing my teeth.

"Ah, so! You American man, you play mouth-organ, you play Bach!"

She fished in her handbag, took out three tickets and showed them to me. Two were for NBC concerts, the third was for one of my recitals. She smiled at me, pleased with her triumph.

"*Now* you like come to my house?"

Well, hell, now we had a relationship, I had to be careful. I was aware by now of the importance of face, saving of.

"You are very nice," I said, "but I must tell you the truth. I only like boys."

She peered into my face.

"No," she said, shaking her head, "maybe you tired. Maybe you not want me. But not true you like boys. You *not* like boys."

"How can you tell?" I asked.

"I know," she said, positively. I invited her to have a drink or a coffee with me. We went to a cafe. She told me she took only white men, never Orientals. "Too much like me," she said. "I shame."

She wanted to know why Toscanini wasn't with the orchestra. Thor Johnson displeased her.

"He too young. He no good!"

I told her that after my recital there was a party for me and invited her to come as my guest. She looked shocked.

"Ah, no," she said, drawing out the "o" sound. "You not want to take me to party. Very bad, your friends see me."

I assured her that *she* was now my friend. I asked her to give me her word she would come backstage after the recital. Reluctantly she promised. She didn't show up, I never saw her again. I even looked for her one night. But again, I had misinterpreted the Japanese mentality. She came from a different stratum. In her eyes she would humiliate me by her presence. I should have known all this.

On a visit to Hiroshima, looking at the memorial to the victims of the atomic bomb, I met some Japanese university students, all of whom knew some English. One said: "In Japan, we think that you Americans would never drop the atomic bomb on a white nation." And how can I contradict him? We did drop it, and it wasn't on a white nation. Truman said that, after giving the order to drop the bomb he never lost a night's sleep over it. Well, goody for him.

I was visiting soloist with André Kostelanetz and the New York Philharmonic at Lincoln Center when the Six Day War broke out between Israel and Egypt. I volunteered to go and play for the Israeli Defense Forces. The U.S. authorities gave me a flat refusal. I returned to England, where I had lived since 1949, and volunteered through the Israeli embassy. They were delighted with my offer and sent me to Israel at once. I was greeted at the Tel Aviv airport by Major Zafrir, special services officer, who asked me if I would play a song, "Sharm-el-Sheikh," that was very popular with the troops. During the battle for Sharm-el-Sheikh, a soldier, Rafi Gabai, had composed this song. By his side, apparently, was a music-publisher because, though the war had been over but a few days, there was a record out already and it was in the charts. I learned the song—it was a very good one—and my first chance to play it was at an air base, El Arish, captured from the Egyptians. It was an important day and a lot of Israeli brass was there, including Yitzhak Rabin, chief of staff and later prime minister. There were about two thousand Israeli soldiers. I stood on a tank and, accompanied by an accordionist, played "Sharm-el-Sheikh." Well, it was like waving the flag. The reception was tremendous, the applause wouldn't stop and I had to play it again. And again. In fact I played it six times. Then I got the audience quiet and told them how deeply moved I was by their reception of my playing, I would never forget it but, I had to tell them, there were other artists who had come to the Sinai to entertain them; I didn't want to slow up the show, "and therefore, my dear friends, please don't ask me to play 'Sharm-el-Sheikh' again." And from the back of the crowd was a shout:

"You'll play it till you get it right!"

Good story, isn't it? I always tell it in my one-man show, it goes down well and is, of course, bullshit. Not all of it though. I *was* asked to play "Sharm-el-Sheikh." I *did* play it at El Arish in the Sinai, but, believe me, I only played it once. The rest is the story of the opera singer at La Scala, taking encore after encore. But it fits so well into my Israeli adventure that I still use it. I might even have come to believe it except that, in 1963, I had written a book, *Jokes and How to Tell Them*, and the opera-singer story is in my book.

That day I met the Israeli air chief General Mordecai Hod, who told me of an interview he'd conducted with a captured Egyptian general. He told the Egyptian officer that he couldn't understand why the Egyptian planes would fly just one mission and that was it for the day, while the Israeli planes, returning from one mission, loaded up and went right out again, doing this all day until the light failed. The Egyptian said he didn't know that about the Israeli air force. Hod was incredulous.

"You didn't know it? But your men knew it, any one of them could have told you. . . ."

Hod said that the Egyptian interrupted him.

"My *men*? I never talk to my *men*!"

I saw some signs of this attitude. In the Egyptian barracks at El Arish the officers' quarters were well built and appeared comfortable. The barracks for the enlisted men hadn't a roof. During the day there would have been no protection from the desert sun. I could see why Egyptian morale wasn't high. Also, round the barracks, there was evidence of panic, shoes taken off and abandoned as a hindrance in getting away.

The Israeli Army had successfully retaken the Old City of Jerusalem, singing "Yerushalayim Shel Zahav" ("Jerusalem the Golden"), as they marched through. The song had become like a second anthem, it had been written recently but had nothing to do with the war. Teddy Kollek, who seems to be permanent mayor of Jerusalem, had held a competition for a song about Jerusalem. It was won by a songwriter, Naomi Shemer. I learned that one as well and also recorded it.

I was longing to see the Old City but civilians were not yet allowed in. I would be going to Haifa and, once there, I'd have no more chance to see Jerusalem. My driver, Alec, suggested I phone General Hod and see if he could fix it. Oh come on, I said, phone the air force commander with a request like that?

Look, said Alec, you met him, didn't you? And he likes you, I know he does. I refused to bother General Hod. Alec went to the phone, asked the hotel operator to get General Hod on the phone. "Tell him Larry Adler wants to speak to him."

The operator called us back with General Hod on the line. Embarrassed, I told him what I hoped to be able to do. Hod told me that he would try to get me a military pass. He would also have a light plane waiting at Amman (Jordan) airport to fly me to Haifa. He could guarantee the plane at Amman but couldn't be sure of getting the pass in time. If the pass didn't arrive, he said, forget it, because there was no way of getting through the lines and into the heavily guarded Old City without a pass.

The pass did arrive (Alec was envious) and I went through the Old City, which I had last seen in 1943. There were signs of heavy fighting; the Jordanians had put up heavy resistance, and buildings were destroyed. Then I came to the great landmark, the wall where religious Jews prayed. There were many Jews there (I dislike the term "Wailing Wall" and the Jews themselves never use it) but all in uniform. I am not religious, haven't been since I was a kid, but I went to stand at the wall; I didn't pray, I have nothing to pray for, but I stood there, in silence, for several minutes. I saw the famous El Aqsa Mosque. (The Arabs, by the way, gave no signs of hostility, just looked at me as they might have at any tourist.)

Finally I had to leave—I had a show to do that night in Haifa— and a jeep took me to the Amman airport. It was eerie. A civilian airport, completely deserted, with the signs and travel posters still up. I was afraid my plane might not be there—I couldn't get to Haifa by ground transport—but I needn't have worried. General Hod's own pilot was there with a small plane. We took off and flew to Haifa. The pilot asked me why General Hod had gone to all this trouble for me? I just didn't know. The whole thing is indicative of Israel. Alec knew it was okay to phone the general, they had once lived on the same kibbutz, and when Hod called back, Alec addressed him at "Motti." "You call a general 'Motti,' just like that?" "Look," said Alec, "I told you. We were on the same kibbutz. If I called him 'General Hod' it would embarrass him and me too."

One night during the trip I was taken to a secret base; so secret, in fact, that they blacked out the windows of my car. When I came onstage I saw about two dozen children sitting in front of the stage. I asked the commander where the children came from. From a kibbutz just up the road, he said. But wasn't this supposed to be a secret base? Oh yes, very secret, very secret indeed. Then how did the children come to be there? He shrugged. "Kids," he said. "What can you do?"

On my 1951 visit I'd played at a children's hospital outside Tel Aviv. One child had had his hands blown off by a grenade. I suggested to him that, if he held a mouth-organ with his wrists, it could be held securely and he could learn to play it. He stared at me morosely and didn't seem to respond. Just before I left the hospital a nurse told me the kid had asked if I would come back to his ward. He had changed his mind and would I give him a lesson? I did, of course, and from then on, when I came to Israel, I'd visit this child. Now, in 1967, he had become a taxi driver, had a full license, driving with his wrists. This was Alec.

In 1973, after the Yom Kippur War, I went to Israel again, but this time they only wanted me to play in hospitals.

There had been heavy casualties; one thousand dead in Israel is like a hundred thousand in the U.S. At the Hadassah Hospital in Jerusalem I played for a soldier who was in plaster of paris from head to foot. He told me that, before the war, he had been a musician, playing clarinet, trumpet and the mouth-organ. Now, he said, he no longer could.

"Well, of course you can't," I said, "but in a few months, they'll take all this crap off and you'll be able to play again."

"It isn't that, Mr. Adler," said the soldier, "I smoke too much."

I was asked to go into a private room where there was a kid of nineteen who had been brought down from the Golan Heights. He was in shock. The nurse asked me to play for him but warned me that I wouldn't get any reaction.

"You will think he doesn't hear you," she said, "but we think he does. So please try."

I played something. The kid lay there, no sign that he heard. The nurse signaled me to play something else. I shrugged but went ahead; it is hard to play to one person who gives absolutely no response. When I finished the second piece the soldier's lips moved, the nurse bent down, then she looked up happily.

"He *hears* you," she said, suppressing her excitement, "and he asks you to play something classical."

I tried to act nonchalant. "Ask him what he'd like."

The soldier spoke, quite clearly this time.

"Beethoven," he said.

"Beethoven wrote several things," I said, and when this was translated the soldier actually smiled! "Which Beethoven?"

He wanted "Ode to Joy," the finale of the Ninth Symphony. I began to play the famous *Alle Menschen werden Brüder,* and as the music was heard outside, soldiers, some in wheelchairs, some on crutches, came into the room and sang it. Then, and though I was there I cannot believe it happened, the soldier sat up in his bed and *he* began to sing. I had to turn away. I was near to crying and I didn't want him to think that I was pitying him.

I checked back before leaving Israel. There was no relapse; that incident started a complete recovery. It is why I am very glad that I am a musician.

CHAPTER
Twelve

THE MOUTH-ORGAN REPERTOIRE isn't huge. The first piece written specifically for it was a Serenade, composed for me by Cyril Scott, who accompanied me on its first (and only) performance at my first recital at Grotrian Hall in 1936. Then, in 1940, the French composer, Jean Berger, wrote a work that exploited every possibility of the mouth-organ besides having exciting South American themes and rhythms. He called it Caribbean Concerto and it had its first performance with the St. Louis Symphony in 1941, Vladimir Golschmann conducting. In 1943, Darius Milhaud composed the Suite for Mouth-organ and Orchestra, and in 1951 Graham Whettam composed a concerto which I played with the Chelsea Symphony. Shortly after that came the work that did more to give the mouth-organ status than any other.

Sir Steuart Wilson, who was a director of the Covent Garden Opera, and whom I had met at one of the musical evenings at Irene Ravensdale's home, told me one day: "I'd like to bring the Old Man over to hear you." The Old Man was Dr. Ralph Vaughan Williams. Eileen and I were living in a rented home in Brompton Square and that's where I played for the Old Man.

"Let me understand one thing," he said. "You exhale to produce C but you inhale to produce D. Am I right?"

Yes, he was.

"Then surely, if you have to change your breath to get a different note, doesn't that make it impossible to achieve a true legato?"

Logically, yes. However, I suggested, I would play a slow melody, the second movement of the Violin Concerto in A Minor by Bach. I would be changing the breath direction constantly. I did this and then asked Vaughan Williams if he could tell *when* my breath changed, in other words, was I able to play a smooth legato or not? The Old Man admitted that he couldn't tell when I was inhaling and when exhaling. Then he suggested that I look over his compositions and select one that I thought would suit the mouth-organ. He would revise that work especially for me. I was delighted, in fact honored, that the Grand Old Man of English music was that much interested in my work. He asked me to give him a diagram showing the assets and the liabilities of the instrument. I wrote out the diagram, which Vaughan Williams told me he pasted on his shaving mirror and studied each morning.

I went to Sweden for an engagement at the China Theater, a music hall. While there I had a letter from Steuart Wilson.

"The Old Man has changed his mind," Wilson wrote, "and has decided to write an original work for you. It's bound to be bloody marvelous because he has told me he's sure you're going to hate it."

When the manuscript reached me I couldn't tell if I liked it or not, indeed I couldn't make it out, it was indecipherable. I moaned to Wilson about this but he said not to worry; a student of Vaughan Williams, Michael Mullinar, could take these hieroglyphics and translate them into legible notation.

Despite my careful exposition of what a mouth-organ could and could not do, Vaughan Williams had written chords and intervals that simply could not be played without using auxiliary lungs. With Michael Mullinar I went to Dorking to play the work for its composer. He had written it as a Romance for Mouth-organ, Piano and Strings but of course I would be playing it only with piano. Before I did play I explained, not without nervousness, that there were a few bits that needed redoing. He cupped his hand to his ear.

"What's that you say? Can't hear you."

I found later that the Old Man had a selective deafness. He heard what he wanted to hear. But I didn't know it then so I repeated what I'd said, only louder. He glared at me.

"So. You don't like my music, eh?"

"No," I bleated, "that isn't it at all, it is just a matter of these few bits. . . ."

"Well, if you don't like it the way I wrote it"—he paused, timing it in a way that Jack Benny would have admired—"I'll change it. If you don't like it after that I'll change it once more. But if, after that, you *still* don't like it, I'm going to rescore the whole bloody thing for *bass tuba*!"

I gave a bad first performance at the Town Hall in New York, in 1952, my first appearance in America since the blacklisting. Although I had studied the music, I couldn't really grasp it; there were parts that were mathematically beyond me, clusters of notes played rapidly, then a rest for a split second, then coming in again; I couldn't seem to count it accurately. I finally got it going fairly well with the piano but when I heard it for the first time with the orchestra I knew I was in deep trouble. At one point the orchestra and I were meant to play two different tempi, one against the other. I couldn't do it. I found myself sliding into the orchestral tempo, which defeated what Vaughan Williams was trying to do.

The second performance with Hugo Rignold and the Liverpool Philharmonic was hardly any better. Then, in the summer of 1952, I was booked to play it at the Proms, at the Albert Hall, with Sir Malcolm Sargent conducting the London Symphony Orchestra. This was my best concert opportunity in London, I could not afford another bad performance. I called Sargent and explained my problem. He was immediately sympathetic, suggesting that he have two private rehearsals with me. At these rehearsals there was a mynah bird who seemed to know whenever I played a bad note; it would let out what sounded to me uncomfortably like a derisive laugh. That bird was no help.

When Sargent saw where my weaknesses lay he pointed them out to me, then said: "Just watch me, my dear boy, I will always bring you in at precisely the right moment, you cannot possibly go wrong."

The performance was one of the best I have ever given. The applause went on and on. I wanted to go back immediately for a curtain call, but Sargent motioned me to wait. He listened critically to the applause, then he tapped me on the shoulder and gestured toward the stage: *"Now,"* he said, and I went out for a bow. He did this every time and the applause mounted in intensity. On about the eighth curtain call Sargent gestured toward the loges. In one of them Vaughan Williams stood up. Now the audience went into the kind of hysteria you associate with Elvis Presley. Sargent went to the side and gestured to Vaughan Williams to come up on the platform, which he did to maniacal shrieks from the crowd. Sargent tapped his baton, nodded to me and indicated that we would play the work a second time. A viola player gave Vaughan Williams his chair and the Old Man sat there through the second performance. (*The Times* wrote that "last night the Vaughan Williams received both its first and its second performance. . . .") This is unique; no new work was ever before encored at the Albert Hall. To be fair, it is a short work, barely seven minutes long. But I think that Sargent, once he heard the enthusiasm of the audience, was able to judge the applause, to manipulate it, to orchestrate it (for once I don't mind that over-worked and misused word) into creating a demand for an encore. *That* is the essence of showmanship; to know when the time is right for such a gesture. I'm sure that had the curtain calls been left to my judgment the applause would have died down and there would have been no encore.

There had been lots of barbed jokes about Malcolm Sargent, I've heard most of them. I know only one way to judge a person, which is, how *I* find them, not by rumors about them. Sargent was not only exceedingly kind to me when I was in a difficult spot, I also found him one of the finest of all conductors when it came to accompanying a soloist.

If I were asked what was the musical high point of my life, I think I would answer that it was the night that I played the Vaughan Williams Romance at the Proms.

After the concert there was a party at my house in St. John's Wood. I was talking to the Australian composer, Arthur Benjamin (his most popular composition was *Jamaican Rhumba*), when Vaughan Williams came and sat down with us.

"Arthur," he said to Mr. Benjamin, "you must write a concerto for Larry."

Benjamin did, and produced a wonderfully melodic work, one that Nathan Milstein later told me was "the Mendelssohn Concerto of the mouth-organ."

I would probably have given another bad first performance of the
Arthur Benjamin concerto in South Africa, but I'd remembered to
take the piano-conductor score, and my accompanist José Rodriguez
Lopez didn't mind running through it with me many times before-
hand so I knew it well by ear before I came to give the public
performance. I played this work at the Proms in the autumn of 1953.
One paper referred to the "excessively long applause" I received.
It didn't seem excessive to *me*.

I told Darius Milhaud that I couldn't read music when he composed a Suite for Mouth-organ and Orchestra for me after hearing
me play the *Rhapsody in Blue* with Pierre Monteux and the San
Francisco Symphony. Milhaud took it calmly. *"Eh bien, mon cher
Larry, you must learn."*

When the Milhaud Suite was finished I tried it and it baffled me.
I'm a melody man and the Milhaud work seemed unmelodic. It
wasn't Milhaud, it was me, I hadn't yet caught up with Milhaud. *I*
didn't even try to get a first performance of the work. Then, in 1947,
a concert with the Concerts Colonnes orchestra, conductor Gaston
Poulet, was offered to me. They'd been told of the Milhaud and
wanted to give it its début.

When I went onto the platform at the Salle Pleyel I was going to
play the work for the first time without the music in front of me. I
thought that was obligatory; in fact it wasn't. No law decrees that the
soloist must play from memory; it was Nicolo Paganini who first
started it, as a gimmick. I could have played from the notes and wish
I had, because, in the third movement, I lost my place, forgot where
I was in the work and panicked. I began to ad lib, playing notes that
Milhaud not only hadn't written but notes he wouldn't have been
caught dead writing. I was sweating but there was no way out. I had
to keep on.

Then, and probably this was sheer hysteria, I saw, in a kind of
vision, not the notes of the piece but a page of the New York *Herald
Tribune;* on it was a notice of the work I was at that moment ruining.
I read this mythical notice with interest (and remember, I was still
ad libbing the music). "Last night," it read, "Larry Adler gave the
first performance of the Suite for Harmonica and Orchestra by Darius Milhaud with the Orchestre Concerts Colonnes conducted by
Gaston Chicken."

Poulet—chicken. It set me off into a fit of giggles. There I was, playing and giggling into the mouth-organ. Poulet must have thought I'd gone mad—but he had to go on conducting that third movement until the end, which came with a loud climax from the orchestra.

The crowd went mad. There were cries of "Bravo!" "Bis!" and they wanted an encore but they damned well weren't going to get one. I knew enough to quit when I was ahead—though I still can't figure how I *got* ahead. There were a dozen curtain calls with me bowing, shaking hands with the leader, clasping Poulet's hand (he was looking at me with something like fear) and acknowledging the reception from the audience.

Milhaud came backstage; I knew I hadn't fooled *him.*

"Larry—what happened to you?"

I told him, omitting the Gaston Chicken part. (Poulet and I were sharing a dressing room.) Whenever I've been in doubt since then, I play from the notes.

Radio Française recorded the concert for broadcast. I had a stroke of luck. My microphone wasn't on. Nobody noticed that the solo instrument sounded remote, mostly inaudible. It was a new work and people thought it was *supposed* to sound that way. I got excellent notices, both on the concert and the inaudible broadcast. Maybe someone is trying to tell me something.

Poulet said not a word to me about my performance. It is customary to murmur charming insincerities but Poulet couldn't bring himself to indulge in such duplicity. He left the dressing room shaking his head in disbelief.

My procrastination got me into trouble again when the BBC commissioned Malcolm Arnold to write a concerto for me. I worked with Arnold as I always do with a composer, showing him what the mouth-organ can and cannot do. Arnold did wonderful things in the second movement to show the chords, intervals and counterpoint that the mouth-organ could produce; he also gave me some technical problems in the third movement runs to be played at greater speed than I'd ever done before. Also a few problems in syncopation to make things even more difficult.

It sounds mad, self-destructive even, but I didn't start to study the work until two weeks before the concert, part of the Proms season at the Albert Hall. (I prefer the Albert Hall to any other in London, just as I prefer Carnegie Hall to Lincoln Center, simply because of the musical tradition of both.)

I play better by ear than from the notes. I must hear the work inside my head and I can only do that by listening to it. With a new work no gramophone record exists; I learn it from the notes or not at all. The performance I gave, with Malcolm Arnold conducting the BBC Symphony, sounded, especially in the last movement with all the pyrotechnics and syncopation that Arnold had written, as if I *hadn't* learned it at all. The work got a good reception, but my performance was poor. I knew it, Malcolm Arnold knew it, and probably the BBC Music Committee knew it too because I was never again asked to the Proms.

When Heitor Villa-Lobos heard me in my annual show with Paul Draper at the New York City Center, he announced that the mouth-organ was the instrument of the future and that he would compose a concerto for me. I met Villa-Lobos, and showed him the problems of writing for the mouth-organ. From then on I heard nothing. Then I read that Villa-Lobos had composed a work for John Sebastian, another mouth-organist. In Paris Villa-Lobos was to give a concert at the Salle Gaveau. I saw him backstage, he was cordial and invited me to lunch next day.

"Maestro," I said, after coffee, "I was surprised to hear that you had composed a concerto for John Sebastian. Didn't you promise to do one for me?"

"But of course," said Villa-Lobos, beaming, "I was willing to write for you. I *wanted* to write for you—and then I waited."

"You waited for what?"

Villa-Lobos's smile was like a sunrise.

"The *money*!" he said.

Had Villa-Lobos given me any indication that he wanted me to commission the work, I would have done so. I commissioned Khatchaturian to write for me. His work would have restored me to the concert field but he died before he completed it.

When I played at the Tango Club in Chicago, I invited Sir Georg Solti to my performance. After the show, he said "What would you like to play with our orchestra?" I couldn't believe he was serious, but his wife said, "Georg never jokes about music." I made a great mistake. I gave Solti my repertoire and he picked the Gershwin

Lullaby. That only ran for seven minutes, so I asked to do another; Solti told me to choose and I said the Romanian Fantasy by Francis Chagrin. This was a really dumb choice. It was a great opportunity for me to play with Solti and the Chicago Symphony Orchestra and I picked a potboiler of a program. I should have chosen Milhaud or the Vaughan Williams. Instead I played encore stuff and the critics rightly gave me hell. It was a stupid mistake. I invited Solti to dinner in London, he came, but he never asked me to be his soloist again.

I don't like "The Tennessee Waltz" as a tune, but it was Harry Truman and James Thurber's favorite. Thurber came one night to the Village Gate and stayed for both my shows. At the late one, he called out for me to play "The Tennessee Waltz" for him. I explained to the audience that, though I considered the tune too sentimental, I'd be happy to play it for Thurber. When I'd finished playing, Thurber stood up.

"I first encountered the name of Larry Adler in print," he said, "and then I heard it said, and then I said it, and it seemed to me a common ordinary name like Abe Lincoln. And then I heard him play and the name was lighted as with the light of stars and I knew it would last as long as music, which is to say forever—and if that isn't sentimental, whatever was?"

I make no apologies for reprinting that. As he mentioned me in the same breath as Lincoln, let me say that I consider Thurber's speech my personal Gettysburg Address.

I lunched with Thurber at the Algonquin, the next day. I said that I would have given anything to have had a tape recorder in the club.

"You mean because of what I said about you?" Yes.

"Have you a pen?" he asked.

I was amazed. "You mean you'd prepared it?"

"I mean I've got a photographic memory. I forget nothing. I remember addresses and phone numbers from my school days in Columbus. It's not that I *want* to remember them, they're of no use to me, it's just that I can't forget them. So get a pen and some paper and I'll repeat what I said last night."

Which he did, and that's how I'm able to reprint it.

Thurber was at my forty-eighth birthday party, given for me by Sylvia Levitt, who had been my first girl friend in New York. I provided the entertainment as well as being the guest of honor and playing a Bach Gavotte. Suddenly Helen Thurber said: "Larry, why do you have to be so bloody highbrow? Get down among the people! Play something we can whistle, for God's sake!''

Thurber, who was nearly blind, got up from his chair and felt his way along until he reached the place where his wife was sitting.

"Helen," he said, biting out each syllable, "you shut your fuck-king mouth!''

It is the only time I heard Thurber swear. He was a language purist and would suffer acute distress whenever Eisenhower held a press conference.

I have had pupils but not many. I am no good with a beginner, I can't teach the first steps in mouth-organ playing. What I *can* do is to take someone who already knows something about playing and sharpen his technique. Most mouth-organists go in for acrobatics, maximum notes in minimum time, which has nothing to do with music. The repertoire is predictable, Monti's "Czardas," "Flight of the Bumble Bee," "Dance of the Comedians," all showoff pieces. I get the player to try a Bach melody, a Siciliano or a chorale such as "Jesu, Joy of Man's Desiring." Few players can handle these slow themes; they can play the notes, but cannot make a musical sound.

One player came to me once a week but stopped when he, a Scientologist, found out what I thought of that movement. I had a class for several summer seasons in Barry, Wales. One man, about eighty, wanted to learn to play "Amazing Grace" to astound his friends at the pub. I taught him that. I also had a pupil who played the diatonic mouth-organ, the kind used in rock and pop groups and usually called the blues harp. This mouth-organ, though the best known and most widely played, is extremely limited. It hasn't a chromatic scale, can't get all the half-tones, the sharps and flats, and thus is impossible for classical, or serious, music. Had this been the only kind of mouth-organ I would never have started to play; the very first piece I played in the mouth-organ competition back in Baltimore, the Beethoven Minuet in G, would have been impossible to play on the diatonic instrument.

This is not to say that there cannot be excellent players on the diatonic mouth-organ. Sonny Terry, to me, is the best of the blues players and we have several times played duets. He gets a sound that I could never hope to duplicate. There have been other fine diatonic players such as Sonny Boy Williamson or Big Bill Broonzy. In general, however, I think the players of the blues harp tend to sound monotonous. There are a few notes on the diatonic mouth-organ that can be *blued,* that is the note can be forced down a half-tone or even more, and these notes are exploited to death by the diatonic players. I have not heard a single one of them, from Bob Dylan to any of the players in the rock, pop, punk or heavy metal groups, who can approach the musicianship of Sonny Terry.

One of the difficulties of the mouth-organ is that too few players can make their own sound. I would say to my pupils, don't be a second Larry Adler, be the first *you.* I found that I couldn't teach anyone to do that; the sound that he creates is what makes any musician unique, but musicianship is, I think, innate. Technique can be taught but not talent.

A player in Japan, whom I met in Kyoto, was technically excellent, he could play anything. What I could not get him to do was to stop imitating me. He would copy my recordings, note for note. If I had played a wrong note, he would faithfully reproduce it.

Any musician worthy of the name has his own sound, it is what makes him unique. I can distinguish Heifetz from Perlman, Rachmaninoff from Ashkenazi, Armstrong from Gillespie, Segovia from Yepes. My own sound is influenced by the musicians I admired, from Rachmaninoff through Miles Davis to Bill Evans, Ellington, Armstrong, Segovia, singers like Ella Fitzgerald and Billie Holiday. I made my own sound but don't know how it evolved, I know only that it is mine.

In Bombay, a young man who worked for Air India auditioned for me. He was good, far better than any other young player I'd heard. I told him I could get him a scholarship at Hohner's school in Trossingen, Germany. I wrote to Karl Hohner, and told him about this young man. Hohner wrote back to say that, as India did not import Hohner mouth-organs, he saw no reason to accept Zafrir as a student. I was outraged and humiliated. I had promised something to Zafrir and I couldn't do it. I wrote to him apologizing and suggested that, if he liked, he could come to London, live in my house and study with me. He wrote back, happy with this new plan; he would quit his Air India job and come to London. I told my children about him and they loved the idea of having Zafrir come to live with us.

Then a letter arrived from Zafrir's father. "The light has gone out of my life. Music is heard no more in my home. My son, Zafrir, is dead."

A drunk driver had run Zafrir down, killing him. I cannot write these words, tell the incident to anyone or even think about it without a shiver. ·What a waste!

Ingrid Bergman, from the first time she heard me play (on the piano) liked my music but was appalled at my laziness. We both lived in Beverly Hills, not far from each other, and Ingrid warned me that, after the German tour when we were back in the States, she was going to make me find a music teacher and begin to study composition. She meant it, too, and nagged at me, making me thoroughly ashamed of myself for not doing more to develop my musical ability. I finally found Ernst Toch, himself a noted composer, and I couldn't have been luckier. Toch was a rare individual who loved teaching, he didn't watch the clock, and the lesson would go on for as long as the pupil seemed interested. He was also a natural teacher; he could explain a point with such clarity that it lodged in the mind, never to be forgotten. I didn't study with him for long, perhaps no more than a year, mainly due to my gathering political troubles, but had it not been for my experience with him I would never have dared to tackle a film score, probably would never have composed at all. As it was, I composed the film scores for *Genevieve, High Wind in Jamaica,* Joseph Losey's film *King and Country,* and *The Great Chase,* which was a collection of chase sequences from the silent days including a splendid train chase from Buster Keaton's *The General.* I did like my score for *The Great Chase,* but *Genevieve* was the best.

It started when I was playing the piano at a London party in 1953. Vivienne Knight, then PR for J. Arthur Rank (and later to marry Patrick Campbell), liked what she heard and asked what it was called. "Oh, I'm just improvising," I said. The next morning she called Henry Cornelius, who was putting together a film comedy about the Veteran Car Club annual London to Brighton run, a film to be called *Genevieve.*

Cornelius took me to lunch at Les Ambassadeurs off Park Lane and said he wanted me to compose the score. I pointed out that, though I'd had some lessons in musical composition, film scoring was a highly technical job that needed an expert. I didn't think I could handle it. Mr. Cornelius said that Vivienne Knight thought I could and that was all he needed to know.

When I read the script I felt I wanted to do the film; when I saw the rough cut, I was positive. The script of this quintessentially British film had been written by an American, William Rose. When I did accept the assignment I told Cornelius that one line in the script had decided me. Cornelius said he'd bet he knew which line it was. He told me and he was right.

It comes early in the film. Dinah Sheridan, married (in the film) to John Gregson, is in the kitchen of their mews house. She calls up to him:

"Alan . . . proper lunch or proper dinner?"

That line decided me; I *had* to do *Genevieve*.

I left it to my agent to work out terms. *Genevieve* was a small film, not expected to get anywhere, and its four leads, Kenneth More, Dinah Sheridan, John Gregson and Kay Kendall, were then unknown. The entire film, in color, cost less than £100,000. Today you couldn't shoot one *scene* for that.

When my agent next spoke to me he sounded gloomy. He had asked for £750. Cornelius pointed out that he didn't have £750. He dropped the ante to £500. Cornelius didn't have that either, he didn't seem to have any cash at all, the company had run out of money.

"Forget it, Larry," said my agent, "this is a small-time outfit. Let it go and we'll find another picture for you later in the year."

"Nobody has ever asked me to compose before. I love the film and I want to do it."

They finally offered a two-and-a-half percent of the producer's share. I accepted that against predictions that I would end up with the price of a hamburger. In fact, within a month of release, *Genevieve* was making a profit. The four leads got £1500 each, a flat fee, with no participation in the proceeds. I was making far more out of the film than the stars; in fact my children went to college on *Genevieve*.

There had been trouble. My friend, Harry Kurnitz, the screenwriter, gave a party at Les Ambassadeurs in London and told the guests, who included some American film executives, that I was writing the score of *Genevieve*. I had a call from Cornelius, could I come over to see him. When I arrived he was obviously nervous. He had a call from a top man at the Rank Organization; the message was

terse—get Larry Adler off the picture. He had been told that if my
name were on the film, it would not get an American release.

"Corny," I said, "you're the one who put me on the film. If you
want me off, just say so and I'm off. I don't want to do anything to
hurt you. Are you telling me you want me off?"

He looked distressed. "No, I'm not telling you that. I put you on
the film. I love the stuff you've already turned in, I don't want to lose
it."

"Okay, then let my agent battle it out with Rank. I'll keep working
on the score."

Cornelius agreed.

I wasn't in all that strong a position. Although terms had been
agreed, no contract had been signed. I had been composing on the
strength of the verbal agreement. A call from my agent reassured
me. A verbal agreement was held to be a contract, we had a deal.
However there was one compromise I had to make if I wanted to
stay on the film. I had to leave billing up to Rank. My agent thought
I should do it, he was sure that when the time came I would be given
proper credit. I accepted this compromise, not without qualms—I'd
never given in to that kind of pressure before.

A few months later I played a nightclub in Philadelphia. *Variety,*
the theatrical trade paper, gave me a good review and there was no
political trouble over the date. My agent used that notice to show
that it was okay to give me proper billing, and when *Genevieve* had
its premiere in London, I had composer credits.

United Artists was to distribute the film in the U.S. I had heard
there might be trouble because of me. My friend, Ben Sonnenberg,
phoned a UA executive. No, no trouble. The man told Ben that they
never messed around with English credits, they took the film as they
got it. *That* seemed to be okay.

Except that it wasn't. The film was booked for a New York run
at the Sutton Cinema on East 57th Street. Six weeks before the
opening Rank received word that the U.S. distributor wanted a print
without my name on it.

They got it. I've never gone into what my own rights were on
this matter. I had already agreed to leave billing up to Rank and
they'd given me proper credit. Had the U.S. distributor the right
to remove my name? It struck me as a shabby thing to do. Few
things have hurt me more than having *Genevieve* open in New

York, with my name taken off. Public Leper Number One. I got some satisfaction when most of the New York film critics gave me credit for the score.

I had a note from Ira Gershwin. "Didn't you tell me that you composed the score for *Genevieve*? The music has been nominated for an Oscar but the composer is named as Muir Mathieson."

Muir Mathieson! Muir had conducted the orchestra but he hadn't written a note of the music. From London I put in a call to Charles Brackett, the president of the Motion Picture Academy. When I told him why I was calling he said, "Larry, I know you're not going to play practical jokes at transatlantic phone rates. But there was no composer listed, we contacted Rank and this is what they gave us— Muir Mathieson."

I explained where Muir Mathieson fitted in on the film. The ballad had been recorded by Percy Faith for Columbia, my own sound-track record was out, also on Columbia, and furthermore, the music was published by Larry Adler Music in England (through Chappells) and by E. H. Morris in the U.S.

"Larry, I accept what you're telling me and I believe you. But you must understand my position. Give me time to check this out and I'll come back to you."

I received a cable two days later. It was confirmed that I had composed the score. However . . . once the nominations were in they couldn't be changed. He promised that if *Genevieve* won, my name would be announced. My brother Jerry, a member of the Academy, went along on awards night and was prepared to tell the world his brother had written the score. But *Genevieve* did not win; the winner was Dmitri Tiomkin with his score for *The High and the Mighty.*

I didn't think that a small film like *Genevieve* had a hope of an Oscar nomination. If I had thought there was a chance I would have acted to protect my name in the U.S.

One odd thing; when *Genevieve* was completed, Rank *hated* it. He put it on the shelf and it looked as if it wasn't going to get a release. It was previewed in Germany and laid a Chinese egg. Nobody seemed to think it was funny.

Then a picture opened at the Leicester Square Odeon for a six-week run. It was a flop and had to come off. The only film free was *Genevieve.* The rest, to coin a cliché, is history. But when I first saw the completed film I was in agony. That dialogue, those sound effects, getting in the way of my beautiful music! I learned a lesson; the only time a film composer ever hears his score the way he wrote it is on the sound stage. From then on the mixers get to work on it and the score is buried under dialogue and effects.

One thing I could not figure out. How could Muir Mathieson have accepted the Academy nomination for composing the score of *Genevieve*? *He* knew who'd written the music. I was standing right beside him playing it on the Shepperton sound stage. I faced Mathieson with that question one day in London.

"Larry," he said, "I just thought the Academy was giving me a special award for services to British film music."

There is a sequel to the *Genevieve* saga. In August 1986, I went to Los Angeles for two appearances with the Los Angeles Philharmonic at the Hollywood Bowl. Shortly before I left London, a letter arrived from my brother Jerry, enclosing a press cutting: Steve Barr, a stranger to me, had noticed a discrepancy in the Hollywood Academy records. Muir Mathieson was credited as composer of *Genevieve* even though Barr had seen a print of the film that listed my name as having composed and played the score. He wrote to the Academy, pointing this out. Two months later, he received a one-sentence letter from an Academy official. The matter had been investigated and Mr. Barr was right. That was all. He wrote again—weren't they going to do anything about correcting the record? A few more months, then: yes, the records would be corrected. Barr persisted and asked if I would be notified, and was told that as I wasn't an Academy member, they had no address for me. Barr later told me he then got my address from ASCAP, but his letter came back. He then contacted Robert Osborne of the *Hollywood Reporter,* who wrote the column that my brother sent me.

I phoned Jerry who contacted the Academy to ask if they could give me my nomination certificate while I was in Los Angeles for the Bowl concerts. They agreed and the nomination certificate was sent in an envelope, no word of explanation or apology, not even an explanatory compliment slip. I have been given my certificate thirty-two years late.

Lou Levy lunched with me at Versailles, one Sunday. Lou was married to one of the Andrews Sisters and had a successful publishing company. He told me he had the rights to the score for a French *série noire* (gangster) film called *Touchez-pas au Grisbi* which starred Jean Gabin.

"Come into town with me tomorrow," said Lou. "I think the title number would be great for you."

When I listened to the music I knew that Lou was right. The tune, *"Le Grisbi,"* was played for me by its composer, Jean Wiener. It is a first-class melody, beautifully constructed. In the film, the tune was played on the mouth-organ by a French player, Jean Wetzel. Shortly after *my* record was released, with Franck Pourcel conducting a rhythm group behind my solo, an executive at Columbia told me there was a good chance that my record of *"Grisbi"* would be nominated for the highest French award, the Grand Prix du Disque. It had never before gone to an American. Sure enough, when the awards were announced, Abou ben Adler (may his tribe increase) led all the rest.

The Grand Prix du Disque awards were made at the Ritz Hotel. Emil Gilels won in the classical section and I in the popular classification. The Paris edition of the *Herald-Tribune* gave me the headline and lead; well, after all I was the local boy. The Grand Prix award certainly boosted sales; *"Grisbi"* led the lists for about eight weeks.

From time to time, I would fly over to America to give a concert. At the Stork Club one evening I was at a table with Leonard Lyons, Paul Small (the agent), Damon Runyon and Walter Winchell. This was when Winchell was still speaking to me, before he joined the witch-hunters. We happened to be talking about popular music and its composers. (Runyon had been operated on for throat cancer so had to write on a pad whatever he wanted to say.) We discussed Harold Arlen, Cole Porter, Kern, Gershwin. Then we got to Irving Berlin and, for some reason, this inspired me to an orgy of pomposity. Berlin, I opined (and you won't find me opining anywhere else in this book), wasn't in the same league as the others we'd been discussing. For example, I said, and now I was opining with gas, if I sat at the piano and improvised, playing whatever came into my head, I could play for, say, two hours. And in all that time, I went on, I'll bet I wouldn't play *one* Irving Berlin tune. At this Runyon took his pad, wrote something on it and passed it to Lyons, who broke up when he read it. Paul Small had the same reaction and Winchell nearly fell off his chair. The pad got to me. Runyon had written, "Poor Irving!"

Harold Arlen is an extraordinary composer, in that he takes more risks than most of the others. Almost every one of his songs contains marvelous surprises, little unexpected key changes, octave drops, melodies with such strength that they hardly need to be harmonized. Arlen is also the best singer of his own songs. Johnny Mercer, Frank Loesser, Hoagy Carmichael were all good but Arlen was unique. He had a throbbing earthy quality; if you could cross Cab Calloway with Cantor Josef Rosenblatt you'd have some idea of what Arlen sounded like. I have heard Judy Garland sing "The Man That Got Away" at Ira Gershwin's house, with Arlen giving her a splendid piano accompaniment. Later in the evening Arlen would sing the same song and, believe me, Arlen was better.

Ira Gershwin had, in 1962, given me, as a birthday present, the manuscript of *Lullaby Time,* a string quartet written by George Gershwin in 1921, which had never been published or even performed. I first played this at the Edinburgh Festival in 1963, then RCA was interested in recording it and suggested an album to consist entirely of unpublished music called *Discovery.* Ira Gershwin gave me two more of his brother's melodies, untitled, which I called "Three-Quarter Blues," and "Merry Andrew"; Morton Gould, who was to conduct, did some research and got two tunes from the Cole Porter estate and one from Jerome Kern's; we got a great tune from Richard Rodgers; Morton Gould contributed two songs of his own and Harold Arlen himself gave me a beauty, "Happy with the Blues," which was my favorite on this album.

Morton Gould had rescored *Lullaby Time* for mouth-organ and strings and I first played this version with the Ulster Symphony at the Belfast Festival in 1967. A program note said that the work had been given to me by George's beautiful widow, Ira. Ira was never a widow and his best friends wouldn't have called him beautiful, so I decided that this should be cleared up. I told the audience: "The work was given to me not by George's widow but by his brother Ira and only a *schmuck* like me would stand up in Belfast and plug a name spelled I-R-A."

In 1981 I was a guest on the Michael Parkinson TV chat show on BBC-TV. Other guests were Lilli Palmer and Itzhak Perlman. At rehearsal Parkinson asked, "Could you two play something together?" We were both agreeable. I suggested a movement of the Bach Double Violin Concerto. Perlman objected. "We'd have to have the music; it would look too formal."

Perlman was right. We tried a few other things, then I suggested "Summertime" from *Porgy and Bess*. We had gone no more than a few bars when I stopped.

"That's it," I said, "let's not kill it in rehearsal. We both know the tune, let's just do it on the show."

And that's what we did. It was the single best thing I think I've ever done on TV. The BBC repeated it and ran it again on *The Best of Parkinson,* a summary of his entire TV career.

When two musicians have rapport, you don't need rehearsal (I'm speaking of jazz improvisation), each is sensitive to what the other is doing. Yehudi Menuhin's duets with Stephane Grappelli are in a different category; Yehudi is like Fred Allen's opinion of Jack Benny: "He couldn't ad lib a belch after a Hungarian dinner." Grappelli, of course, is a natural jazz man, one of the best, but Menuhin had to have every note written out. This is no crime, it just isn't jazz.

The duet with Itzhak Perlman had a serendipitous sequel (I've been waiting, all through this book, to use that word; I also hope to get *gallimaufry* in before I'm finished).

A story in *The Times,* by John Hennessy, reported that the skating team of Torvill & Dean (it was the first time I'd seen their names in print) had won the compulsory section of the European ice dance championships in 1981, their routine being based on my recording of "Summertime." "What Adler did for Gershwin," Hennessy wrote, "Torvill & Dean now did for Adler." I gathered from *The Times* headline that between us we had brought summertime to England, a feat in itself. I was delighted by this and wondered how it had come about. That question was answered in John Hennessy's book *Torvill & Dean* (why can't *I* think of titles like that?). Hennessy quotes Christopher Dean:

"We were all quite adamant that it [a blues routine] should be completely different from anything the others might offer. We tried to think of the obvious thing and go the opposite way, so we came up with the idea of going back to the roots, a sort of sad lament rather than an upbeat sexy blues. We had no clear vision of the music at that time, except that it should be a strong single instrument. Someone suggested it ought to be an unusual instrument—something like a harp, I think, he had in mind. But

a few months beforehand I'd seen a Michael Parkinson pro-
gramme on television in which Larry Adler was a guest and he'd
played a great harmonica with a violinist. [A violinist! Itzhak
Perlman's not going to like *that*.] That memory remained with
me and the next day we went to the Nottingham Library and
pulled out a Larry Adler LP.

"The track that most appealed to us both was Gershwin's
'Summertime,' very striking and evocative. Our main doubt was
that it was so well known that somebody else might use it.
Choosing a piece of music is fraught with the same difficulty as
a woman choosing a hat. We experimented with other music
and other instruments, but we kept coming back to Larry Adler
and 'Summertime.' Our minds were finally made up by the
strong sound the record made over the system at the rink."

Well, if that isn't serendipity, what is? Everyone has seen Torvill &
Dean skate-dancing to my record of "Summertime" except me.
Sometime I'd like to play it with them live (what a silly word; could
I play it any other way?) and this is to be taken as a hint.

Irene Ravensdale, baroness in her own right, and the first woman
to sit in the House of Lords (surprising that feminists didn't agitate
to have the name changed), was a very dear friend. She gave me my
twenty-first birthday party, also my forty-second. She was the daughter of Lord Curzon, viceroy of India, in whose autobiography Irene
isn't even mentioned. Oswald Mosley was a brother-in-law. At my
forty-second birthday party the guests included Malcolm Sargent,
Jascha Heifetz, Benno Moisewitsch, Cyril Smith, and Phyllis Sellick,
William Primrose, and a lot of others. I played a duet with Heifetz,
and Sargent criticized me for carrying my mouth-organ in the rather
unattractive wooden case it had come in, with garish colors. "Good
God, man, you're an artist. You should have a proper case for your
instrument," he said. They got together and had a beautiful case
made for me at Hill's in Bond Street, which had a Stradivari in its
windows. Inside the finished case each of the musicians had a silver
disc with his signature. I was proud of that case, which didn't prevent
me losing it, as I've lost so many valuable things. I can't get worked
up over the loss of possessions. Years later I tried to get a duplicate
of that case made at Hill's, but the original order had been lost and
they said they wouldn't know how to make another such case.

IT TOOK ME A WHILE to realize that Eileen was in love with Henry Cornelius. It first hit me when, in St. John's Wood, I had played some of the score of *Genevieve* for Cornelius and Graham Whettam. Whettam had no car and Eileen and Cornelius maneuvered *me* into being chauffeur while Cornelius stayed behind with Eileen. I was aware, then, that something was going on. I did nothing about it.

We recorded the score at Shepperton. I was to leave for the U.S. after the recording. Eileen asked her best friend, with whom I had been having an affair, to drive me to the airport while she stayed with Cornelius. Well, *that* seemed clear enough.

Later Eileen said she needed time to make up her mind, to stay with me or to end our marriage while she went to Cornelius. She wanted me to give her two weeks. I went to Paris, and at a party given by Kendall Milestone I met Perdita. Lord knows, I was vulnerable, but Perdita wasn't difficult to fall for. Handsome rather than beautiful, she was witty and we had the rapport of shared humor. She had a boyfriend who, before he could marry her, wanted her to turn

Catholic. I made it my mission to prevent that happening. I saw Perdita often and, before long, knew I loved her.

I had to return to London. Eileen had decided that it wouldn't work with Cornelius and, if I agreed, she was willing to keep our marriage going. Well, now *I* was in love; however I took the weak way out, to stay together "for the sake of the children." I know now that that is a mistake. The children know—believe me, they *know*— and would prefer that the marriage break up rather than both parents stay together in a state of warfare.

Eileen's relationship with Cornelius continued while I tried to pretend that it was over. It did not work, though. We lived in the same house but it was an unhappy and uncivilized state of affairs, bad for both of us.

Why should it matter to me that Eileen continued her affair? Was I not involved with Perdita? The answer is pride, nothing more.

I met an impresario, A. Strok, who gave a new meaning to "old school." He had booked Caruso, Paderewski, Cortot, Casals, and he made me an offer, a tour of Indonesia, Australia, New Zealand, Tasmania, Hong Kong, Singapore and Japan. It sounded wonderful. I wanted Perdita to come with me. Eileen asked me *not* to invite her. It was not that *she* wanted to go along, she didn't, but she sounded as if it were important to her and, weakly, I agreed.

It ruined my relationship with Perdita. The tour lasted four months, it wasn't fair to ask her to wait around. For a long time she did, but her letters, usually very funny, grew sad, as if she knew we had no future together. However, the tour had its compensations. Charles Moses, director of the Australian Broadcasting Corporation was more colorful than any of the artists; he kept an axe in the office and, when he felt like it, would go out and chop wood. He invited me to do a ten-minute talk on the ABC radio program, "Guest of Honour." I agreed, and then forgot about it.

The program was carried live on Sunday night at nine. On Sunday morning the producers phoned, wanting the script. There was no script. I whipped one off, ad-lib, and sent it over. It was aimed at young people, asking them to be individuals, not groups, to think for themselves rather than conform, to challenge every opinion, doctrine or dogma to see if it made sense to them. That night I broadcast the talk.

It was if Savonarola had made a personal appearance. The talk was on the front pages of the papers, excerpts were on the news bulletins, and about 30,000 letters came in, the biggest mail any talk had received. The ABC gave me four secretaries and I spent days on the mail. I had touched a nerve. Had I prepared the speech properly it would not have had the same impact. The ABC asked me to write a weekly column in their magazine, and in every town there were students, editors or reporters from school papers, who wanted to talk to me.

I was surprised how little opposition there was. A few papers made fun of me but there was an avalanche of agreement. Some kids wrote that they wished they could discuss such things with their parents but couldn't make contact. A few years later, I gave a follow-up talk. By then the ABC had television, I didn't have as big an audience; it still drew big mail but below the first talk.

In Singapore I repeated the talk. Besides my recital there I played the Cathay Cinemas, owned by Loke Wan Tho, who became a close friend. He liked my broadcast but criticized it.

"The trouble with Americans," he said, meaning me, "is that they think that what's good for them is good for everyone. In this part of the world that doesn't work; our culture, our habits, our customs are all different from yours. You Yankees have to learn to leave people alone: stop being missionaries."

I was asked to make a tour of eight clubs and ask people to have chest X-rays, as the incidence of tuberculosis was high. I got a phone call: "My name is Malcolm MacDonald. Did you know that, of the eight clubs you're visiting, seven will not admit Chinese or Malays, even as guests?"

"Well, that's easy," I said, "I'll visit the eighth one." He chuckled, "I rather hoped you'd say that. It's the Garden Club, I'm the chairman, and I look forward to seeing you there."

Malcolm MacDonald, the commissioner-general, was the son of the former prime minister, Ramsay MacDonald. We got on well, he liked jokes. When he introduced me he said that, as a schoolboy, he had wanted to be a mouth-organ player. "But I heard Larry Adler so I decided to go into politics." Then he whipped out a chromatic mouth-organ, the same kind as mine, and played the "Eton Boating Song," with me joining in on the second chorus. He definitely had a future.

*   *   *

In 1965, by now divorced, I appeared at the Edinburgh Festival, where I was interviewed by Sally Cline, a journalist from *Queen* magazine. Later I was playing a date in Glasgow when I got a call from the Paddington General Hospital in London. Sally Cline had been brought in after attempting suicide. The main source of identification seemed to be her notes on me, in her bag.

Although I knew her only from the interview, I went to the hospital, but she had discharged herself. I finally located her; I was touched by her distress. I tried to help and, inevitably, a relationship developed. Sally was bright, funny, extremely clever, but we were not right for each other. I am not sure why we weren't; these things are not easily explained. However, we got married.

Our relationship was not made any easier by Sally having a difficult pregnancy; she suffered with hyperemesis from the first month, retching and vomiting. One day she said, bitterly, "I don't think it's a child growing in me at all—it's an animal."

"It's a marmoset," I said, and just as Eileen and I had called Carole "Twombly" during the pregnancy, this new child was "Marmoset." Katelyn is the name she uses at school but she still likes me to call her "Marmoset."

Sally wanted me present at the birth and I went to classes where they taught one to be helpful when the time came. I am squeamish and didn't like Sally's idea, but she insisted. I was really a help, making her laugh. However, the event itself was—I hate the word —traumatic. It had a bad effect on me and killed my sexual feeling for Sally. I don't know how it affects other fathers, but judging by me, it's a bad idea. There ought to be a way to find out if a prospective father is the right type to have around at the birth.

After Marmoset was born, we bought a house in Little Venice, in Robert Close, but I wasn't making enough money to run it. For a while things weren't bad and we started a Sunday bagels-and-smoked-salmon brunch for our friends. When we had to sell the house Sally moved to Brighton. Things were bad between us: we were soon both having outside relationships. One day there was an extremely painful confrontation and I went to London. I called my friend from Chicago days, Betty Field, and said I'd quarreled with Sally; could she put me up? Betty invited me as an extra man for a party she was giving that night for Lady Selina Hastings, even though she had an eligible young man for the guest of honor.

The eligible young man didn't seem to be interested in Selina or any other female, what could Betty have been thinking of? However, one man was very much interested in Selina. I'd tell you who, but there ought to be some suspense in this story.

Having met her I couldn't get her out of my mind. I thought about her at some point in every hour. Her smile, especially, was of a quality that melted me. What I am writing is inadequate, but I have to make do with what I've got.

Yet I made no effort to phone her or to get in touch with her at all. I was free to do so. The incident with Sally had made a reconciliation impossible, one could not come back from that kind of confrontation. No newcomer could threaten my marriage; there no longer *was* a marriage.

Then one morning Betty was phoned by Selina and I heard her say that she was sorry but she wasn't free to have lunch the next day. I snatched the phone and said: "This is Larry Adler—Betty may not be free tomorrow but I am." I didn't give Selina much option and she invited me to lunch.

There were other guests there, including a publisher who seemed to consider Selina his personal province, which I resented. To my joy Selina invited me to lunch again the next day. I had been meaning to leave for Copenhagen for an engagement with Edmondo Ros and his orchestra; I canceled my flight and booked it for the following day. I mentioned to Selina that I had written a book, *Jokes and How to Tell Them*.

After the second lunch—probably before—I was hooked. Love at first sight is for kids, women's magazines—and me. I was in love. After I had packed for Copenhagen, I phoned Selina, said I had the joke book with me and would like to show it to her. This was a feeble excuse and she knew it. I came over and found Selina was entertaining Rosamond Lehmann, the novelist. I waited her out and let Selina know that I wanted to stay. She made me up a bed in her guest room. I asked her to come back to talk to me. She did and I told her I was not out for an affair; even if it were possible I would refuse it. Selina was important to me and I would not damage that importance by anything so casual. I meant what I said and Selina knew it. I got up early the next morning to catch my plane. I left a rose on her pillow without waking her. Selina said that she was impressed by the rose, but less so when she realized it came from her own vase.

From Copenhagen I wrote Selina a ten-page letter, by hand. This may not sound impressive but I never write anything except my signature; my handwriting is childish, near illegible, and my hand tires easily. So a ten-page letter is something. It was a love letter. I wrote that, when I returned, I would court her, that I was serious. If she accepted that, she must know what it involved—no more dates with anyone else. It was a mad letter, an arrogant one, but I meant what I wrote.

I phoned her, and asked her to come to Copenhagen. She considered the idea but didn't come. She answered my ten-page outburst with a friendly letter which told me nothing.

These things are hard to write about; when it concerns people close to me, important in the immediate past (if there is any such thing), then the words come slowly, forced out of me, and I am reluctant to write of them at all.

Also, memory seems trickier. I find myself less confident about the present past. (I may start a whole new time measurement.) I am not unusual in this. I was at Bertrand Russell's ninetieth birthday party. Russell was partly deaf and my American voice was easier for him to hear than the British ones, thus he spent a lot of time talking to me. I told him that I remembered an article he wrote for *Look* magazine in the forties in which he said that in certain circumstances it would be all right to drop the atomic bomb on the USSR. He grinned delightedly. Yes, he said, that was him, all right, he did write that.

"Except that you're taking it out of context. I proposed an international control of atomic energy and that the Soviets should join such a body. If she refused to join them, I suggested, the *threat* of dropping the bomb should be used."

"That shocks me," I said, "because you seem to be saying that the end justifies the means."

"Well, if it doesn't, I don't know what does!" And he bellowed with laughter, slapping his side, enormously pleased with his quip.

Then he talked about memory. He had no difficulty, he said, recalling the article he'd written thirty years before. "But it is hard for me to remember what happened last week."

It's nice to know that I share characteristics with Bertrand Russell because I'm having the same trouble.

I meant what I wrote in the letter I wrote to Selina. I intended to

court her, I was in love with her. I was also worried about my
motives; a lot of goodies went along with Selina.

Once, while on tour in the U.S., I bought *Self-Analysis* by Karen
Horney. I did what Professor Horney advocated, writing down my
thoughts and dreams, using the Freudian method of free association,
no matter how ridiculous the finished product might be. It had
seemed, at the time, that I was able to get at the truth of some
puzzling things, my true feeling about Ingrid Bergman, for example.
I decided to try self-analysis again. I sat up night after night, thinking
of Selina and writing down whatever occurred to me. I did this for
several weeks. And it was clear to me that it was Selina that I loved;
I could not ignore the material and social factors, but had they not
been there I knew that I would love Selina for herself. I never told
her about this experiment.

I was not at ease with Selina's mother. She didn't approve of me
and why should she? I was married, I had a child by that marriage,
I was in my late fifties. As she said to me: "You must admit, you're
not a very viable proposition."

It was easier with her father, who gave the impression that he liked
everybody.

Selina told me we'd met twice before, once when her stepsister got
married and another time at a cocktail party. I can understand not
remembering her on the first of these occasions, when she had been
a child, but I can't imagine meeting the mature Selina and not being
aware of her. At our first meeting, she had gathered that I was quite
famous. The only famous Larry she knew of was a television character, Larry the Lamb, so she assumed that must be me.

I often went to see Selina without giving her any notice that I was
coming. She might be set to go out for the evening, but when she
saw the real distress I was in, she would cancel her date and devote
the evening to calming me instead. She always could. It wasn't just
that she was kind, sympathetic, with understanding that would have
done credit to a psychiatrist, she was also very funny. She could, with
a phrase laced with a touch of acid, make me see the ridiculous side
of myself and get me to laugh.

There was a marquis who seemed keen on Selina and who didn't
regard me as opposition. He sent Selina impassioned notes, accompanied by travel tickets to Tunis, and seemed to take it for granted
that Selina would show up at the airport. Selina decided the best way

to handle him was to invite him to lunch with her mother and me, so that he could see that I was more than a visitor. When he arrived he asked Selina to look out of the window. There was a new Daimler limousine with Selina's initials on the door, this was his idea of a friendly gift. Selina told me that at that moment her loyalty to me was tested severely.

After lunch I found myself alone with the marquis, who told me that his business and political acumen was in such demand that Arab rulers would pay him one million pounds to have a single conference with him. I tried to look impressed. Later he married and invited Selina and me to the wedding reception at the House of Lords, his attitude to Selina implying "You see what you missed, foolish girl!"

Selina and I took several Caribbean cruises on the *Canberra,* and one on the *QE2* through the Panama Canal to Los Angeles.

At Grenada we looked up a friend of Mack Kriendler, the boss of "21" in New York. This friend had a villa on the beach rented from a Captain Brownlow. There was to be a demonstration on the beach in front of the house at three P.M. Captain Brownlow had made the beach in front of his house strictly private and wouldn't even let people walk along it. The demonstration was to try to prove that Brownlow was acting illegally.

By a quarter to three there was a large crowd, all black, on the beach in front of the house. I came out on the verandah. I have a habit of standing when relaxed, with my left hand under my left armpit, my right hand under my right armpit; it looks odd but I find it restful. I was standing that way when someone on the beach called, "Hey, man, how do you do that?" I came down the steps and showed them; they tried to do it, none could; meanwhile the demonstration came and went unnoticed.

The shows on the ship were easy: two in one night, in different ballrooms, that was it for the week. Same routine with a new program for the second week. Cabaret and lecturers were changed every fortnight. Curiously, only the cabaret artists were paid, the lecturers were given the cruise. Selina operated my tapes. The tapes had my musical accompaniments, one cassette per number. This gave me excellent accompaniment and meant that I didn't have to rehearse with the musicians, and also, my program was flexible. I could change it as I liked.

* * *

Once, when Selina wasn't well, I took her to see a doctor. She told me he warned her against me, saying that I was destructive to women. He has a case. I don't think it's deliberate, I just can't seem to keep a relationship going. I am selfish, I know that. I haven't ever been able to be true to one woman, but I came nearest to it with Selina, mainly because no woman could be other than second to her. But I wasn't perfect. There was a need to show off, to be admired, to test my masculinity (which I always doubted anyway).

Neither Selina nor I wanted children so I decided to have a vasectomy. I recorded a radio program, "Quote, Unquote," and immediately after checked into University College Hospital for the operation. I had mentioned this on the program, saying that a vasectomy means never having to say you're sorry, which got me into the *Penguin Book of Quotations.*

The operation was absurdly simple and only good sense prevented me from riding home on a bicycle after it was over.

Selina and I helped each other in our writing. I was able to weed out redundancy, tautology and cliché in her work, while she tried to teach me form. She didn't succeed. She also did a great deal of work on the preliminary drafts for this book, taking material, doing a scissors-and-paste job on it, organizing chapters with suggestions on what each should contain. I am ashamed that I did not take advantage of Selina's work; I let it drift. Selina was hurt by my negligence.

It is that carelessness, laziness, procrastination that was the main contributor to the breaking up of the best relationship I ever had. It is ungallant, after two marriages, to say that my best relationship was with a lady I never married. If I come out a heel, so be it. My rapport with Selina, the direct contact, the shared humor, was something I'd never had before. Had I met her five years before, I wouldn't have been ready for her, wouldn't have been able to appreciate her. I *did* appreciate her and I owe her the eight happiest years of my life. But I was brought down by my own faults. I was content to coast. Selina was not content, and didn't like the coasting and I think it soured her on me.

It would do my ego good if I could say that the breakdown of the relationship was Selina's fault. My ego will have to wait. I say this not to show what a nice fellow or good sport I am. It was I, and not Selina, who caused the breakdown of the relationship.

This is painful and difficult to write. Nobody likes to admit failure.

I had the best relationship of my life and I will never have its like again.

The title of this book works once again. By the time of publication in England, in 1985, I had met a restaurateuse, Tatiana von Saxe Dilley, in line with my avocation as a restaurant critic. It seems unlikely even to me but, in my review of her restaurant, The Cafe Delancey, I had this line: "Tatiana, will you marry me?" She replied by letter that she had already fallen in love with me. We were both lying, we had briefly met only twice, but I set to work remedying this omission. Tatiana had another business, Mainline, where she would design the logo of a company onto a hard fabric to be used as a cover for diaries, address books, etc. I asked her to design a special cover for my book that I could give to friends. I truly admired her work, I did want the book covers, but I'm sure that my main purpose was to get to know her better. I hope by the time the U.S. edition of this book appears the complicated name of Tatiana von Saxe Dilley will be shortened to the so much simpler Tatiana Adler.

CHAPTER

Fourteen

WHEN SELINA SUGGESTED SEPARATION she had already asked Olga Maitland to take me on as a temporary tenant. Olga has a successful career with her diary column in the *Sunday Express.* She has become even more widely known as chairman of "Women and Families for Defense." I totally oppose Olga politically but am devoted to her as a good and loyal friend. Being her tenant would give me a chance to work on this book. Olga agreed; I moved into a basement room in her house and did no work on the book at all. It is amazing, the number of excuses I've found to avoid writing.

What got me going were two factors, one mechanical, one human. In Hong Kong I saw a typewriter that seemed to be in every shop window. It was a Brother EP 20, an electronic typewriter, weighing five pounds, two inches thick, noiseless, no traveling carriage, and you could write on a plane with it without disturbing anyone. It fascinated me and I bought one. Then, on the *QE2,* which I had joined at Hong Kong, there was a passenger, Gloria Leighton. Gloria sized me up as one of nature's procrastinators, also saw that the book was likely to be the last major project of my life, and made it *her* project to get me going. She succeeded; without her help, her encouragement, above all her incessant nagging, I don't think, even with the miracle typewriter, I'd have done all this work; it *is* work.

It may be an American trait but I've always had a strong dislike of queueing. I will miss a film rather than queue for it. I will not stand in line for a restaurant table. On flights where seats aren't reserved, I always get the worst seat because I won't join the crowd waiting for the gate to open so that they can board first. This annoys others I'm with and at least once it got me into serious trouble. When I lived with Selina at Albany, in Piccadilly, Jackson's, the grocery shop, was just across the street. I would go in to buy something, but if there was a queue at the cash desk, I would hold up the article to the cashier and go out, paying later when there was no queue. I was known at Jackson's and that was my regular routine.

Once I bought a packet of their toffee. There was quite a queue. I held up the toffee, signaled to the cashier, and walked out. Outside a lady accosted me, told me she was the store detective and asked me to come back into the shop. I explained my custom at Jackson's but she wouldn't accept it. We went to the manager, who assured her that I was a well-known customer and that I often did what I had just done. The lady wouldn't accept that either and insisted that the police be called. When the manager explained things, *they* tried to get her to call things off, she wouldn't. She didn't work for Jackson's, but for a security company, and she would make it a private prosecution. The policeman gave me a helpless shrug and said that, as she wouldn't withdraw the charge, he would have to take me to the police station. There I was formally charged and then allowed to go. As it happened, we had friends to lunch. When I got back to Albany Selina asked why I was so late. I whispered that I had been arrested, charged with shoplifting. "Oh, is that all?" she said.

Among our guests was Sir John Foster QC, an old friend since the days when he had been legal adviser to the British embassy in Washington in the late thirties. I asked John to stay after the others left and told him what had happened. To my surprise he advised that I plead guilty. "What for?" I asked. John's idea was to get it over with as quickly as possible; why have the additional publicity of a trial? No, I said, I would plead *not* guilty. In that case, said John, he would testify on my behalf. When the day came, he gave me a fine character deposition, as he had years before in my libel case, but I think in an English court he carried more weight.

The store detective testified that I, as I had never denied, had walked out of Jackson's with a packet of toffee not paid for. The fact that I was known to the staff, and that the manager had confirmed my story, carried no weight with her. My solicitor, Benedict Birnberg, asked her what she would do if she saw the queen walk out of Jackson's in the same way.

"I would arrest her," said the detective, which got the best laugh of the day.

I took the stand. The magistrate asked me if I would do a similar thing at Harrods?

"Of course not," I answered. "They don't know me at Harrods —they do know me at Jackson's."

The magistrate then said that he didn't think there was any case to send to a jury. That was it; it was over.

Outside Bow Street Magistrate's Court, John Jackson, a friend from the *Daily Mirror* whom I was more used to seeing at Wimbledon, asked if I had any hard feelings against the detective. She was certainly far from being my favorite person but I said no, that I bore her no grudge, she was doing what she thought to be her job. I just thought she showed excessive zeal. Would I pose for a photograph with her? I didn't really want to, but she was standing right there and I, as I have proved several times in this book, am a coward. I couldn't be rude to her. I even, so help me, gave her a mini-mouth-organ.

A year later I was phoned by a *News of the World* reporter. The detective had complained that, since the case, she couldn't get further work as a store detective. The reporter asked my reaction to that. I said that I was sorry, that I didn't like to think of anyone being unemployed. The reporter was disappointed; I think he hoped I'd gloat.

Even if I have been painfully slow in finishing this book, during the last few years I have been doing a lot of writing, including book reviewing. When Leo Rosten wrote *The Joys of Yiddish,* I asked Richard Crossman, then editor of the *New Statesman,* to let me review it. He did, and I headed my piece "Sealink," saying that if I build a room, including floor and walls, what is still missing? De sealink; ufcawss! This isn't hilarious humor, but Kingsley Amis told me it was the funniest review he'd ever read. I like to write my own titles; reviewing Gershon Legman's book, *The Rationale of the Dirty Joke,* my heading was "Nobody Knows de Troubles Obscene."

I am partial to puns. Reviewing Arthur Rubinstein's autobiography, I disapproved of the way he named his many affairs and suggested he could have subtitled the book, *The Lay of the Last Minstrel.* Harold Evans, then editor of *The Sunday Times,* said he was considering a regular column for me but it didn't happen, though I took Alan Brien's place twice as guest columnist.

At a book party I saw Humphrey Lyttleton, who besides being England's leading trumpeter, was also restaurant critic for *Harpers and Queen* and had been so for several years. I said, casually, "Great job you have, Humph. I envy you."

Two months later Lyttleton phoned me and asked if I'd be interested in taking his job. He was tired of eating out, my remark had given him the incentive he needed. He had already mentioned the idea of me to Willie Landels, editor of the magazine, and Landels liked it. I met Landels at the Press Club and we shook hands on it; I was now, with no previous experience, the *Harpers and Queen* restaurant reviewer.

I had one full page, about 1200 words, to write each month. The pay wasn't large, and were I to pay my own restaurant bills, I'd lose money on each piece. *Harpers and Queen* didn't pick up the tab so I depended on restaurants inviting me. This is an obvious weakness. If you are getting a free meal, are you obliged to give a good review? I thought not and, in accepting an invitation, made it clear that I would write what I found. This was usually accepted. (Maybe they didn't believe me.)

I was new to the field. I was used to dining out but not to writing about my meals. I knew little about wine, perhaps "nothing" would be more honest.

After my second article had appeared I had a call from Jacques Léal, who ran Chanel in London. He said he liked my writing, and invited me to the Mirabelle. Léal looks so much like a diplomat that you can almost see a ribbon diagonally across his shirtfront. It was soon obvious that he was a connoisseur and a gourmet. I asked him why he wanted to meet me when he knew so much more about food and wine than I did. "I don't need a critic to analyze the composition of the sauce," he said. "I simply get the impression, when I read your articles, that if *you* enjoy a restaurant, so will I."

And that is what I aim for. No use throwing technical knowledge at you, I haven't any. I'm not a cook (though, thanks to Paul Draper's tuition, I can make excellent scrambled eggs), so what I do is list what I've eaten and comment on it.

I enjoyed writing for *Harpers and Queen* but I involved them in a libel suit and they dropped the column. Then I met Peter Carvell at a Dunhill fashion show. He told me he was starting a new giveaway magazine, *Portrait,* and suggested a restaurant article. I have now written for them for three years as well as producing a restaurant column for the *Kensington and Chelsea Newsletter.* I particularly liked writing a weekly column, "A Yank in London," for *What's On,* until it folded. It was fun because my editor didn't censor me and I could go in for exotic puns, for jokes, for lambasting sloppy journalism; I had an open brief. I have recently begun writing a weekly column for the *Jewish Gazette* in Manchester.

I was really angry when I did a piece for *Eating Out in London* and saw, when the piece appeared, that the editor had *added* to my copy. She had me, "splashing out" on a meal and inviting someone to "this neck of the woods." I hate clichés as I hate hell, all Montagues and probably thee, except I don't know thee. An editor has the right to cut; no editor has the right to add. Most editors can't write, anyway.

I informed the editor that the day I wrote a phrase like "this neck of the woods" would be the day I hailed "Sonny Boy" as the world's greatest melody and nominated Richard Claydermann as the finest living pianist. I closed with this:

> Shoot, if you must, this old grey head
> But don't add words I never said.

For eight years or more I have conducted what started as a feud and is now an addiction, in the form of a correspondence with the British satirical magazine *Private Eye.* It involved letters from me, attacks by them. Around the world I find that I'm known, especially by the press, as the *Private Eye* letter writer.

It began at a *Private Eye* lunch when I mentioned that I'd offered the *Sunday Times* journalist, Alan Brien, £35 if he could get a Nixon joke involving an obscenity into his column. He tried but it was taken out. I told the joke:

During Watergate, Ron Ziegler, Nixon's press adviser, says he has a great idea.

"We're gonna get you circumcised, that'll get all the Jews behind you, you really need 'em, it'll make headlines."

So they send for a *mohel,* the man who performs the operation. He's in the bedroom three hours with Nixon, finally comes out, exhausted.

"It's impossible," he says, "I can't do it. There's no end to this prick!"

Auberon Waugh was at the lunch and in the next issue of *Private Eye* he ran the joke, then wanted £35 from me. I told Waugh my offer was to Alan Brien to get the story into a national newspaper. There were no kudos attached to getting it into a satirical magazine. Waugh then attacked me in his column. Should I sue? It seemed pompous. I wrote a funny letter. Another attack, another letter. This has gone on for over eight years. I'm almost one of the family. Richard Ingrams, the editor, actually paid me a fee (£100) to play on their Christmas record. On the twenty-first birthday party at the Reform Club, I received an official invitation (though the columnist, George Gale, accused me of gate-crashing), and Richard Ingrams asked me: "Why haven't we had a letter from you lately?" The feud continues.

Writing letters to *Private Eye* is only one of the occupations I've invented to stop me working on this book. In 1977, the week before Wimbledon, I watched the Stella Artois tennis tournament at Queen's Club. I was in the bar with C. M. Jones, probably the man who had done most to advance British tennis. Jimmy Jones is an excellent teacher—he runs a tennis school with Angela Buxton and if I have a backhand it is due to him. He introduced me to Jack Yardley, who asked if he'd be seeing me at Wimbledon. No, I said, I had no tickets and there was no chance of getting anything.

"I'm inviting you," said Yardley, "and you don't need a ticket."

He wasn't kidding. Jack was the head groundsman at Wimbledon, in charge of all the courts. I met him at noon on opening day at the gate. I thought entrance to the grounds was fine and hoped that perhaps Jack Yardley would get me on to number two or three court. I didn't know Yardley. First he took me to center court to watch the Centenary Celebrations, with veterans like Lew Hoad, Don Budge, Jean Borotra, Bobby Riggs, Jaroslav Drobny, Jack Kramer, all Wim-

bledon champions. Then, when the ceremony was over, he told me
to come back at a quarter to two as the first match was due to begin
at two. He put a chair down, canvas back, like a film director's chair,
just where the turf begins, so that center court players almost had to
climb over me to get on court.

In the press bar, when I went for a drink, reporters asked me how
I had got that seat? What could I say? Jack Yardley had invited me,
that was all I knew. Okay, I was a celebrity but that couldn't be it.
Wimbledon doesn't lack famous names. I saw most of the center
court matches that day and Jack also took me to number one court,
where the matches sometimes outshine center court. At the end of
play I had a drink with him in the Player's Bar. I told him it was the
nicest gesture anyone had ever made to me; I was a tennis fanatic and
nothing could have pleased me more than to sit in that seat in that
place to watch the best of all tennis tournaments.

"What are you thanking me for?" asked Jack, "this is only the first
day."

I was there in that seat every day of the tournament; when Virginia
Wade came out for her match she saw me sitting in my seat.

"My God, Larry, what are you *doing* here? *Nobody's* supposed to
be sitting here!"

"Ginny, I'll tell you after the match." I certainly couldn't explain
then why I was where I was.

After the last match, I had a final drink with Jack.

"Jack, I've asked David Gray, John Jackson, Fred Perry, everybody; you've never done a thing like this for anyone."

"That's right."

"Well, why me? Is it my intelligence, my beauty, my wit? I could
understand all that but there must be something else."

And finally he told me—he had waited until the last day. He was
a thwarted mouth-organist and had nearly been a nonthwarted one.
He had as a teenager auditioned for the Borrah Minevitch Harmonica Rascals. Minevitch accepted him, but his father wouldn't let him
tour and that was the end of Yardley's career as a mouth-organist.
As I too had auditioned for Minevitch when I was fourteen and
hadn't made it, Jack could reasonably claim that he was a better
mouth-organist than I was.

From then on I was at Wimbledon every day of the tournament
each year; except in 1980 when I had a nightclub date in New York

that began during the second week of Wimbledon; and at that, I nearly turned it down.

At the end of the 1981 season Jack retired to Hull where the club bought him a house. But I thought I'd risk a trip to Wimbledon in 1982 and just see what happened. I was let in through the main gates and was welcomed to the Player's Bar but had no seat. I hadn't met the new head groundsman—I haven't met him yet—but it was unlikely that he too would be a thwarted mouth-organist.

Ten minutes before the tournament started a man came over to me. "Have you a seat?" he asked. I admitted I hadn't.

He told me to come to the competitor's box, on center court. So that's where I sat for the tournament in 1982 and again in 1983 and 1984. I can't explain my incredible luck but I'm not going to knock it.

It's the single greatest perk I've ever had.

It is almost too pat that my last concert prior to finishing this manuscript was with the symphony orchestra in Wheeling, West Virginia. That's where Senator McCarthy launched himself with the speech in which he announced: "I hold in my hand the names of sixty-seven (the figure varies with who tells it) card-carrying members of the Communist party presently employed in the State Department." In fact McCarthy had no names. It didn't matter. He could tell the gullible press that he would have a shocking tale to reveal next day. "MCCARTHY VOWS NEW REVELATIONS SHOCK."

After my orchestra rehearsal I walked the few blocks to the McClure Hotel, where McCarthy made his speech. A shabby-looking building, it is being demolished. The various TV and radio interviewers all made a point of disclaiming any honor for Wheeling that involved McCarthy. They seemed ashamed of the notoriety it brought them. That's good, but there was no such sense of shame at the time.

Why couldn't just one journalist have asked, "Where's your evidence?" Faced with that, McCarthy must have backed down because, in truth, he had none. How do you finish an autobiography? There is always, "Today I died." Don't laugh; when Elvis Presley died a PR man said: "Great move, public-relationswise." I suppose there should be a summing up, though I feel Somerset Maugham cornered *that* market. One thing, this autobiography is really auto. No ghosts, no as-told-to's, no transcribing from tapes. One journalist, told that I was writing an autobiography, asked, "Who's it about?" Me, that's who.

I do love to write, I also respect language, considering it a precious thing, being like liberty in demanding eternal vigilance. I have seen language gradually being eroded, helped on its way by too many journalists and broadcasters. When I play music I know only one way to play: my best. I rarely achieve it but that's what I aim for. To me the crime in music is to play down. By extension I think that a journalist or broadcaster who writes or talks down is a whore.

Clarity is all; why complicate prose by trying to gussy it up with gimmicks? The vocabulary of sex is limited and it surprises me that there is still a market for pornography. Sure, as a kid I read *Lady Chatterley's Lover* for the dirty bits. (And there were two shops on Broadway that advertised "the filthy parts of the Bible," said parts underlined to save you the trouble of looking them up.) Neville Cardus thought that his sex life could be set down on the back of a postcard. I feel the same way. In autobiography I despise the bed-droppers, listing every sexual partner, especially if the name is famous. Naming names is repugnant, sexually as well as politically. I hope that no one who trusted me will feel I have betrayed their confidence.

I love a good joke, detest a bad one, the latter including all stereotyped humor. If the point telegraphs itself, it isn't funny. Jokes that begin with a question aren't funny. Irish jokes, Polish jokes, that depend for humor on the stupidity of the subject aren't funny. No Jewish joke that starts with Abie, Ikey or Beckie is funny. Chinese or Japanese jokes depending on the letters R or L (this is the flied lice syndrome) are deeply unfunny. Any such rule can be overthrown by a touch of wit, but wit, in such jokes, is rare. Dialect is generally pejorative, it is usually laid on like cement around a Mafia victim. The British should be forbidden by law to tell American jokes and vice versa.

All of this is valid unless it involves Henny Youngman. They broke the mold *before* they invented Henny. He is quite the most *endearing* comedian in the business. He is also the kindest of men, as I have reason to know.

I read about Dial-a-Joke, which was Henny Youngman's invention, and which took in about $700,000 in calls the first month after it was launched. Henny got a straight fee: he should have had a royalty.

I didn't know Henny well. We had been on the bill together at the Chicago Theater, and I remember his advice, "Always be sure you have enough 'fuck-you' money." I wish I'd taken that advice. I never had it when it was needed.

I wrote to Henny from London, asking how Dial-a-Joke worked. He didn't just answer my letter, he sent the tapes and explained the entire operation. Show business, populated by egomaniacs, isn't noted for selfless gestures, and I was moved by Henny's consideration.

On my next New York trip, I phoned to thank him. He invited me to come with him to the Rainbow Grill on the roof of the RCA building in Radio City, where Lainie Kazan was opening that night.

"Come with me," he said. "Who knows, you might make a good contact." I knew by now that was typical Henny.

At the Grill we met my old friend and first PR man, Hal Davis. Hal suggested to the Grill management that they book me. They did, too, and a four-week booking was extended to ten weeks.

By now I think of Henny not only as a friend but as a good-luck charm. He goes out of his way to make good things happen, he comes to see my show when I'm in town, I always see his. My first call when I am in New York is usually to Henny. "Meet me at the Friars Club for lunch. Come in person," he advises, or else it's the Carnegie Deli, where Henny is treated as royalty.

His answering service comes on with "Henny Youngman, king of the one-liners."

My favorite Henny Youngman joke involves more than one line. A man visits a psychiatrist. "What's the matter with me, Doc, I'm unpopular. Nobody wants to talk to me." The psychiatrist says, "Next!"

And a last great thought? What advice would I give to young people? I would say think for yourself, accept no dogma, resist the pressure to conform. Better be a lonely individualist then a contented conformist. To anyone in authority who tells you what's good for you, ask: "How do you know?" Test the validity of the most dogmatic of beliefs. To many, faith is enough. Not for me. I respect the truth, if the truth is there to find. What I have said is what I have told my children. But just because Daddy says it, Daddy isn't always right. Daddy has no monopoly on wisdom. So I can end as I began —it ain't necessarily so.

Index

Abbot, Merriel, 101
Abbott and Costello, 8
Adler, Carole (daughter), 80, 87–88
Adler, Eileen (*née* Walser; first wife):
  LA meets, 69–73; marriage, 74;
  tours with LA, 77; children, 79–80,
  99–100; teases LA, 84; moves to
  California, 87; relations with
  Carole, 87–88; moves to England,
  136; and Henry Cornelius,
  190–91; divorce, 193
Adler, Hilliard Gerald ("Jerry";
  brother), 2, 184
Adler, Jacob ("Zadie"; grandfather),
  2, 7
Adler, Mrs. Jacob ("Bubbim";
  grandmother), 2
Adler, Katelyn (daughter), 193, 198
Adler, Peter (son), 99–100, 162–63
Adler, Sadye (mother), 2–3, 50, 74
Adler, Sally (*née* Cline; second wife),
  193, 198

Adler, Wendy (daughter), 80,
  99–100
Albert, Eddie, 123
Alec (Israeli driver), 167–68
Alfonso XIII of Spain, 59–60
Alhambra Theatre (Paris), 57
Allen, Fred, 188
Allyson, June, 94
"Alone Together," 32
Ambrose, Bert, 54
American Legion, 148–49
Amis, Kingsley, 203
Anderson, Eddie ("Rochester"),
  102–3
Anderson, Maxwell, 114
April, Elsie, 48, 51
Argyll, Margaret, Duchess of (*née*
  Whigham), 53–54
Arlen, Harold, 32, 186–87
Arnaz, Desi, 123
Arnold, Malcolm, 176–77
Arnold, Thurman, 149

Ash, Paul, 15, 17
Astaire, Adele, 27, 28, 30, 31
Astaire, Fred, 27–32, 64
Asther, Nils, 8
Attorney general's list, 127–28
Australian Broadcasting Corporation,
    191–92
Ayer, Sir A. J., 83

Bacall, Lauren, 124
"Bach Goes to Town," 79
Baker, Phil, 123–24
Banducci, Enrico, 147
Barber, Samuel, 86
Barber, Stephen, 157
Barr, Steve, 185
Barrymore, Ethel, John, and Lionel,
    95
Belasco, Leon, 26
Belfast Festival (1967), 187
Bel Geddes, Norman, 33
Benchley, Robert, 84
Ben-Gurion, Paula, 163
Benjamin, Arthur, 174–75
Bennett, Robert Russell, 91
Benny, Jack: on Boy Scouts, 9–10; in
    USO, 88, 93–94, 106–7, 109–12,
    113–17, 120; friendship with LA,
    90, 110–11; in North Africa,
    102–6, 107–8; LA writes for,
    104–5; and Ingrid Bergman,
    113–14; in Germany, 116–18; and
    LA's political trials, 139; in
    Palestine, 155; in Korea, 157; Fred
    Allen disparages, 188
Benny, Mary, 90, 106
Berger, Jean, 171
Bergman, Ingrid, 88–90, 113–16,
    117–18, 181, 196
Berkeley, Busby, 62–63, 64
Berlin, Irving, 32, 49, 186
Berry Brothers, 47
Bessie, Alvah, 147–48
Bliven, Bruce, Jr., 83

Blue, Ben, 48
"Blue Bowery," 27
"Blue Skies," 49
"Body and Soul," 49, 95
Bogarde, Dirk, xvi
Bogart, Humphrey, 123–25
Bolero (Ravel), 36–38, 52, 54, 55,
    58–59, 82, 93
Boleslavski, Richard, 39
Bolger, Ray, 82
Boomer, Lucius, 76
Boyer, Charles, 95, 115
Boyer, Lucienne, 57
Brackett, Charles, 184
Braggiotti, Mario, 62
Branga, Roger, 36
Brien, Alan, 203, 204
Bronx Symphony Orchestra, 82
Broonzy, Big Bill, 179
Brownlow, Captain, 197
Bruce, Lenny, 1, 49, 147
Bruce, Virginia, 29
Brusiloff, Nat, 11, 12, 13, 15, 19
Buchwald, Art, 148
Buckley, William, 136
Budberg, Baroness Moira, 77
Burgbacher, Kurt, 119
Burns, David, 73
Burns, George, 45, 104–5
Burrows, Abe, 92, 128, 144–45
"But in the Morning, No," 49
Butterworth, Charles, 33

Caen, Herb, 80
Caesar, Sid, 105
Cahn, Sammy, 19
Caldwell, Taylor, 97–98
Cantor, Eddie, 4, 25, 31, 35, 51
Capone, Al, 20–22
Caprice Viennois, 54, 60
Caravita, Francisco di (Prince
    Sirignano), 61
Cardus, Neville, 208
Caribbean Concerto (Berger), 171

Carmichael, Hoagy, 32, 187
Carroll, Earl, 25–26
Carvell, Peter, 204
Cassells, Jeff, 123
Cassini, Igor, 126, 138
Caston, Saul, 59
Cavalcade (Coward), 19
Chagrin, Francis, 178
Chaplin, Charles, 98–99
Chappell's (music publishers), 51–52
Cherkassky, Shura, 6–7
Chicago Symphony Orchestra,
  177–78
Chicago Theater, 35–37
Christiansen, Arthur, 68, 72–73
Ciment, Michel, 144
Clair de Lune (Debussy), 94
Clark, Bill, 17–18, 20–21
Claydermann, Richard, 204
Cline, Sally. *See* Adler, Sally
Cochran, Charles B., 48–49, 50–52,
  54–56, 66, 77
Cochran, Evelyn, 52–53, 55
Cohn, Roy, 146, 184
Coletti, Sergeant, 120
Collins, Frank, 53
Columbia Concerts, 137
Columbia Pictures, 153
Columbia Records, 54, 184
Committee for the First Amendment,
  122, 124–25, 131
Community Concerts, 137
Constantini, Countess, 59–60
"Continental, The," 54
Cooper, Gary, 38, 90, 115
Coots, J. Fred, 32
Cornelius, Henry, 181–83, 190–91
Covarrubias, Miguel, 84
Coward, Noel, 32, 52
Crawford, Joan, 64
Cronkite, Walter, 99
Crosby, Bing, 47
Crossman, Richard, 202–3
Crum, Bartley, 129–30
Cupero, E. V., 3
Curzon, Lord, 189

Dahl, Gertrude, 29
Dali, Salvador, 99
Dave's Blue Room, 24, 30
Davies, Marion, 38
Davis, Benny, 32
Davis, Bette, 63, 73
Davis, Hal, 81–82, 209
Davis, Meyer, 141
Dean, Christopher, 188–89
Dempsey, Jack, 31
Denniker, Paul, 14
Detroit Symphony Orchestra, 78–79
Deutsch, Armand, 97–98
Dewey, Thomas, 126, 129
Diamond, Jack ("Legs"), 29, 30
Dietz, Howard, 32
Dilley, Tatiana von Saxe, 199
Discovery, 187
Donne, John, 154
Donovan, Bill, xiv–xv
Draper, Paul: teams up with LA, 28,
  77, 122; recitals with LA, 78; tours
  with LA, 88; substitutes for LA,
  99; politics, 126, 130, 134,
  136–37, 138–39; at New York
  City Center, 137–38, 177; Israel
  tour with LA, 161; cooking, 204
Dreyfus, Louis, 52
Duchin, Eddy, 26, 80
Duryea, Dan, 93
Dylan, Bob, 180

Eating Out in London, 204
Ebsen, Vilma and Buddy, 33, 34
Edinburgh Festival (1963), 187
Edward, Prince of Wales (later Duke
  of Windsor), 54, 76
Edwards, Gus, 23, 25, 27, 32
Eisenhower, Dwight, 116–17, 127, 179
Elkan, Vogel (music publishers), 59,
  93
Ellington, Duke, 33, 45–48
Ellis, Vivian, 51, 52
Enesco, Georges, 95–96

Etting, Ruth, 17, 23, 51
Evans, Bill, 47
Evans, Harold, 203

Fain, Sammy, 32
Fairbanks, Douglas, Jr., 95
Faith, Percy, 184
Falla, Manuel de, 54, 60
Farben, I. G. (Frankfurt), 116
Farley, James, 126
Farquharson, Myrtle, 71
Feather, Leonard, 47
Feffer, Itzik, 135
Ferry, Felix, 59
Field, Betty, 193–94
Field, Marshall, 101
Fields, Dorothy, 31, 50
Flagg, James Montgomery, 34
Flying Colours (show), 33–34
Fogelson, Samuel, 87
Fong, Jue, 20
Ford, Henry, 78
Ford, John, 63
Fore, Virginia, 8
Forster, E. M., 22
Fortas, Abe, 149
Foster, Harry, 54
Foster, Sir John, 139, 201–2
Fox, Dorothy, 26–27
Foy, Bryan, 40–42
Foy, Eddie, Jr., 27, 41–42
Francis, Kay, 64
Frankau, Ronald, 54
Franzmathes, Mr. (State Department
    official), 151–52
French, Ward, 137
Fresnay, Pierre, 48
Friedenwald, Dr., 12–13

Gabai, Rafi, 166
Gabin, Jean, 185–86
Gable, Clark, 64, 95

Gale, George, 205
Garbo, Greta, 95, 99
Gardner, Ava, 95
Garfield, John, 128
Garland, Judy, 87, 187
Gauty, Lys, 57–58
Geller, Uri, 42
Geneviève (film), 181–85, 190
George V of England, 55
George VI of England, 69
Gerry Society, 16
Gershwin, George, 32, 48, 49–50,
    52, 64–65, 87, 90–91, 187–88,
    189
Gershwin, Ira, 91, 124–25, 184, 187
Gervasi, Frank, 104
Geva, Tamara, 33
Gibbons, Carroll, 53, 74
Gilels, Emil, 186
Gilford, Jack, 149–50
Gillespie, Dizzy, 47
Giovanni (stage pickpocket), 67
Glaenzer, Jules, 49
Glaser, Joe, 47
Gleason, Jackie, 8
Goering, Hermann, 57
Goldwyn, Samuel, 97
Golenpaul, Dan, 145–46
Golschmann, Vladimir, 171
Good Boy (show), 12–13
Goodman, Al, 34
Goodman, Benny, 79, 114
Gordon, Max, 32–34
Gordon, Joseph Wechsler
    ("Waxey"), 34
Gould, Morton, 187
Grafton, Samuel, 101–2, 138
Grand Prix du Disque, 186
Grandlund, Nils T. (N.T.G.), 49
Grappelli, Stephane, 188
Grauman, Sid, 35–38, 46
Grauman's Chinese Theater, 35–36
Graves, C. L., 50–51
Great Chase, The (film), 181
Green, Johnny, 49, 95–96
Gregory, Paul, 27

Gregson, John, 182
Grossinger's Hotel, 156
Guinan, Texas, 31
Gustav V of Sweden, 59–60

Hall, Henry, 55–56, 62
Handy, W. C., 32
Harmonica. *See* Mouth-organ
Harpers and Queen, 203–4
Harriman, Margaret Case, 83–84
Harrison, Rex, xvi, 73
Hasegawa, Charlie, 159–60
Hastings, Lady Selina, 193–201
Hauptmann, Bruno Richard, 109
Hayden, Sterling, 128
Hays Office, 97
Hearst, William Randolph, 38
Heifetz, Jascha, 189
Hellman, Lillian, 142–43, 148
Hennessy, John, 188–89
Hepburn, Katharine, 95
Herbert, A. P., 51–52
Hero, Stephen, 97
Herzog, Chief Rabbi (of Jerusalem),
   162
Heyerdahl, Thor, 44
High Wind in Jamaica (film), 181
Hilton sisters (Daisy and Violet), 8
Hines, Earl, 47
Hitchcock, Alfred, 90
Hod, Mordecai, 167–68
Hodges, Johnny, 46
Hohner, Ernst, 119
Hohner, Karl, 119, 180
Hohner Company, 9, 119
Holiday, Billie, 33, 47–48, 180
Holliday, Judy, 128
Hollywood Ten, 136, 147
Holmes, Teddy, 51–52
Holtz, Lou, 18, 23–24
Hoover, J. Edgar, 133, 146
Hopper, Hedda, 93
Horowitz, Julie, 106
Horowitz, Vladimir, 62

Houdini, Harry, 42, 43
House Un-American Activities
   Committee, 25, 125, 126, 128,
   133, 136, 141–44
Howard, Tom, 27
Hubbard, Lucien, 39
Hume, Paul, 127
Hungarian Rhapsody, Second (Liszt),
   107
Huston, John, 125

"I Can't Give You Anything But
   Love," 31
"If I Had a Girl Like You," 24
"If You Would Always Be Good to
   Me," 29
"I Got Rhythm," 32
I Led Three Lives (film), 126
"I'm Glad I Waited," 27
Ingrams, Richard, 205
Irwin, Lou, 15
Israel, 155–57, 161–63, 166–70
Iturbi, Amparo, 96
Iturbi, José, 93, 95–97
Ives, Burl, 128
"I Wanna Be Loved by You," 13, 17

Jackson, John, 202
Jackson's (shop in Piccadilly), 201–2
Japan, 158–60, 163–66
Jazz Singer, The (play and film), 8–9
Jerusalem, 167–68
Jessel, George, 8–9, 95, 105, 133
Jews against Communism, 131
Joan of Lorraine (play), 114
Johnson, Samuel, 154
Johnson, Thor, 164
Johnston, Arthur, 46, 73
Johnston, Hugh, 148
Jolson, Al, 4, 9, 24–25, 31, 38, 77
Jolson Story, The (film), 24–25
Jones, C. M. ("Jimmy"), 205

Jones, Jim, 42, 44
Joyce, Peggy Hopkins, 31

Kahn, Albert, 135
Kahn, E. J., Jr., 42, 83, 99, 158
Kalcheim, Nat, 50
Kane, Helen, 12–13
Karlov, General and Madame, 120–21
Kaye, Danny, 105, 125
Kazan, Elia, 128, 141–44
Kelly, Gene, 125
Kelly, Nell, 36, 38
Kelly, Patsy, 33
Kemp, Hal, 36
Kendall, Kay, 182
Kent, George, Duke of, 54, 71–72
Kent, Marina, Duchess of, 71–72
Kern, Jerome, 32, 90, 186
Khachaturian, Aram, 177
Khan, Taley Mohammed (Nawab of Palanpur), 75
King and Country (film), 181
King of Jazz (film), 48
Knight, Vivienne, 181–82
Kollek, Teddy, 167
Korea, 157–58
Kostelanetz, André, 166
Koster, Henry, 93–94, 97
Kreisler, Fritz, 54, 60, 65
Kriendler, Mack, 139, 145, 197
Kurnitz, Harry, 182–83
Kurosawa, Akira, 164

LaGuardia, Fiorello, 137
La Jana, 51
Lake, Harriette (later Ann Sothern), 27
Landels, Willie, 203
Landis, Carole, 109, 111
Lane, Burton, 32
Lanin, Paul, 30

Lardner, Ring, 14, 28, 31
Lastfogel, Abe, 36, 62, 81, 95, 101, 133–34, 135, 143–44, 146, 157
Lastfogel, Frances, 81
Laughton, Charles, 41, 70, 73, 77, 79
Laughton, Elsa, 41, 70, 77, 79
Laurents, Arthur, 92
Léal, Jacques, 203–4
LeBaron, William, 45–46
Lee, Anna, 101, 107
Legman, Gershon, 203
"Le Grisbi," 186
Lehmann, Rosamond, 194
Leigh, Vivien, 73
Leighton, Gloria, 200–201
Leningrad Symphony (Shostakovich), 86
Lerner, Alan Jay, xvi
LeRoy, Mervyn, 97
Leslie, Lew, 48
Levant, Oscar, 91
Levin, Harry O., 4
Levitt, Sylvia, 62, 178
Levy, Lou, 185–86
Lewis, Fulton, Jr., 138
Liberty, 5, 12
Liebman, Herman, 146
Lindbergh, Ann Morrow, 108
Lindbergh, Charles Augustus, 108–10
Lindsay, Howard, 144
Lipstone, Louis, 35–36
Liverpool Philharmonic Orchestra, 173
Loeb, Philip, 33
Loesser, Frank, 187
Loke Wan Tho, 192
Lombard, Carole, 93
Lombardo, Guy, 45–46
London Symphony Orchestra, 173
Lopez, José Rodriguez, 175
Losch, Tilly, 51
Losey, Joseph, 181
"Louisiana Hayride," 33
Loyalty Order, 127–28
Lullaby Time (Gershwin), 187

Lyon, Jacques, 58–59
Lyons, Leonard, 80–81, 186
Lyttleton, Humphrey, 203

MacArthur, General and Mrs.
  Douglas, 111
McCarthy, Joseph, 33, 126, 128, 135,
  145–46, 149–50, 154, 207
McCullough, Hester, 126, 128, 134,
  135, 136, 148, 149, 153
McCullough, John T., 139
MacDonald, Jeanette, 39, 96
MacDonald, Malcolm, 192
MacFadden, Bernard, 31
McGranery, James Patrick, 127
McHugh, Jimmy, 31, 32
McKern, Leo, 66
McLaglen, Victor, 63
Maharishi Mahesh Yogi, 43
Maitland, Lady Olga, 200
Mannix, Eddie, 39
Many Happy Returns (film), 45–47
Marian ("Kiki"), 28–29
Marmor, Judd, 92
Marx, Groucho, 23, 105
Mary, Queen of England, 55
Maschwitz, Eric, 56
Mastbaum Theater (Philadelphia), 25
Mathieson, Muir, 184, 185
Matusow, Harvey, 149–50
"Max Gordon Raised the Money,"
  33–34
May, Dr., 92
Mayer, Louis B., 39, 90, 94–95, 98
"Meadowland," 148
Meir, Golda, 161
Men Only, 56
Menuhin, Yehudi, 93, 188
Mercer, Johnny, 63, 187
Merman, Ethel, 16, 31, 49
Metro-Goldwyn-Mayer, 39, 95–96,
  98
Mikhoels, Solomon, 135
Milestone, Kendall, 190

Milestone, Lewis, 123
Milhaud, Darius, 171, 175–76
Milland, Ray, 45
Miller, Marilyn, 27, 30
Miller, Max, 54–55
Millstein, Nathan, 174
Milton, Vera, 25–26
Minevitch, Borrah, 12–15, 206
Molotov, Vyacheslav, 127
Mona (friend of Paul Draper), 46,
  47
Monte Carlo Sporting Club, 59, 61
Monteux, Pierre, 53, 175
Moore, Monette, 33
More, Kenneth, 182
Morgan, Helen, 145
Morris, Ernie, 13
Morris, Newbold, 137
Morris (William) Agency, 38, 62,
  126
Morros, Boris, 16
Moses, Charles, 191
Mostel, Zero, 142
"Mountain Greenery," 49
Mouth-organ: LA first plays, 9–11;
  early acts with, 13–18; as novelty,
  32; LA assesses standards and
  players, 84–85, 179–80; wartime
  supply difficulties, 119–20;
  repertoire, 171–77; LA teaches,
  179–80; diatonic, 179–80
Mozart Oboe Quartet, 161
Mullinar, Michael, 172
Music for Millions (film), 93–94

Nahum, Baron, 53, 68
National Broadcasting Company, 86,
  104, 105, 144. *See also* NBC
  Symphony
National Conference of Christians
  and Jews, 131
NBC Symphony, 86, 164
New York City Center, 137–38
New Yorker, 29, 83–84, 86, 115

Nicholas, Mr. (State Department official), 151–52
"Night and Day," 63
"Night over Shanghai," 63
Nixon, Richard M., 204–5

O'Brien, Margaret, 94
Odets, Clifford, 141–42
O'Donnell, John, 129
Of Thee I sing (show), 32
Olivier, Laurence, 66, 73
Operator 13 (film), 38
Ormandy, Eugene, 78–79
Orsatti brothers, 39
Osborne, Robert, 185
Owen, Frank, 68

Paderewski, Ignace, 5
Paganini, Nicolo, 175
Palmer, Lilli, 187
Palmer House (Chicago), 47, 51, 99, 101
Paramount Theater (New York), 14, 15–16, 81
Parker, Dorothy, 72
Parkinson, Michael, 187–88
Parks, General, 116–17
Parks, Larry, 24–25, 128
Parnell, Val, 73
Partington, Jack, 15–17
Pasternak, Joe, 94–96
Patton, George S., 117
Pegler, Westbrook, 129, 137, 138
Perelman, S. J., 23
Perlberg, Bill, 38–39
Perlman, Itzhak, 187–88
Peter (of Peter and Zelda), 18–20
Philadelphia Orchestra, 59
Piazza, Ben, 38–39
Pommer, Erich, 73
Porgy and Bess (musical), 64, 91, 188
Porter, Cole, 49, 52, 186, 187

Porter, Paul, 149
Poulet, Gaston, 175–76
Pourcel, Franck, 186
Powell, Dick, 17, 62
Powell, Eleanor, 93
Prague, 115–16
Prentice, Charles, 53
Presley, Elvis, 207
Primrose, William, 189
Printemps, Yvonne, 48
Private Eye, 204–5
Progressive party, 126, 128–29
Puleo, Johnny, 12–13
Punch, 50–51
Pyle, Ernie, 102

Queen Mary, 62

Rabin, Yitzhak, 166
Rachmaninoff, Sergei, 4, 5, 68
Radio Rogues, 35
Raft, George, 62, 93
Randi, James, 42, 43, 44
Rank, J. Arthur, 181, 184
Rank Organization, 182–84
Raphaelson, Samson, 8
Ravel, Maurice, 36–37, 51, 55, 57–59, 93
Ravensdale, Irene, Baroness, 171, 189
Red Channels, 127–28
Reinhardt, Django, 47
Reisman, Leo, 26
Reith, John (later Baron), 51
Renoir, Jean, 90
Revel, Harry, 32
Rhapsody in Blue (Gershwin), 48, 49, 62, 91, 175
Rickard, Tex, 31
Rignold, Hugo, 173
Ritchie, Bob, 39
Ritual Fire Dance (de Falla), 54, 60

Robbins, Jerome, 128
Robeson, Paul, 130
Robey, George, 54
Robinson, Bill ("Bojangles"), 23
Robinson, Edward G., 128, 146–47
Robitschek, Kurt, 57
Rodgers, Richard, 32, 49, 52, 71, 187
Rodriguez Lopez, José, 175
Rodzinski, Arthur, 86
Rogers, Ginger, 15, 64
Rogge, O. John, 136
Rokach, Israel, 156
Romance for Mouth-organ, Piano and Strings (Vaughan Williams), 172–74
Romanoff, Mike, 100, 125
Roman Scandals (film), 35
Romberg, Sigmund, 32
Roosevelt, Eleanor, 79, 126, 127, 163
Roosevelt, Franklin D., 79, 109, 126
Ros, Edmondo, 194
Rose, William, 182
Rosenblatt, Josef, 4
Ross, Harold, 83–84
Rosten, Leo, 202
Rothe, Marshall, 133–34
Rothstein, Arnold, 26, 31
Roumanian Rhapsody (Enesco), 95–96
Roxy Theater (New York), 122–23
Royal, John, 106
Royal Albert Hall (London), 50, 173, 176
Rubenstein, Ida, 37
Rubinstein, Arthur, 4, 203
Runyon, Damon, 186
Russell, Bertrand, 195

Saerchinger, Cesar, 62
St. Louis Symphony, 171
St. Martin's Lane (film), 72–73
Salesman Sam, 51
Sally (friend), 34

Samuels, Fred, 18
San Francisco Symphony, 175
Saratoga Trunk (film), 115
Sargent, Sir Malcolm, 79, 173–74
Schallenberg, Mrs. (neighbor), 2
Schary, Doré, 98
Schmidt, Lars, 89
Schubert brothers, 48
Schultz, Rabbi, 131
Schwartz, Arthur, 32, 33, 34
Schwarzwald, Jacques, 115
Scollay Square Theater (Boston), 22–23
Scott, Cyril, 171
Sebastian, John, 177
Segal, Vivienne, 49
Sellick, Phyllis, 189
Senate Internal Security Committee, 128, 154
Sensations of 1944 (film), 92–93
Serenade (Scott), 171
Serotkin, Annie (aunt), 3
Sha'arei T'filoh Synagogue, Baltimore, 6
"Sharm-el-Sheikh," 166
Shaw, Artie, 81, 87
Shaw, Wini, 101, 107, 110, 120–21
Shawn, William, 83
Shearer, Norma, 39
She Done Him Wrong (film), 16
Sheil, Bishop Bernard J., 132–33
Shemer, Naomi, 167
Sheridan, Dinah, 182
Sherkot, 51
Shore, Dinah, 79, 106
Shorvon, Joseph, 92
Shostakovich, Dmitri, 86
Silvers, Phil, 8, 105
Simmel, Ernst, 87, 88, 90–92
Simon, Simone, 63–64
Sinatra, Frank, 125
Singer's Midgets, 8
Singing Marine, The (show), 62–63
Skating Whirlwinds, 66–67
Skolsky, Sidney, 24
Skouras, Spyros, 142

Small, Paul, 186
Smiles (show), 27–31
Smith, Cyril, 189
"Smoke Gets in Your Eyes," 51, 55
"Smoking Reefers," 33
Snyder, Jack, 107
Sokolsky, George, 125, 137, 138
Solti, Sir Georg, 177–78
Sonnen, Fred, 9–11
Sonnenberg, Benjamin, Jr., 80,
    82–83, 146, 148, 149
"Sonny Boy," 77, 204
"Sophisticated Lady," 46
Sothern, Ann (formerly Harriette
    Lake), 27
Spiegel, Sam, 153
Spingold, Nate, 153
Stanwyck, Barbara, 90
Steel Pier (Atlantic City), 25
Stein, Bill, 78, 80
Stein, Jules, 76
Steinberg, Earl, 8
Sten, Anna, 97
Stephens, Billy, 51
Sterling, Sir Louis, 70
Stevens, William, 139
Stone, Andrew, 92–93
Story, Ronald D., 44
Strassner, Joseph, 69
Streamline (revue), 51–53, 55
Strok, A., 191
Strube, Gustav, 10
Suite for Mouth-organ and Orchestra,
    171, 175
Suleiman, Sheikh, 162–63
"Summertime" (Gershwin), 188–89
Sun (Chicago), 101
Swaffer, Hannen, 69
Swan and Leigh, 67
Swanson, Gloria, 38
Sweeny, Charles, 53–54
Szold, Henrietta, 156

"Tachanka," 120
Talmadge, Norma, 87

Taylor, Henry, 35
Taylor, Robert, 95
Temianka, Henri, 97
Templeton, Alec, 79
Terry, Sonny, 84, 179–80
Thalberg, Irving, 39
Thau, Benny, 39
"These Foolish Things," 62
Thielmans, Jean ("Toots"), 85
Thomas, Norman, 145–46
Thomas Hair Treatment campaign,
    81–82
Three Daring Daughters (film),
    95–96
Thurber, Helen, 178–79
Thurber, James, 92, 105, 178–79
"Tiger Rag," 63
Tilden, William T., 99
Tilton, Martha, 109, 111,
    113–16
"Time on My Hands," 28
Times (London), 50, 188–89
Tiomkin, Dmitri, 184
Toch, Ernst, 181
Tokyo Symphony, 159–60
Tolstoy, Leo, xvi
Torvill, Jane, 188–89
Toscanini, Arturo, 58, 62, 164
Touchez-pas au Grisbi (film), 186
Tracy, Spencer, 95
Transcendental Meditation, 43
Trinder, Tommy, 65, 68
Truman, Harry S., 95, 117, 126–29,
    166, 178
Truman, Margaret, 127
Trumbauer, Frankie, 48
Tucker, Charles, 65, 74
Tucker, Sophie, 93
Tune Inn (revue), 66–67, 70
"21" Club, 30

United Artists, 183–84
United Services Organization (USO),
    88, 93–94, 101, 103, 106–7, 109,
    113, 155

Vallee, Rudy, 14–15, 17, 24
Vanities (show), 25
Variety, 23, 31, 35, 47, 183
Vaughan Williams, Ralph, 141, 171–74
Venuta, Benay, 98
Villa-Lobos, Heitor, 177
Violin Concerto in A minor (Vivaldi), 53, 78, 82, 159–60
Vogel, Melvin, 10, 11
Von Däniken, Eric, 44
Von Hartz (editor), 102
Vrbacki, Konstantin, 120

Wade, Virginia, 206
Walker, Jimmy, 31
Wallace, Henry, 126, 128–29, 134
Waller, Thomas ("Fats"), 33
Walser, Eileen. *See* Adler, Eileen
Walsh, Raoul, 38
Walsh, Thomas, 150–51
Wanger, Walter, 38–39
Warner, Ann, 63
Warner, Jack, 62–64
Warner, Sturgis, 151–53
Warner Brothers, 9, 62–63
Warren, Harry, 63
Washington Star, 44
Watson, "Sliding Billy," 8
Waugh, Auberon, 205
Wayne, Naunton, 51
"Wear a Straw Hat in the Rain," 73–74
Webb, Clifton, 33
Wechsler, James, 144–45
Weitman, Bob, 81
Weitz, John, xiii–xv
Weizmann, Chaim, 156–57
Welles, Orson, 38
Werblin, "Sonny," 76
West, Mae, 16, 36, 46
Westmore, Wally, 64
Wetzel, Jean, 186
What's On, 204
Wheeler, Bert, 40
Whelan, Tim, 73
"When Day Is Done," 15, 17, 48

Whettam, Graham, 171
Whigham, Margaret. *See* Argyll, Margaret, Duchess of
Whistler, Rex, 51
Whiteman, Paul, 48, 49
Whittemore, Reese, 6
Wiener, Jean, 186
Wiggin, Fred, 136–37
William Morris Agency. *See* Morris (William) Agency
Williams, Ralph Vaughan. *See* Vaughan Williams, Ralph
Williamson, Sonny Boy, 179
Wilson, Charles, 136
Wilson, Sir Steuart, 171–72
Wimbledon, 205–7
Winchell, Walter, 24, 31, 34, 133–35, 186
Windsor, Edward, Duke of (formerly Prince of Wales), 54, 76
Windsor, Wallis, Duchess of, 76
Wisner, Frank, 67
Woltman, Frederick, 135
Wood, Sir Henry, 68
Wood, John, 173
Wood, Robert, 109
Woollcott, Alexander, 29
Woolsey, Robert, 40
Worth, Billie, 33
Wozzeck (Berg), 64
Wyatt, Woodrow, 157
Wyler, William, 97

Yardley, Jack, 205–7
Yorty, Sam, 146
Youmans, Vincent, 27–28, 29, 31
Young, Loretta, 95
Youngman, Henny, 105, 208–9
"Young Man of Manhattan," 28, 31

Zacchini, Hugo, 84
Zafrir (Indian harmonica player), 180–81

Zafrir, Major, 166

Zhukhov, General, 117

Ziegfeld, Florenz, 27–29, 31, 48

Ziegler, Ron, 205

Zimbalist, Freddie, 13

Zimmerman, Ethel (later Ethel Merman), 16

Zinkeisen, Doris, 51